The Oil Has Not Run Dry

Footprints Series
Jane Errington, Editor

The life stories of individual women and men who were participants in interesting events help nuance larger historical narratives, at times reinforcing those narratives, at other times contradicting them. The Footprints series introduces extraordinary Canadians, past and present, who have led fascinating and important lives at home and throughout the world.

The series includes primarily original manuscripts but may consider the English-language translation of works that have already appeared in another language. The editor of the series welcomes inquiries from authors. If you are in the process of completing a manuscript that you think might fit into the series, please contact her, care of McGill-Queen's University Press, 1010 Sherbrooke Street West, Suite 1720, Montreal, QC, H3A 2R7.

1 *Blatant Injustice*
The Story of a Jewish Refugee from Nazi Germany Imprisoned in Britain and Canada during World War II
Walter W. Igersheimer
Edited and with a foreword by Ian Darragh

2 *Against the Current*
Memoirs
Boris Ragula

3 *Margaret Macdonald*
Imperial Daughter
Susan Mann

4 *My Life at the Bar and Beyond*
Alex K. Paterson

5 *Red Travellers*
Jeanne Corbin and Her Comrades
Andrée Lévesque

6 *The Teeth of Time*
Remembering Pierre Elliott Trudeau
Ramsay Cook

7 *The Greater Glory*
Thirty-seven Years with the Jesuits
Stephen Casey

8 *Doctor to the North*
Thirty Years Treating Heart Disease among the Inuit
John H. Burgess

9 *Dal and Rice*
Wendy M. Davis

10 *In the Eye of the Wind*
A Travel Memoir of Prewar Japan
Ron Baenninger and Martin Baenninger

11 *I'm from Bouctouche, Me*
Roots Matter
Donald J. Savoie

12 *Alice Street*
A Memoir
Richard Valeriote

13 *Crises and Compassion*
From Russia to the Golden Gate
John M. Letiche

14 *In the Eye of the China Storm*
A Life Between East and West
Paul T.K. Lin with Eileen Chen Lin

15 *Georges and Pauline Vanier*
Portrait of a Couple
Mary Frances Coady

16 *Blitzkrieg and Jitterbugs*
College Life in Wartime, 1939–1942
Elizabeth Hillman Waterston

17 *Harrison McCain*
Single-Minded Purpose
Donald J. Savoie

18 *Discovering Confederation*
A Canadian's Story
Janet Ajzenstat

19 *Expect Miracles*
Recollections of a Lucky Life
David M. Culver with Alan Freeman

20 *Building Bridges*
Victor C. Goldbloom

21 *Call Me Giambattista*
A Personal and Political Journey
John Ciaccia

22 *Smitten by Giraffe*
My Life as a Citizen Scientist
Anne Innis Dagg

23 *The Oil Has Not Run Dry*
The Story of My Theological Pathway
Gregory Baum

The Oil Has Not Run Dry

The Story of My Theological Pathway

GREGORY BAUM

McGill-Queen's University Press
Montreal & Kingston • London • Chicago

© McGill-Queen's University Press 2017

ISBN 978-0-7735-4826-8 (cloth)
ISBN 978-0-7735-5477-1 (paper)
ISBN 978-0-7735-9996-3 (ePDF)
ISBN 978-0-7735-9997-0 (ePUB)

Legal deposit first quarter 2017
Bibliothèque nationale du Québec
First paperback edition 2018

Printed in Canada on acid-free paper that is 100% ancient forest free (100% post-consumer recycled), processed chlorine free

Funded by the Government of Canada | Financé par le gouvernement du Canada | Canada

We acknowledge the support of the Canada Council for the Arts, which last year invested $153 million to bring the arts to Canadians throughout the country. Nous remercions le Conseil des arts du Canada de son soutien. L'an dernier, le Conseil a investi 153 millions de dollars pour mettre de l'art dans la vie des Canadiennes et des Canadiens de tout le pays.

Library and Archives Canada Cataloguing in Publication

Baum, Gregory, 1923–, author
The oil has not run dry : the story of my theological pathway / Gregory Baum.

(Footprints series ; 23)
Includes bibliographical references and index.
Issued in print and electronic formats.
ISBN 978-0-7735-4826-8 (cloth). ISBN 978-0-7735-5477-1 (paper)
ISBN 978-0-7735-9996-3 (ePDF). ISBN 978-0-7735-9997-0 (ePUB)

1. Baum, Gregory, 1923–. 2. Theologians – Canada – Biography. 3. Catholics – Canada – Biography. 4. Church renewal – Catholic Church. I. Title. II. Series: Footprints series ; 23

BX4705.B254A3 2016 241'.042092 C2016-905364-4
C2016-905365-2

For Philip and Colleen: The Joy of Friendship

Contents

Significant Dates

20 June 1923: Gerhard Baum, born in Berlin, Germany, brought up Protestant in a family originally Jewish.

May 1939: left for Great Britain on a children's transport.

May 1940: was interned in Great Britain as a German national and a few weeks later sent to internment camps in Canada, first in Farnham, Quebec, and then in Sherbrooke, Quebec.

April 1942: released from the camp and, in September, became a student at McMaster University in Hamilton, Ontario, obtaining a BA in mathematics and physics in June 1946.

July 1946: baptized in the Roman Catholic Church.

September 1946: studied at Ohio State University in Columbus, Ohio, obtaining an MA in mathematics in September 1947.

September 1947: entered the Augustinian Order, received the new name of "Gregory."

1950–59: student of theology at the University of Fribourg, Switzerland; ordained a priest in 1954; obtained a doctorate in theology in 1956; served in a parish in Neuchâtel and continued studies.

1959: returned to Canada and began teaching theology at St Michael's College at the University of Toronto for seminarians and lay students until 1986.

1960: appointed by John XXIII *peritus* (specialist) at the Secretariat for Promoting Christian Unity, a preparatory commission of the Second Vatican Council; attended meetings in Rome several times a year and attended the four sessions of the Council between 1962 and 1965.
1969–71: studied sociology at the New School for Social Research in New York City.
1976: resigned from the priesthood and the Augustinian Order, continued teaching at St Michael's College.
1977: married Shirley, an old friend, a teacher, a former nun who, after thirty years of married life, died peacefully in 2007.
1986: became a professor in the Faculty of Religious Studies at McGill University in Montreal and was soon invited to join the editorial committee of the francophone review *Relations*, published by the Jesuit-sponsored le Centre justice et foi.
1999: retired from McGill University and was invited to have an office at le Centre justice et foi.

The Oil Has Not Run Dry

There was food every day for Elijah and the widow of Sarepta.
The jar of flour was not used up and the jug of oil did not run dry,
in keeping with the word of the Lord spoken by Elijah.
– 1 Kings 17:15
New International Version NIV Bible

PART 1

My Theological Pathway

Friends of mine have encouraged me to look back over my life, record the important experiences that have affected my thinking, and tell the story of how my faith and my theology have evolved. For a long time I hesitated to do this. I do not think of myself as an important thinker. I had the good fortune of meeting great theologians. As a member of the board of directors of the international review *Concilium*, I have worked with Yves Congar, Gustavo Gutierrez, Hans Küng, Karl Rahner, Edward Schillebeeckx, and David Tracy. These are original thinkers, whom I admire from a distance and from whom I have learned a great deal.

I think of myself as a practical theologian moved by the troubling issues of the present who tries to interpret and respond to them in the light of the Gospel. To do this work, I reflect on the sources of the Christian faith, listen to the voices in the Catholic community, study the debates among theologians, and converse with concerned secular thinkers, male and female. When I arrive at an insight I regard as significant, I feel the urge to develop it in an article or a book addressed not to specialists in theology but, rather, to the wider circle of educated Catholics and their Protestant and secular friends. I regard myself as a theological essayist, disturbed by what is wrong in the world and convinced of the transforming power of the Gospel. I am deeply troubled by the calculated injustices built into the dominant institutions and the suffering they inflict upon men and women all over the world, yet my faith in God's promises forbids me to despair.

Praying, thinking, and writing as a theologian, I foster a critical culture in church and society and support movements of social change that reduce human suffering, making society more pleasing to God. Working as a theologian I often have the feeling, possibly quite illusory, that I am leaning against an evil wind. Today a good number of people, believers and non-believers, are convinced that cultural resistance is what their ethical commitment demands of them.

While I mourn the suffering inflicted upon the innocent, my own life has been so protected and so privileged that I cannot help but be embarrassed. I often think of myself as the widow of Sarepta (1 Kings 17:7–19) who, at a time of famine, was chosen by God to be fed: God sent the prophet Elijah to reward her for her generosity with a meal that never diminishes and a jug of oil that does not run dry. I have chosen *The Oil Has Not Run Dry* as the title of this book. The older I get – I am now over ninety – my sense of gratitude is becoming ever more intense.

To give expression to this gratitude I have decided to reply positively to my friends and write the story of my theological pathway. This book is not an autobiography. I refer rather briefly to my childhood, my emigration, my internment, my education, my life in the church, and my academic career. What I wish to report at greater length are the experiences that have affected my theological thinking. I record the events and encounters that made me ask new questions and obliged me to rethink the meaning of Catholicism in the contemporary world.

Since I have kept no records of the past, my report lacks precision. When I entered the monastery in 1947, I decided not to keep letters or photos of the past; and, in subsequent decades, as an academic at the university, I continued the custom of not keeping any records. I dropped into the wastepaper basket my correspondence, my papers as *peritus* at the Second Vatican Council, the essays I wrote, and the courses I taught. This changed in the 1990s when I began to use a computer and left my writings to its good memory. A few years ago, unskilled as I am, I pushed a wrong button and wiped most of them out. But I do have copies of the books I wrote and the long list of the articles and chapters of books I published over the years. More important, I have all the issues of a small review, the *Ecumenist*, which I founded in 1962 and edited until 2003, when I left the editorship in the hands of David Seljak, professor at St Jerome's College in Waterloo, Ontario. I have often said to my friends that editing the *Ecumenist* has been a major source of my mental health since whenever I was frustrated by events in the church or society – and this happened very often – I would study the issue, write an article on it, and publish it in my own review. The articles I wrote for the *Ecumenist* over five decades constitute a record of the evolution of my theological thought.[1]

Writing the present book, I depend largely on my own memory. I try to verify what I remember, using my books and articles, yet I have no way of testing whether my memory of what the past events meant to me is reliable. I am aware that memory is always affected by present concerns: it recalls and forgets in accordance with our open or hidden preoccupations. Still, I write about my thoughts and feelings of the past as I remember them. Since this book is not the story of my life but, rather, an account of the evolution of my faith and my theology, when recalling my childhood I discuss the experiences that predisposed me to become a believer. Of my emigration and arrival in Canada I record the events that contributed to my trust in God. Then I speak of the impact that St Augustine's *Confessions* had on me in 1946. The subsequent sections of Part 1 present the theological themes that preoccupied me and demanded rethinking and development on my part. In Part 2, a friend of mine asks me questions about my life and my ideas, to which I give my answers.

1

My Childhood in Berlin

I was born in 1923 in Berlin into a wealthy German bourgeois family of Jewish origin and Protestant culture. My name was then Gerhard Baum – Gregory was given me later when I joined the Augustinian Order. In the nineteenth century, middle-class German Jews sought complete assimilation into German culture: they turned to Reform Judaism, which abandoned the ceremonial and dietary laws of the tradition, or they became Christians without necessarily becoming believers.[1] Most of them became patriotic Germans, supported liberal values, identified with the capitalist class, and, after 1870, were proud of the Kaiser. My grandfather on my father's side was an industrialist, and my grandfather on my mother's side was the owner of a private bank. My father, Franz Siegfried Baum, a university-trained engineer, became an officer in the German Army in the First World War and assisted Dr Fritz Haber of the Kaiser Wilhelm Institute, professor of chemistry and inventor of poison gas, to organize the gas attacks on the British. Because the wounds my father received during the war never completely healed, his physical resistance was weak, and he died after an appendix operation in 1924, when I was one year old. I have no memory of him.

My mother, Bettie Baum, née Meyer, looked after me and my three-year-old sister. In an article in *Canadian Dimension*, I wrote, "because I had a wonderful mother who loved me and left me free, I was always, all my life, accompanied by an inner smile." My mother was a warm-hearted, intelligent, and cheerful woman with a passionate interest in art and literature. Since we had a cook, a maid, and a nanny, my mother had the time to read books, travel, and explore her love of the arts. She used to read poems to us from a book of German poetry edited by Echtermeyer (I remember his name after all these years); she also read to us from the New Testament, a large leather-bound volume illustrated with etchings by Daumier. We had long conversations with our mother, usually for an hour after the mid-day meal, sitting around the table while she drank her coffee. That I was a poor student in school did not bother her: she had a quite unfounded confidence in me.

Eventually my mother married again, this time to a man with whom she had little in common, so the union did not last very long. My stepfather was good to me, yet he never became my father, nor I his son. In 1939, both of us left Germany and headed in different directions, leaving my mother alone in Berlin. My stepfather and I drifted apart. In 1957, when he had become a wealthy businessman in New York, he made inquiries about me; found me as a graduate student in Fribourg, Switzerland; and regretted that I had become a priest in the Augustinian Order. He wanted me to join his business firm and, naively, asked me if a substantial financial gift would persuade the church to release me. Belonging to quite different cultural worlds, we did not communicate in words: we simply smiled at one another.

That my real father had organized the gas attacks in the First World War did not bother his family. In our ignorance, my sister and I were proud of our father's achievement: he had received the Iron Cross for his services. It was only much later that I learned that gas attacks, eventually employed by all powers during the First World War, violated the international Hague Conventions of 1898. I learned that Fritz Haber's operation had been criticized at the Kaiser Wilhelm Institute by Otto Hahn, another well-known scientist, and that Haber had replied that he organized gas attacks "to shorten the war and save human lives" – the argument President Truman gave when he permitted the use of the atomic bomb. Haber's wife, Clara, a doctor of chemistry and a dedicated humanist, tried to stop her husband from conducting the gas attacks, and, severely distraught by his stubborn refusal, she committed suicide in 1915. Despite the attempt of Britain and France to have Haber taken to court as a war criminal, he was given the Nobel Prize for his research in chemistry in 1919. It is a tragic irony that Haber, a nominal Protestant of Jewish origin, became the inventor of the cyanide-based gas Zyklon B, which was subsequently used in the Hitler regime's death camps to exterminate the Jews.

I was brought up in a humanistic home. What counted was *Bildung*, an education in German culture, literature, and history. The great value was *Humanität*, a term used by German philosophers of the eighteenth century. Today I recognize the ambiguity of this educational ideal since it allowed the educated middle class to feel superior to working people and the poor and to remain ignorant of their plight. I have no memory of critical political conversations in my family. My sister and I did not even know that our grandparents were Jewish. Our birth certificates recorded that our parents were *Dissidenten*, the official German designation for people who chose to be religionless and hence did not pay the taxes the government demanded of Christians and Jews to support their religious and educational institutions. In school I received Protestant religious instruction, and at home we celebrated Christmas and Easter. It was only in 1935, when Hitler introduced the Nuremberg Laws – the new racial legislation – that we became a Jewish family.

Despite the Hitler regime, the memories I have of my life in Berlin are happy ones. I was surrounded by love and friendship; I adored the city; I was taken to the theatres, operas, museums, and cinemas; and often travelled with my mother.

Some of my friends tell me that I have a tendency, possibly unconscious, to remember only the happy moments of my life and to erase the unpleasant and painful ones. This may be true. Perhaps I am running away from being unhappy. I remember that my mother often told my sister and me how happy her childhood had been and how sorry she was that our childhood was troubled, living as we did under the Hitler government. I always replied to her, quite honestly I think, that I regarded my childhood as a happy one. I did not dwell on the dark moments, enjoying instead the love, the friendships, and the culture that surrounded me. As a young man and an adult I kept this attitude. I de-dramatized the painful experiences of my life in order to be free to appreciate the good and promising events. In the 1960s, as I report further on, I became profoundly touched by the suffering of "the poor and oppressed" as the Bible calls them: I became politicized, made an emancipatory commitment, and changed my theological orientation.[2] Yet refusing to let the great sadness invade my entire being, I tried to live the daily paradox of combining troubled concern for others with grateful acceptance of personal joy. That is why, as an old man receiving dialysis three times a week and slowly becoming deaf, I am able – with God's help – to have an interesting, committed, and happy life.

Did any experiences in my early life in Berlin have an effect on my life as a Christian believer and theologian? On the surface, our life at home was quite secular. Yet my mother was aware of a deeper dimension, an unspoken mystery in human life, that summoned people to become good, generous, and creative. She was greatly moved by the novels of Dostoyevsky. Because of her special love of medieval art, she travelled through Germany, with my sister and me packed into her car, to visit Romanesque and Gothic churches and monasteries and to admire their architecture, their clustered windows, and their works of art. I was enthralled by the beauty of these religious buildings. I loved the medieval cathedrals and sculptures, while being less fond of Baroque architecture. Over all these years my heart still warms when I look at photographs of the marvellous sculptures that decorate the cathedrals of Naumburg and Bamberg. In the northern parts of Germany, the Gothic churches and monasteries were made not of stone but of red bricks (*Backsteingothik*, in German), manifesting a simplicity, a calm beauty, and a spiritual sobriety that I found – and still find – deeply moving. I think that for my mother these religious buildings and their art were symbols of an unspoken Otherness, distinct from the world of every day, yet accompanying people in their daily lives. Though she never articulated this feeling, I think that I picked it up and shared it.

In 1939, when her second husband, my sister, and I fled Germany in different directions, my mother, who had never done manual work, felt called to become a nurse in Berlin's Jewish Hospital. In 1942, she thought of seeking refuge in the house of friends, but she fell ill, caught meningitis, and died peacefully in the hospital. She was forty-five years old. When I returned to Berlin for the first time in 1951, I asked at the hospital whether some nurses had survived the war and were still working there. A woman present at the reception desk asked me why I wanted to know this. When I told her my mother's name, she cried out, "You must be Gerd!" (my name was Gerhard, but everyone called me Gerd). She, the head nurse, had been my mother's friend; she told me how much my mother was loved for her service and her kindness. If my mother had lived, she might have survived the war as some nurses and doctors of Berlin's Jewish Hospital were not arrested: its staff and its facilities were used by the military to take care of wounded soldiers.

I wish to mention two profound experiences I have never forgotten. At the age of seven or eight, I cried in school when the teacher of religion, a pious Protestant, spoke to us in moving terms of the death of Jesus on the cross. At the age of eleven or twelve, sitting in my stepfather's big car – a Horch – and waiting for him to return from an errand, I saw through the windshield an old man, a street cleaner, bending down to pick up some dirt from the street – a picture that grieved me deeply. I was seized by a wave of sorrow over the shocking inequalities among humans and the humiliation inflicted upon the poor and misfortunate. This painful insight was new for me: I had not been introduced to it by members of my family. Several years later, a short poem by Hugo von Hofmannsthal reawakened this sorrow in me. The first strophe describes people happily walking on the deck of a ship admiring the sun and the sea, and the second strophe depicts the slaves in the hull of the ship, rowing chained to their oars. Even if the two moments of grief and the poem did not affect my life at the time, I never forgot them: they were imprinted upon my memory and, decades later, became meaningful for me in my turn to liberation theology. I then felt that these moments of grief had a religious significance. To be wounded by the suffering of others is a gift of the Holy Spirit.

2

Coming to Canada

Members of the German Jewish bourgeoisie foolishly refused to recognize the danger in which they lived. They thought of National Socialism as a *Kinderkrankheit*, a childhood disease, that would soon fade away. Having no political analysis, they were confident that Germany's humanistic culture was not seriously threatened. Hitler and his followers, they thought, were not authentically German. Lessing was German, so were Herder, Mendelssohn, Schiller, Goethe, and Kant. It was only after the burning of the synagogues and the massive arrest of Jews on 9 November 1938 that these German Jews recognized that they had to leave the country, if that was still possible. Most countries did not accept refugees at that time. My stepfather, now divorced from my mother, had international business connections that allowed him to leave. My sister went to England to work as a maid. When a friend of mine, Harry Nagler, a boy of my age, told me on the telephone that there was still room on a British Kindertransport, the program bringing refugee children to safety in Great Britain, I put my name on the list and left Berlin with a group of children at the end of May 1939

Looking back I realize that this forced emigration, the loss of home and family, and the radical insecurity regarding the future were heart-rending experiences for both adults (who lost the achievements of their lives) and for small children (who lost the support of their parents). For boys and girls of my age the experience was different. As I remember it, we made the transition without lamenting and without self-pity. Adult life was just beginning for us. I did not ask questions about the past or the future, I simply lived one day after another, content with doing what was necessary. I think that I lived my life unreflectively and found refuge in thoughtlessness. Philip McKenna tells me that psychologists call this "dissociation": to protect themselves in situations of crisis, people focus on doing the essential, blocking out the threatening details.

In England I worked on a farm. That the farmer and his wife were Christian Scientists fascinated me. In the evening after work I would read the Bible and Mary Baker Eddy's *Science and Health with Key to the Scriptures*, and on Sundays I accompanied the famer and his wife to their church. I had a vague faith in God but did not believe the special message of Christian Science that evil was an illusion, a product of "mortal mind" or unenlightened consciousness. Yet reading and thinking steadied me. I had no training, no education, no plan for the future, but this did not bother me. My blindness allowed me to be cheerful.

In May 1940, nine months after the beginning of the war, the British government, witnessing the German invasion of France, became afraid of a possible invasion of Britain. The decision was made to intern the German refugees, in case some of them were siding with Germany and were ready to welcome invading troops. When the police came to the farm to pick me up, I was in the barn shovelling manure. I leaned the shovel against the wall, went out to meet the officers, and happily left with them in their car.

The internment was a great experience for me. I met hundreds of Germans – Christians and Jews, communists, socialists, liberals, and anarchists – all refugees from the Hitler regime. My group was first put into a camp near Liverpool, then spent a few weeks on the Isle of Man, and was eventually shipped off to Canada. We landed in Trois-Rivières, stayed for several days in the city's stadium located on a hill, and then spent a few weeks in a camp that was being built near Fredericton, New Brunswick. I was eventually sent to Camp A at Farnham, a small town south of Montreal, where I spent well over a year, and finally landed in a camp at Sherbrooke, where I spent several months.

Though I could write an entire book about my life in the camps, I will only make a few remarks about the education I received there. Camp A represented the real Germany for me: Christians and Jews, groups of Protestant ministers, Catholic priests and brothers, Jewish rabbis and thinkers, and representatives of the political parties suppressed by Hitler. We lived tightly in wooden barracks and were surrounded by high barbed-wire fences, but we were secure, well fed, and had time for our own activities. The older men created a camp school for the boys where the classes were taught, at first without books, by distinguished German professors. William Heckscher, a professional educator, wrote to McGill University asking permission for the camp school to prepare us for the junior matriculation. At this school, surrounded by many friends, I, who had been a poor student in Berlin and deprived of education in England, discovered that I was reasonably intelligent. For older men, separated from their families, whose career in Britain had been interrupted, the internment was a hardship; but for us, the boys, it was an exciting opportunity. I woke up intellectually in the camps.[1]

Reflecting on my life, I recognized with amazement that good things happened to me without my doing. I had been rescued from Hitler's Germany and released from tedious farm work to become a student. An experience I had in the camp still makes me wonder. A high British officer had arrived to persuade the young and not so young inmates of the camp to volunteer for the Pioneer Corps in Britain. The task of the Pioneer Corps was to assist people in repairing their homes damaged by German bombs. I went to see the officer and told him I was ready to volunteer, yet, after a short interview, the contents of which I have forgotten, he told me to stay in Canada. I was puzzled by this – and at the same time grateful to him.

The Canadian government eventually realized that we were refugees and not enemy aliens. It decided, since there was no room for us in Canada, that we would be sent back to Britain after the war to be released in the country that had interned us. To everyone's surprise, the boys of the camp school were visited by a woman, a social worker named Constance Hayward sent by the YWCA, who thought it was shameful that these young men lived in a camp instead of studying at a Canadian university. She told us that she would work for our release. When the government declined her request, she proposed that she would find Canadians willing to pay for our education, hoping that then the government would release us. Her proposal, supported by Senator Cairine Wilson, was accepted. A Jewish refugee committee found sponsors for the Jewish boys, and Constance Hayward persuaded Archbishop McGuiggan of Toronto to sponsor the Catholic boys. As I was a Protestant, she found a remarkable Protestant woman to sponsor me, Emma Kaufman, a member of a wealthy family from Kitchener, Ontario, who had spent several decades in Japan building the YWCA in that country, financed in part by her own resources. Having returned to Canada when the war started, she now became my sponsor. I was released, after almost two years, at the end of April 1942.

Thanks to Emma Kaufman's generosity, I was able to study mathematics and physics at McMaster University in Hamilton, Ontario. My relationship to my sponsor was respectful; it was never intimate – neither she nor I wanted this. My great effort was to get used to a culture that was new to me and to do well in my university studies. I enjoyed my life at McMaster and kept in touch with the former camp boys now studying in Toronto. In the summers I would make some money working on a farm or in a factory.

Looking back to my four years at the university, I now feel a little ashamed. I was so involved in my own life, my studies, and my inner conflicts that I failed to sorrow over the killing, the bombs, the destruction, and the horrors taking place in Europe at that time. I was an unthinking person, not awakened to the wider context in which I lived. One summer I did some work in a cottage for a Canadian couple whose only son, a soldier, had just been killed in the war. It did not occur to me at the time to be troubled by the sadly paradoxical fact that he, a Canadian, had left his country to fight fascism and had died, while I, a refugee from fascism, lived in his country and was safe. These generous people never said a word.

3

The Impact of *The Confessions of Saint Augustine*

While a student at McMaster University, I was vaguely interested in religion. I thought of myself as a believing Protestant, attended Sunday worship in different churches, and was an active participant in the McMaster Christian Union, a student organization associated with the international Student Christian Movement. My closest friend, Walter Hitschfeld, whom I had met in the internment camp, was a student at the University of Toronto. Walter was a Catholic from Vienna. Through him I met an older German refugee, Egbert Munzer, a Catholic, who had worked for the German government under Chancellor Heinrich Brüning. Since Egbert Munzer had refused to take the oath of loyalty to Hitler, an obligation imposed on the members of the administration in 1933, he decided to leave Germany. He now taught courses at the University of Toronto. He regarded me as a young friend, and I enjoyed his company and learned a great deal from him. He married a lovely woman, Margo, a refugee from Berlin, with whom I developed a great friendship that lasted several decades.

An important event in my life took place on 1 January 1946, the day I began to read a famous book Walter had given me for Christmas, *The Confessions of Saint Augustine*. This book had a powerful impact on me. It made me recognize God's presence in my life and urged me to cultivate the interior life in which God deigns to address believers and their communities. Reading it was a turning point in my life.

What was it that impressed me so profoundly in this book written in North Africa at the end of the fourth century? Young people are often deeply touched by special persons, their ideas or their actions, without being able at the time to analyze the reasons for their enthusiasm. I felt that *The Confessions* assigned new meaning to the Gospel, lifted me to a higher world, and gave me the taste for the spiritual life. "Taste and see that the Lord is good" (Ps. 34:8). God's presence became more real to me than ever before. Reflecting sixty-five years later on the religious enthusiasm that *The Confessions* engendered in me, I observe four themes that touched me at the time and that, much later, came to guide my theological thinking.

The first theme concerns pluralism. Augustine lived in the late Roman Empire, a pluralistic society in which people were exposed to a variety of religious and philosophical currents and had to make up their own minds about what they believed. This plurality of beliefs and values, very much like the pluralism of modern society, made the life of individuals, particularly among the educated, into a spiritual adventure – searching, discerning, and committing themselves – that assigned priority to personal convictions, lifting them above tribal loyalties and cultural pressures. Beliefs and values were not inherited; they were chosen. Among the educated, each person had his or her own story to tell, very much like seekers in modern society. Even if Augustine's story of his conversion dealt with religious currents of the fourth century, he spoke to me in my own situation in the twentieth century. He was my contemporary.

When I studied the *Summa Theologica* of St Thomas in the 1950s, I noticed that this great thinker presented his theology without referring to his personal history. He had never wrestled for his faith since it had been given to him by his Catholic culture. By comparison, Augustine was "modern."

The second theme concerns the nature of God. *The Confessions* reveals that the God in whom Augustine came to believe was, for him, an inexhaustible source of vitality. Reading the Christian message as a series of moral obligations easily creates the impression that God is the great restrainer, the super-ego in the sky, limiting personal freedom and frowning upon our moments of happiness. For Augustine, finding the God proclaimed by the church was the opening of doors and the starting point of a life of endless creativity. He found in his faith both peace and passion. He left behind the failings that had marred his life until then, escaped from the prison of self-centredness, and became a free man deeply in love with God. In reliance on this God, he became a bold thinker, inventing new ways of proclaiming the Gospel to his society. As a gifted writer, Augustine was able to persuade many readers that God was the Really Real, the invisible redemptive mystery, the unique source of life, truth, and love. Turning to God in faith was the beginning of a spiritual adventure.

The third theme concerns the relation between God and the cosmos. St Augustine was troubled by the cosmological images of the Bible that placed the throne of God in the heavenly kingdom above the earth. Heaven and hell were here spoken of as cosmic spaces. Following the Platonic tradition, Augustine came to think of God as eternal Truth, Goodness, and Beauty beyond human comprehension – in which the world and, more intimately, human beings participated in some measure. This God was not enthroned in a space called heaven; this God had created space and time, transcended the world, and was at the same time immanent in it. St Paul had already moved beyond these cosmological divine images when he approvingly quoted, and gave new meaning to, the Hellenistic aphorism: "In God we live, and move and have our being" (Acts 17:28).

In *The Confessions*, Augustine also admits that he had been troubled by biblical passages that made God appear violent and vengeful, and that he was greatly relieved when he listened to the sermons of Bishop Ambrose in Milan, who gave to these passages a non-literal, allegorical meaning. Augustine was not a literalist.

The fourth theme concerns God as saviour. Augustine wrote *The Confessions* to give thanks to God for the spiritual gift that opened his eyes to the truth and made his heart capable of love. He recognized that his urgent religious quest had been a response to a divine summons, that he had been able to find God because God had found him first. According to Augustine, the Good News preached by Jesus and explained by the Apostles reveals that people enter into the light not as a result of their own effort but, rather, in response to a gratuitous divine call addressing them in their lives. Already in *The Confessions* Augustine is the doctor of grace. The good things of significance that happen to us are unmerited gifts. Intelligence and will power alone do not allow us to discover the meaning of our existence. Faith is the response to God's Word. Augustine held that operative within us is a mystery, a hidden presence, a divine word that allows us to find the way and see the light. For Augustine, God was saviour, rescuing us from our self-destructive propensities.

Under Augustine's influence I came to look upon my short personal history as a series of rescues – granted me out of the blue – that made me marvel and be grateful: my wonderful mother, my flight from Germany, the internment that made me a student and brought me to Canada, the university education sponsored by a generous woman, and the encounter with God through Augustine's *Confessions*. The conviction that God is my rescuer has never left me. In English, we call Jesus "Saviour"; in German, we call him *Heiland*, a beautiful word that refers to his power to save and to heal. Many years later, I became deeply troubled by the question: Why me and why not others?

At the end of his life, Augustine wrestled against the theology of Pelagius, a spiritual guide in Rome who held that personal will, aided by grace, is the source of holiness, hinting that, by trying hard, one could be saved. Augustine believed that this interpretation, subsequently named Pelagianism, contradicted the message of the New Testament. Salvation was a free gift of God, surprising and unmerited. He recalled the words of Jesus: "You have not chosen me, but I have chosen you" (John 15:16), and "I am the vine, you are the branches ... without me, you can do nothing" (John 15:5). St Paul also wrote that God had loved and redeemed us while "we were still his enemies" (Rom. 5:1). Augustine won the argument. In reliance on his writings, several church councils condemned Pelagianism and affirmed the gratuitous divine initiative present in the acts of faith, hope, and love.

While I did not know this history when I read *The Confessions*, I caught Augustine's message that all good thing begin in God. This conviction has remained with me. I have always been uncomfortable with sermons that scold people for breaking the commandments and that urge them to become more obedient, without reference to the Good News that we are enabled to do good through a power not our own. Troubled by certain sermons I heard in church, I would go to my room, open the *Denzinger*, the collection of official church documents, and read the ancient conciliar texts that condemned Pelagianism.[1] Even when my theology become socially concerned and action-oriented, I never abandoned the Augustinian emphasis on the divine initiative. Here is a paragraph from my book *Religion and Alienation*.

> Social engagement is not deprived of the mystical dimension that is part of the Christian life. According to the ancient teaching, especially of St. Augustine, the good we do is God's free gift to us. In this Christian perspective, action equals passion. While we see, we are being enlightened; while we act we are being carried forward; while we love we are being saved from selfishness; and while we embrace all people in solidarity, we are being freed inwardly to cross one boundary after another. Every step towards greater humanization is due to the expansion of a new and gratuitous life in us. We are alive by a power that transcends us.[2]

Many years later, I discovered that St Augustine also had a dark side. Because the attachment to sexual pleasure had prevented him from thinking clearly, he adopted – after his conversion – a purely instrumental understanding of sexuality: it was a means of procreation and nothing else. He regarded the pleasure that accompanies begetting in married life as close to sin. Another decision of St Augustine has had terrible consequences in the church's history. As a Catholic bishop, he had called upon the state to close the doors of a dissident church and force its members to submit to Catholic teaching. At that moment he believed, contrary to his own theology, that violence can be of service to the truth. Yet discovering the dark side of St Augustine's ideas did not weaken my admiration for his theology as expressed in *The Confessions*.

In 1946, I was a fourth-year mathematics and physics student at McMaster University. Because of courses taken in the preceding year, I had much free time in the last semester, which allowed me to read theological literature, engage in conversation with believing Protestants and Catholics, and explore my own spiritual vocation. The library at McMaster University provided me with Protestant literature and Egbert Munzer's collection of books on German Catholic thought. I admired both traditions: their prayers, their theological thoughts, and their great thinkers and bold witnesses. My desire was to become a disciple of Jesus. Eventually, in the summer of 1946, I decided to become a Catholic.

I don't know all the reasons that persuaded me to make this choice. I was troubled by the Catholic Church's support of fascist governments in Spain and some other countries; however, living in Ontario, where Catholics were a minority and still had to defend themselves against prejudice, I realized that the church exerted no political power. I looked with esteem at the Catholic political party in Germany, the Zentrum, committed to social justice and democracy, which had collapsed when Hitler came to power in 1933. As a German refugee cut off from his roots, I was attracted to Catholicism because it allowed me, living in Canada, to join a European tradition and become identified with a new cultural home. My mother's love of medieval religious art and architecture may also have had something to do with my decision. I was, moreover, attracted by the possibility of joining a religious order. Since I recognized myself as homosexual, I had no intention of exploring my capacity for intimate love and looked upon monastic life as an appropriate form of discipleship. Through Egbert Munzer, I became acquainted with an Augustinian monastery near Toronto, recently founded by German priests and brothers who had left Germany when Hitler closed the Catholic schools. They spoke German at the monastery. Moved by an inner call, I decided to apply for membership in the Augustinian Order.

In my book *Man Becoming* I wrote a paragraph describing my spirituality in the early years of my life in the monastery.[3] I had embraced Karl Barth's Protestant theological stance, which contends that wisdom and salvation are in Jesus Christ alone and nowhere else. This was more exclusivist than Catholic teaching at the time. I remember how scandalized I was when my friend Walter took me to a lecture at St Michael's College given by Professor Anton Pegis on the famous article of the *Summa Theologica* (I–II: 89, 6), where Thomas Aquinas argues that divine grace is offered to every child as he or she enters the age of reason. I was disturbed by this thesis because I then held that divine grace was communicated exclusively by the gift of faith and baptism. I did not realize then that St Thomas drew upon an ancient patristic theme, echoing the Prologue of the Fourth Gospel, that God's Word, which is in fact God, addresses every human being that comes into this world (John 1:9). The narrow interpretation I then had of the Christian message raised many anguishing questions for me at a later time.

After receiving my BA at McMaster in the summer of 1946, I went to Ohio State University to work on a master's in mathematics, which I obtained in the summer of 1947. I then joined the Augustinian Order. I spent two years in our monastery at Racine, Wisconsin, where I studied Latin, Greek, and scholastic philosophy, followed by one year of the novitiate at Monastery, Nova Scotia. The Augustinian Order then sent me to the University of Fribourg in Switzerland, where I was to study theology and prepare myself for the priesthood. I remained nine years in our monastery of Fribourg, from 1950 to 1959. First, I received my theological education and was ordained a priest; second, I worked on my doctoral dissertation on an ecumenical topic and did pastoral ministry in Neuchâtel; finally, in the last two years, I worked on a book on the church's relationship to Jews and Judaism, a topic to which I return further on.

My life in the Augustinian Order was a happy one. I enjoyed the worship, the prayer, the common life, and the time to study, reflect, and wrestle with important questions. The passion and discipline of monastic life slowly transformed me, a scattered young man, into a determined person with a focus. At the University of Fribourg, we studied the *Summa* of St Thomas Aquinas: we did this for four years, both in the morning and in the afternoon. It was a great experience to become familiar with the complex thought of a major systematic theologian, a man of great genius, who, in his theology, creatively appropriated the philosophical and theological traditions of the past.

Thomas Aquinas developed his theology in dialogue with Aristotle. Yet our professor of dogmatic theology, the Dominican Adolf Hoffmann, paid special attention to the Platonic and Patristic themes present in the theology of St Thomas. He emphasized in particular the *via negativa*, or negative theology, taught by the church fathers. The ancient Christian thinkers insisted that the God of whom the Bible speaks is an ineffable and incomprehensible mystery. Following the third century theologian known as Denys the Areopagite, Thomas taught that everything we say of God must at first be negated. Since all our concepts are derived from experiences in the finite world, they do not fit when applied to the Infinite One. We know what "good" means when applied to people, books, or meals, yet when "good" is applied to God it is no longer true. Thus, taking into account the finite sense our experience gives to this word, it is more correct to say "God is not good" than it is to say "God is good." This does not mean, of course, that God is evil: it means, rather, that when the notion of good, meaningful when applied to finite beings, is predicated of God, it must be vastly expanded and thus escapes the grasp of the human mind. Similarly, if "is" is said of a person or a thing, it is more correct to say that God "is not" rather than that God "is." The transcendental ideas of goodness and being apply to God not as such, but only *secundum quid*, after a fashion, according to a certain analogy. God remains an incomprehensible mystery. The discourse about God is made up of paradoxical affirmations and includes, more especially, silence.

Emphasizing the *via negativa* refutes the idea proposed by some philosophers of the Enlightenment that Christian faith is an anthropomorphism, that God is simply the projection of human personality onto the sky. According to Thomas, we know *that* God is, but not *what* God is. God does not belong to a genus: God is not a being, not a person, not a substance – except according to a distant likeness, the difference always being greater than the similarity. What we know about the Godhead is what it is not. Even after God's self-revelation in Jesus Christ and the church's faith in God as Father, Son, and Spirit, God remains the incomprehensible and ineffable mystery transcending the cognitive power of the human mind. God is Father, Son, and Spirit only according to a certain likeness. For St Thomas, the faith of Christians reaches through and beyond the words *ad rem* to divine reality, the Really Real. We don't believe in doctrine: we believe – through and beyond doctrine – in God. Despite the highly rational or even scientific character of the *Summa*, Thomas remained the humble believer who, with Augustine, regarded theology as *docta ignorantia*, learned ignorance. When we are elevated to the prayer of union, Thomas writes, we embrace God *sicut ignotum*, as the Unknown One.

Negative theology is part and parcel of the Catholic tradition. It was endorsed by the Fourth Lateran Council in 1215 recognizing that, for every concept applied to God, the difference is always greater than the similitude.[4] Still, the ineffable One, whom we are unable to think, addresses us, thus initiating a dialogue of salvation. In his preaching Jesus has revealed to us that the invisible God, the creator of all that is, is also redeemer or savior, rescuing us from sin, the prideful self-destruction operative in our lives and our societies. Relying on Christ's words, we believe that God loves us, but what this love means escapes definition, remains mysterious, and is explored in the religious experiences of believers. Because I have experienced divine rescue so many times in my life, God as savior or reconciler is, for me, the dominant image.

I already mentioned that St Thomas held, on the basis of the Prologue to the Fourth Gospel and the Patristic tradition of the East, that, in Jesus Christ, God has embraced the whole of humanity and offers the grace of salvation to all. Yet this insight did not affect the whole of St Thomas's theology, nor did it influence the church's official teaching until the Second Vatican Council. We read in *Gaudium et spes* (no. 22): "Since Christ has died for all humans and since the ultimate vocation of humans is in fact one and divine, we ought to believe that the Holy Spirit in a manner known only to God offers to every person the possibility of being associated with the paschal mystery (Christ's death and resurrection)."

I remember an extraordinarily liberating sentence from the *Summa*, the location of which I have forgotten. Thomas wrote *Deus non ligatur sacramentis* (God is not bound by the sacraments). The full implications of this affirmation impressed me decades later when theologians and the Second Vatican Council presented the church as the great sacrament of salvation. That God is not bound to this sacrament implies that there is salvation outside the church and that God's compassion is truly universal, leaving no one out.

I was grateful for my Thomistic education, even though I did not become a Thomistic theologian.

4

The Discovery of Ecumenical Dialogue

My wish was to write a doctoral dissertation on an ecumenical topic. In the 1950s this was a controversial topic in the Catholic Church. In 1928, Pius XI had condemned the ecumenical movement started by Protestant and Anglican Christians.[1] If they truly seek Christian unity, he wrote, let them return to the Mother Church and start obeying me. Under Pius XII, Catholic theologians were still forbidden to attend ecumenical meetings. Still, some Catholic theologians in France, Germany, and Holland had become involved in ecumenical dialogue and cooperation. Already, in 1937, the great theologian Yves Congar had written his pioneering volume *Chrétiens désunis*. Yet the mainstream of Catholic theology was still unable to offer a positive interpretation of the Protestant traditions. My respect for Protestant thought, acquired at McMaster University, made me an ardent ecumenist. I eventually wrote my dissertation on the evolution of papal teaching on the ecumenical quest for Christian unity, documenting the gradual recognition, on the part of recent popes, that contemporary Protestants were not heretics. The popes acknowledged that Protestants had not rejected the ancient creeds and that, since they had inherited their faith from their ancestors, they were not personally guilty of heresy. Pius XII reluctantly recognized their genuine Christian faith, though he continued occasionally to deny it.[2]

Looking back I am somewhat ashamed of my unimaginative dissertation, written in a conformist spirit without anticipating the change of the church's official teaching a few years later. Still, I argued against certain narrow Catholic writers in North America who held that Protestants were in error and deprived of divine grace, and that Catholics should make an effort to convert them to the Catholic faith. My rather mediocre dissertation, published as a book in 1958 (and subsequently translated into French), persuaded Cardinal Bea's Secretariat for Promoting Christian Unity, at the Second Vatican Council, to have me appointed as a *peritus*, a conciliar theologian.

The exciting aspect of my doctoral studies was the participation in ecumenical dialogue and the discovery that dialogue transforms the consciousness of the participants. I describe this transformation in my essay in *Journeys* and on several other occasions.[3] Ecumenical dialogue is not a purely humanistic engagement providing the participants with new information. It is a spiritual process that changes the self-perception of the partners. The starting point is an act of love prompting us to be silent, to listen to others, to try to understand their aspirations, and to look at reality from their perspective. In the past, we listened to dissident Christians in order to detect their errors and to find arguments to correct them. Ecumenical dialogue was something quite new. In his book *I and Thou*, Martin Buber shows that listening with empathy to "the other" makes us aware of the mystery in "the other" and enables us to perceive what is deepest in him or her – a recognition that changes us, the listener, and liberates "the other." In ecumenical dialogue, listening to the others and putting oneself in their shoes is a gesture of love and humility. We discover that we have been prejudiced towards them but are now ready to open ourselves to the truth. We also discover how we are seen by others and thus gain a critical insight into ourselves. Some of the ideas of the others appeal to us, and, upon reflection, we become aware that they are part of our own tradition, even if, in the past, we largely neglected them. Because ecumenical dialogue expands commonly held truths and values and, at the same time, clarifies the differences between the participants, it allows everyone to reappropriate his or her own tradition in a new light.

Many Catholic theologians have become aware that, throughout its history, the church's reaction to communities deemed heretical was not guided by careful listening. The young Joseph Ratzinger made the bold suggestion that the stubbornness of the Church may be the principal cause of Christian disunity.[4] The Church of Christ, Ratzinger argues, was meant to be plural, embracing regional churches situated in different cultures and welcoming liturgical, spiritual, and theological pluralism. When a Christian or a Christian community had a new spiritual insight and the church, stuck in the past, refused to respect it and make room for it, the frustrated party often decided to leave the church and, in doing so, not only made its own position one-sided but also deprived the church of a precious truth. The ecumenical imperative, Joseph Ratzinger argues, demands that the Catholic Church make room within itself for the various Protestant traditions. He recognized that, in the 1960s, the Catholic Church was not ready for the internal pluralism that was its appointed destiny. This readiness, he believed, might come in the future.

In proposing this bold theory Ratzinger was probably thinking of the origin of the Lutheran Church at the time of the Reformation. A major point of disagreement between Lutherans and Catholics at that time was the doctrine of justification by faith. The issue produced passionate debates in the absence of respectful listening. Dialogue had as yet not been discovered. Yet, after the Second Vatican Council, in a culture that promoted dialogue, a Catholic-Lutheran theological commission produced a joint declaration, eventually signed by the two churches in 1999, expressing their agreement on "justification by faith," even if there remains a difference of emphasis.[5]

The Second Vatican Council's decree on ecumenism recognizes the transformative impact of ecumenical dialogue and acknowledges the ecumenical movement as the work of the Holy Spirit.[6] In this decree, the Catholic Church redefines its perception of dissident Christians: they are Christians in the full sense, members of Christ's mystical body through faith and baptism, and their churches are institutions used by the Holy Spirit to save and sanctify their members, thus participating in the ecclesial mystery. At the same time, the Catholic Church continues to see itself, in a not clearly defined sense, as the one, true Church of Christ.

The extraordinary creativity of the Second Vatican Council is largely due to the ongoing intra-ecclesial dialogue: bishops and theologians were listening to one another, freely confessing what God's Word meant to them in their historical situation, and were carried by the hope that the respectful exchange of ideas would lead to new insights acceptable to all. This dialogue, in which God's Word was present, made possible the *aggiornamento* of the Catholic Church. Pope Paul VI was so impressed by the ideas and the energy generated by the dialogue at the council that he wrote the encyclical *Ecclesiam suam* (1964), proposing that, in the future, dialogue would guide the church's relationship to the world as well its internal life. Paul VI wrote:

> How greatly We desire that dialogue with Our own children may be conducted with the fullness of faith, with charity, and with dynamic holiness. May it be of frequent occurrence and on an intimate level. May it be open and responsive to all truth, every virtue, every spiritual value that goes to make us the heritage of Christian teaching. (no. 113)

The pope wrote this in 1964 during the council, yet he did not apply it in subsequent years. In 1968, he published his encyclical *Humanae vitae* on human sexuality, without consulting the bishops of the church and in disagreement with the recommendations made by the study commission appointed by him. Since then the popes have gradually returned to the monarchical understanding of the papacy:

authority in the church again became a top-down exercise of power. Pope Francis, elected in March 2013, has returned to the spirit of the Second Vatican Council. For him, dialogue between the rulers and the ruled is an essential dimension of the church's pastoral mission.

5

The Anti-Jewish Rhetoric of Christian Preaching

Let me return to the years prior to the Second Vatican Council. In 1956, after receiving my doctorate in theology, I was invited by the association of American seminarians at the University of Fribourg to give a series of lectures on the Catholic Church's relationship to Judaism and the Jews. I had never reflected upon this topic before. At first, I followed the traditional Catholic discourse, saying that the Jews had been rejected and the Gentiles chosen, that the younger brother had been preferred to the older, Isaac to Ishmael, Jacob to Esau, yes, and even Abel to Cain. I was soon shocked by the book *Jésus et Israël*,[1] which challenged the Christian tradition.

Its author, Jules Isaac, a French historian, was a secular Jew with a sense of the spiritual. While his wife and daughter were arrested and sent to the death camps in the East, he was able to survive the war hidden by his friends. Searching for the sources of the hatred of the Jews, he made a careful study of the New Testament and the early Christian preaching, finding in them expressions of contempt for the Jews and disdain for their religion. Isaac shows in his book that this hostility was at odds with the attitude of Jesus himself as recorded in the synoptic gospels: Jesus saw himself as a Jew, obeyed the commandments, followed the rituals, and worshipped in the temple. Written during the war, *Jésus et Israël* was published in 1947.

When I read the book ten years later, I was disturbed and destabilized by the discovery of the church's anti-Jewish discourse and its cultural consequences. I felt that the ground on which I stood was about to collapse. Despite the Jewish background of my family, I had been totally insensitive to the anti-Jewish discourse associated with Christian preaching almost from the beginning.

Profoundly troubled by Jules Isaac's book, I asked myself how the message of the life of Jesus, which I believed was a story of love, had become a story of hate. As I continued my studies, I verified Jules Isaac's thesis that the proclamation of the Gospel had been accompanied almost from the beginning by words and images spreading disdain for Jews and vilifying their religion. Even the great theologians taught that, because the Jews had refused to believe in Jesus and/or because they wanted him crucified, they had been rejected by God and their religion no longer gave them access to salvation. Still, I remained convinced that the New Testament itself, the revelation of God's unconditional love, was pure and in no sense the origin of hatred and contempt.

I decided to write a book in which I would denounce the anti-Jewish discourse of the Christian tradition and, at the same time, demonstrate that the New Testament itself was not the source of this hostility. I was no exegete, my training was in theology, yet I thought that, by making use of the recognized biblical commentaries, I could shed light on a dimension of the New Testament, to which biblical scholars at that time had paid next to no attention. In my book *The Jews and the Gospel* I interpret the passages insulting to Jews in the synoptic gospels, the fourth gospel, and the letters of St Paul either as condemnations addressed by a prophet to his own people – a literary form found in the Hebrew Scriptures – or as rebukes uttered in a particular situation implying nothing about Jews in general.[2] At the same time, I was deeply troubled by Paul's remark in the First Letter to the Thessalonians and its impact on Christian teaching throughout the ages:

> The Jews have put the Lord Jesus to death, and the prophets too, and persecuted us also. Their conduct does not please God, and makes them the enemy of the whole human race, because they are hindering us from preaching to Gentiles to save them. Thus all the time they are reaching the full extent of their iniquity, but retribution has finally overtaken them. (1 Thess. 2:15–16)

In the fourth gospel, Jesus occasionally addresses the Jews as though he does not belong to them and speaks about "their Law" as though he does not observe it himself (John 8:17). He also tells the Jews that they refuse to believe him because their father is the devil (John 8:45). I reluctantly acknowledged that these passages, written decades after the destruction of Jerusalem, reflected the conflict and animosity between the church and the synagogue at that time.

When, in 1973, Rosemary Ruether asked me to write a preface to *Faith and Fratricide*,[3] her book on the Christian roots of anti-Semitism, I examined her interpretation of the harsh biblical texts and, with a heavy heart, changed my mind, conceding that already the New Testament contained the seeds of contempt for the Jews and their religion. The shadow sin falls even on the inspired Scriptures.

I have just reread, after fifty years, the introduction to my *The Jews and the Gospel* and am reminded of how deeply disturbed I was by the discovery of the church's theological anti-Semitism. It shook the very ground on which I had built my life. I now felt that I could remain a Catholic theologian only if I committed myself to working for the reform of the church's preaching about Jews and Judaism. The Jewish origin of my family now acquired significance for me. As a youth I had told myself that Hitler defined me as a Jew, even though I had never been Jewish. Now the consciousness of my Jewish origin impelled me to wrestle against the church's anti-Jewish rhetoric. Though I knew nothing of post-biblical Judaism, I realized that contempt for it had cultural consequences that made innocent people suffer. The denigration of the Jews in the church's preaching and even in its liturgy had produced a Christian culture hostile to Jews, and, while this religious anti-Judaism was different from the racist anti-Semitism of the nineteenth and twentieth centuries, a certain continuity between the two cannot be denied. Today Christians are deeply ashamed that it took the Holocaust to open the eyes of the church to the seeds of hatred spread by its preaching. I think that my Jewish background gave me the will and the energy to become a critic of the church's disdainful discourse with regard to all outsiders: dissident Christians, followers of other religions, and secular humanists. Awakened by Jules Isaac to the truth about the Christian tradition, I discovered the critical function of theology, which I further explored – as we shall see – a decade later in my study of sociology.

That I had been unaware of the church's anti-Jewish discourse and its socio-political consequences, and needed Jules Isaac's book to open my eyes, reveals something important about my own cultural inheritance: the discomfort felt by the German Jewish bourgeoisie, whether secular or baptized Christian, with regard to their Jewish origin. They saw themselves as Germans active in making German culture flourish, and they saw no positive relation at all between themselves and the Jewish tradition. They tended to look down upon the unassimilated Jews of Eastern Europe and despised the Yiddish language spoken by them, without realizing how close this attitude was to anti-Semitic prejudice. Because of this inheritance, I think, I did not have the sensitivity to recognize the church's anti-Jewish rhetoric for what it was. I needed Jules Isaac's awakening call.

In public lectures I have often expressed my regret that I never sent my book to Jules Isaac and told him how much his work meant to me. The Toronto lawyer Norman Tobias, a believing Jew with a doctorate in religious studies, wrote a dissertation on Jules Isaac's impact on the Catholic Church, which is about to be published as a book.[4] Working in the archives of Jules Isaac in France in 2014, he discovered that I had actually been in touch with the French scholar. Tobias found that, in the spring of 1961, I had sent a copy of *The*

Jews and the Gospel to Isaac, who mentioned his reaction to it in a letter to a friend: "I have just received a book that I draw to your attention, *The Jews and the Gospel* by Gregory Baum. To my great surprise, I am front and center stage from the very first page, but in a most sympathetic light; it was the reading of *Jésus et Israël* that is the impetus of this Catholic work." Tobias found that Isaac sent me a letter of thanks, to which I replied on 26 July 1961, telling him that his *Jésus et Israël* opened my eyes and that, in my endeavour to purify the preaching of the Gospel of the malevolent fables of the past, I am his follower.[5]

It is troubling to realize that I would have willingly taken an oath that I have never been in touch with Jules Isaac. This reminder of the fallibility of my memory compels me to acknowledge a certain concern for the reliability of some of the things I recount in this book. That said, I have done my best to be accurate and truthful.

Opposition to Christian anti-Semitism, I soon discovered, was a topic closely related to the ecumenical movement. Since anti-Jewish prejudice was mediated by the Catholic as well as the Protestant traditions, Catholic and Protestant theologians disturbed by this inheritance now cooperated in wrestling against it. Working on my book in the late 1950s, I became acquainted with a small movement of Christian thinkers who reacted to the Holocaust by urging the Christian churches to rethink their relationship to the Jews and to modify their official teaching. A first international meeting had taken place in 1947 at Seelisberg in Switzerland, bringing together over fifty Protestant and Catholic Christians, all of whom were troubled by the anguishing question of whether or not there was a causal relation between the Church's theological anti-Judaism and the racist anti-Semitism that began in the nineteenth century and climaxed in the Holocaust. Present at Seelisberg were also a number of Jewish thinkers, including Jules Isaac. The participants discussed the passages of the New Testament that have been read as expressing hostility to Jews, and they elaborated concrete proposals – the so-called

Ten Points of Seelisberg. These proposals were addressed to the churches and were to aid them in teaching the biblical message in a manner that fostered respect for Jews and their religion.[6] They were promoted by centres of Christian-Jewish cooperation in France, Germany, England, and Holland and, a few years later, influenced the teaching of the Second Vatican Council.

I mentioned earlier that, in 1960, John XXIII appointed me a *peritus* of the Secretariat for Promoting Christian Unity, one of the commissions set up to prepare and accompany the Second Vatican Council. At our first meeting in Rome in November 1960, Cardinal Bea told us that the pope, whom he had just met, had asked the secretariat to prepare, in addition to its ecumenical texts, a draft document on the church's relation to the Jews. Many years later, I read that Jules Isaac, then an old man, had had an interview with John XXIII in August 1960, during which the pope had promised that the council would renew the church's relationship to the Jews. Cardinal Bea asked us to give him names of theologians familiar with this issue, whom he might appoint as *periti*. After the meeting I told the cardinal (speaking to him in my mother tongue) that I had just written a book on the topic; I also gave him the name of John Oesterreicher, a priest scholar and the founder of the Seaton Hall Institute for Judeo-Christian Studies, who, in the 1930s, had already started to wrestle against Christian anti-Semitism. From a biography of Cardinal Bea,[7] published in 2000, I learned that the cardinal, a German Jesuit, had been acquainted with the Seelisberg movement, had been in conversation with many Jewish personalities, and was passionately committed to reforming the church's teaching on the Jews.

It is not my intention to tell the long story of how the statement on Christian-Jewish relations was composed by the secretariat, discussed at the council, opposed by certain groups in the church, rewritten several times, and eventually made part of a wider statement, the Declaration of the Church's Relation to the World Religions (*Nostra aetate*). The literature on this topic is ample.[8]

I just wish to mention one important point: *Nostra aetate* recognizes that the ancient divine covenant mediated by Moses continues to be a source of truth and grace for Jewish people today. This is new teaching. The early Christian writers had argued that, because of their refusal to believe in Jesus Christ, the Jews had fallen into darkness and lost their spiritual inheritance; yet taking into account the Pauline passage "The gifts and the call of God are irrevocable" (Rom. 11:28), the early Christian writers held that the Jews would not lose themselves in the world but, even while living in darkness, would remain God's first-loved people, destined to turn to their messiah and be saved before the end of time. *Nostra aetate* offers a different interpretation of the Pauline teaching. Because God's call is without repentance and because the Jews remain God's first-loved people, the Second Vatican Council teaches that God's ancient covenant with the Jews remains valid and is for them the source of truth and grace. Jews find their salvation in Judaism. This teaching implies that there is no theological justification for a Christian mission to covert Jews to Christianity.

This conciliar interpretation of the Pauline passage "God has not abandoned his people" (Rom. 11:1) is new. None of the books and commentaries I consulted when writing *The Jews and the Gospel* had interpreted this passage as implying the ongoing validity of the ancient covenant. At the council we read the Pauline message following a post-Holocaust hermeneutics – that is to say, avoiding any biblical interpretation that would humiliate and do harm to the Jews of today. I fully accepted the new teaching. In the revised edition of my book, now entitled *Is the New Testament Antisemitic?* and published in 1965, I inserted the new interpretation, indicating in a new preface the pages on which I had made these changes.

While I was grateful and overjoyed that the Second Vatican Council had changed the church's teaching on Jews and Judaism, I remained deeply troubled by the anti-Jewish rhetoric present in Christian preaching through the centuries. It revealed to me the ambiguity of the Christian religion and, more widely, of religion in general. The truths and virtues promoted by religion are accompanied by the potential for producing contempt for outsiders. Every religion divides humanity into "us" and "them" and looks upon the outsiders as inferior. Every religion is tempted to see itself as uniquely true and to promote itself by slandering the religion of others. Many years later, I mentioned in a book of mine that I had learned the pejorative meaning of ideology not from Karl Marx but, rather, from my study of the church's anti-Jewish discourse – the distortion of truth in favour of the interests of an institution.

Some ancient Christian authors were aware of the church's ambiguous historical reality, especially when it became the official religion of the Roman Empire. The church was holy because Christ had adopted it as his body, forgave its sins, and continued to renew it; at the same time, the church was unholy because it allied itself with the rulers and served their interests. In an essay published in 1961, provocatively entitled *Casta Meretrix* (The Chaste Whore), Urs von Balthasar records the paradoxical language used by a number of church fathers to reveal the ambivalent nature of the church. Luther's paradoxical *simul justus et peccator* (both holy and sinful) may be meaningfully applied to the church itself.

I remember an occasion when Joseph Ratzinger made startling use of this paradoxical language. I have often spoken of this in my lectures, but I don't believe I have ever written it down. At noon, after the session of the council in St Peter's Basilica, I usually went to the press conference in English where we, the theologians, would interpret for the press what had happened at the morning session. Sometimes I joined a group of German *periti* who remained in the basilica, standing in a circle under its great cupola. On one occasion, in a context I do not remember, Joseph Ratzinger said, pointing to the copula: "We read there in giant letters *Tu es Petrus* (Thou art Peter, Matt. 6:18); to make this theologically correct, one would have to add *Retro Satana* (Get thee behind me Satan, Matt. 16:23)." Ratzinger used the ancient Catholic paradoxical language to say that Peter, the appointed rock whose purpose is to protect the Church's unity, is also a potential obstacle for the realization of this unity.

6

The Second Vatican Council

In 1959, I returned to Canada from Fribourg. My appointment was to give weekend retreats at Marylake, the Augustinian monastery north of Toronto. I was almost immediately invited to teach at the Basilian seminary on the campus of St Michael's College, and the Augustinians were good enough to allow me to live on the campus in downtown Toronto. I soon became a professor at St Michael's College and remained there till 1986.

A year after my arrival, in 1960, I received a letter signed by Pope John XXIII appointing me as a *peritus* at the Secretariat for Promoting Christian Unity. I was amazed. I was also happy and grateful. I supposed it was my dissertation published as a book that persuaded Cardinal Bea, the president of the secretariat, and his assistant, Monsignor Willebrands, to have me appointed.

Working at the secretariat before and during the Second Vatican Council was a dramatic happening, a spiritual experience, a theological adventure, an unmerited privilege, and an unforgettable time of intense living. We at the secretariat were excited by the council's grappling with a new self-understanding of the Catholic Church. We participated in the conciliar debate over the meaning of divine revelation in modern society and over the nature of the church's mission in the world.

At the council, the Catholic Church, listening anew to God's Word, was in conversation with itself. Composing the conciliar documents involved a continual exchange of ideas among the bishops and the appointed theologians. We all listened, studied, worked hard, and prayed. There was great freedom of thought. For us at the secretariat, the conversation included the non-Catholic Christian observers who had been invited to attend the council. Once a week we held a meeting with them, listened to their observations, and reported them to Cardinal Bea, who regarded the observers as part of the Christian family and paid attention their ideas.

Many years later, I described the intense dialogue and communication going on at the Second Vatican Council as a form of "effervescence." This term was used by the French sociologist Émile Durkheim to account for the heightened consciousness and enhanced vitality that occur at solemn gatherings of tribes whose members live dispersed over a wide territory. It was the heightened religious awareness that allowed the bishops to introduce bold changes into the church's official teaching. I will never forget the heightened consciousness I experienced with my theological colleagues, having the council in mind from morning to night – as we celebrated an early mass, engaged in dialogue with bishops, examined proposed conciliar texts, carried on conversations with the non-Catholic Observers, and, above all, worked at the secretariat on the formulation of our draft documents – feeling all the time that this was a moment of grace, a kairos, a tryst of the Holy Spirit.

It is not my intention to tell the story of the Second Vatican Council, nor to describe my own work as a theologian at the Secretariat for Promoting Christian Unity.[1] I simply wish to mention the experiences that made me look upon the council as a turning point in the history of Catholicism.[2] As the secretariat had been assigned to produce draft documents on three controversial topics – religious liberty, ecumenism, and interreligious cooperation – it decided to take into account the new self-understanding emerging among many

Catholics and produce draft documents that modified the papal teaching of the past. These documents generated heated debates at the council. They were discussed, criticized, and several times rewritten; yet, at the end, they received the approval of the overwhelming majority of the bishops.

As I am writing these lines, I remember the first meeting of the Secretariat for Promoting Christian Unity in November 1960, when Cardinal Bea impressed upon us the importance of convincing the Catholic bishops of the turn to ecumenism. To reach them, the cardinal wanted the members of the secretariat, upon returning to their respective countries, to publish articles, give public lectures, write to newspapers, and speak on radio and television about the new Catholic openness to ecumenism. "If we have an impact on public opinion in the Church," the cardinal said, "the bishops will listen." He himself would give public lectures and publish them in *La documentation catholique*. He invited us to use his speeches as "umbrellas" to protect us if our message was challenged by conservative ecclesiastics.

The dialogue, the discussion, and the debates at the Second Vatican Council eventually convinced the overwhelming majority of the Council Fathers to modify the church's official teaching on the above-mentioned controversial topics. Transcending the condemnation of religious liberty pronounced by the popes of the nineteenth century, the declaration on religious liberty proclaimed the freedom of religion as firmly rooted in natural Law. Transcending the age-old designation of dissident Christians as schismatics or heretics, the decree on ecumenism recognized them as Christian believers, members of Christ's mystical body, and it recognized their Churches as institutions used by the Spirit to save and sanctify their adherents, even if the Catholic Church continued to see itself, in some undefined way, as the one true Church of Christ. Transcending Pius XI's condemnation of the ecumenical movement, the decree on ecumenism now blessed this movement, recognizing it as a work of the Holy Spirit and calling upon Catholics to join it. The declaration on the church's relation to the non-Christian religions, *Nostra aeate*, acknowledged that the ancient Covenant made with the people of Israel has retained its validity and is the source of divine grace for Jews in the present. *Nostra aetate* deplores the anti-Semitism of the past and the present, and it asks Catholics to cultivate friendship, dialogue, and cooperation with Jews. It also expresses the church's respect for the world religions: they share many truths and values with the Catholic Church and may even be affected by the rays of the Eternal Light that is fully revealed in Jesus Christ. This is an extraordinary leap from the idea expressed in 1919 by Benedict XV's apostolic letter *Maximum illud*, which holds that pagans "live in ignorance of God, and thus, bound by chains of blind and violent desires, are enslaved in the most hideous of all forms of slavery, the service of Satan."[3] The doctrinal development recorded in these three documents is supported by biblical reflections that take into account the present-day context; it is at the same time related to the church's emerging self-understanding as witnessed in *Gaudium et spes*, the conciliar document on the church in the modern world.

The conciliar statements that modified the teaching of the magisterium actually preserved and deepened the church's unchanging doctrine that God the Father loves all human beings, that God the Son has redeemed the entire human family, and that God the Spirit, blowing where it will, is ever renewing the face of the earth. The Second Vatican Council reaffirmed the substance of Catholic faith and upheld the ancient creeds. New and contemporary was this openness of the church to the pluralistic world, a development that seemed to us at the Secretariat for Promoting Christian Unity as a conversion made in fidelity to God's Word, under the impulse of the Spirit and in conformity with the church's mission in the world. On the deepest level there was unbroken continuity.

Some Catholics have criticized the Second Vatican Council because it was preoccupied with rethinking the church's nature and mission and said next to nothing about God, a topic of much greater importance. It is true that no conciliar documents deal with the mystery of God and the questions raised about God by contemporary men and women. Yet these critics did not notice that several conciliar documents contain significant passages announcing the liberating message of God's redemptive immanence in the world. Rereading the Scriptures and the Catholic tradition, the council recognized that God is present in human history as Creator and Redeemer not only in the church, where the Gospel is proclaimed, believed, and celebrated, but also in a more hidden way, in the world religions and wise secular traditions that offer insight and grace to every human being. Despite the sin of the world, which casts a shadow even on the church, the Gospel proclaims that God is graciously at work in people's lives, offering rescue, truth, hope, and love. According to the conciliar teaching, this is true even for atheists: they, too, are summoned in their lives to love their neighbour, transcend utilitarian self-interest, and forget themselves in the service of others.

The new perception of God has changed the church's relation to the world and its attitude towards outsiders. For many centuries Catholics believed that human beings, wounded by the inherited sin, were destined to eternal punishment unless they listened to the church's message and became believing Catholics. This was known as *Extra ecclesiam nulla salus* (no salvation outside the church). Catholics believed that pagans, Jews, and heretics lived in the shadow of darkness, destined for punishment in hell. This teaching was confirmed by the Council of Florence in the fifteenth century. Catholic missionaries in foreign lands were convinced that the Gospel they preached promised to rescue the pagan population from divine condemnation. Catholics believed that babies who died without baptism were excluded from God's grace since they had inherited the sin of Adam. Since assigning their souls to the fires of hell seemed callous, theologians invented a special state, called limbo, where these souls suffered no physical torment, their only punishment being the exclusion from God's love. While a current in the Catholic theological tradition did recognize the gift of God's grace beyond the church, the church's official teaching and the dominant Catholic piety regarded the church as the single community that offered God's forgiveness to sinful humanity. The church was the body of Christ, in which humans found their salvation.

The teaching of the Second Vatican Council offered a different interpretation of Catholicism. In Jesus Christ, the council now recognized, God had embraced the whole of sinful humanity. In the vocabulary of St Thomas, Christ was not only the head of the church but also the head of humanity, and the grace of the head (*gratia capitis*) addressed each human person.[4] The church is the unique community wherein the mystery of salvation is believed, proclaimed, and celebrated, but this mystery, this transcendent enlightening and transforming power, is mediated by the wisdom inherent in the world's religious and cultural traditions. Because God embraced the whole of humanity in Christ, there is no reason to worry about the fate of babies who die without baptism. After the council, the church's official teaching dropped the entire idea of limbo.[5]

The church's mission to proclaim the Gospel so that the world may believe is now accompanied by another mission – the social mission to extend its solidarity to humanity, especially to the poor, the oppressed, and the afflicted, and to cooperate with people of good will in the struggle for justice and peace. The church's social mission serves the common good of humanity so that God's will may be done on Earth. How the Church's two missions are related to one another is an issue that the Second Vatican Council did not resolve. As we see further on, this issue is still being hotly debated decades later.

Catholic theologians try to reconcile the new teaching with the church's older tradition. They try to show in what sense the new interpretations are a continuation of the teaching inherited from the past. I have consistently argued that, in response to troubling questions raised by the Holocaust, the atomic bomb, and the carpet bombing of civilians – as well as by the universal protests against colonialism and economic domination – the Catholic Church, listening anew to God's Word in Scripture, heard the divine call to extend its love to all human beings. The *agape* of the New Testament now includes solidarity with the victims of human malice and social injustice. Catholics now emphasize an aspect of the Gospel that previously attracted little attention. I refer to this as "shifting the focus of the Gospel."[6] Yet shifting the focus – that is, making central God's unconditional love for humanity – obliges the church to reinterpret its entire teaching in the light of this focus.

When we discussed these matters at the board of directors of *Concilium* (of which I was a member from 1970 to 1990), Hans Küng made a proposal that convinced many of us and that he subsequently explored in several books. He adapted the idea of "paradigm shift," introduced by Thomas Kuhn to interpret the changes of explanatory models in the evolution of the natural sciences, to theology. Küng argued that, when the inherited form of Catholicism was no longer able to respond to the challenges of modern society, thoughtful Catholics became restless, searched for new answers, reread the Scriptures, studied contemporary thought, and had new religious experiences. They came to be gripped by a new perception of Catholicism. What occurred, Küng argued, amounted to a paradigm shift within the Catholic tradition, an internal restructuring of the totality, a shift that was subsequently endorsed by the Second Vatican Council. Here the substance of faith remains identical, but the form and the face of Catholicism have changed. The council reinterpreted the church's teaching and practice, remaining faithful to its divine origin but permitting it to transmit the Gospel effectively in today's troubled world.

Needless to say, the meaning of paradigm shift in the history of the sciences is not the same as it is in ecclesiology. A paradigm shift in the sciences is produced by researchers who discover that the inherited theory no longer explains the experimental findings, while a paradigm shift in the Christian Church is a gift of the Spirit: it is something that happens, provoked by new questions, sustained by new religious experiences, and clarified by theological thought.

Since Hans Küng made the proposal over forty years ago, the idea of paradigm shift has been widely accepted in the field of religious studies and has been used to render an account of the changes experienced by religions as they enter into radically altered historical circumstances. Küng himself has applied this idea in his major historical studies of Christianity,[7] Judaism,[8] and Islam.[9]

According to Thomas Kuhn, the proposal of a new paradigm in the natural sciences provokes the opposition of scientists attached to the inherited theory. The emergence of a new paradigm of Catholicism has had a similar effect: it has provoked an opposition among many Catholics – bishops, priests, and lay men and women attached to the Catholicism of yesterday. Küng's theological proposal is useful because it offers a persuasive explanation of the new vision of Catholicism that emerged at the Second Vatican Council as well as of the subsequent conflicts within the Catholic Church. I must mention in this context that, in order to obtain the approval of the majority of bishops at the council, certain conciliar documents that clearly expressed the new paradigm were modified by the insertion of passages that reflected the older paradigm. Thus, the conciliar documents are not free of internal contradictions. Catholics attached to the Catholicism of yesterday appeal to the inserted passages and interpret the church's turn to the world simply as an exercise in public relations, a diplomatic gesture to create good will.

In the year 2000, Cardinal Joseph Ratzinger, at that time president of the Roman Congregation of the Doctrine of the Faith, published the instruction *Dominus Jesus*, claiming that the Second Vatican Council had not modified the church's self-understanding. Catholics must remember, he wrote, that religious pluralism exists only in fact (de facto), while in principle (de jure) there exists only one religion – Roman Catholicism. The cardinal also argued that interreligious dialogue tends to undermine the church's evangelizing mission.

Catholics involved in this dialogue, he insisted, must not forget that the ultimate aim of these encounters is the conversion of their partners to the Catholic faith.

When he became Pope Benedict XVI, Joseph Ratzinger continued to worry that Catholics were interpreting the conciliar teaching as a moment of discontinuity of the Catholic tradition, transcending the church's teaching throughout the ages. In a speech delivered to the Roman Curia, he criticized the reading of the conciliar documents guided by "a hermeneutic of discontinuity" and recommended instead "a hermeneutic of reform" sensitive to the common ground of the new and the older teachings.[10] I would argue that Hans Küng's idea of paradigm shifts in religious traditions recognizes the underlying continuity in the emergence of the new. Earlier, I mention that the new conciliar teaching is grounded in the church's ancient Trinitarian theology. To describe the continuity in the evolution of the church's teaching, I have often used the terms "difference" and "retrieval," taken from the vocabulary of the Frankfurt School: the new teaching is "different" from the old, yet it is verified by "retrieving" an ancient teaching read in a new light. The idea that God embraced the whole of humanity in Jesus Christ is different from the doctrine *extra ecclesiam nulla salus*, but the new teaching retrieves the ancient meaning of divine Incarnation held by several church fathers and the message of the liturgical antiphon *Ubi caritas et amor, Deus ibi est* (Where there is love and charity, there is God). Further on, we see that, over the years, Pope Benedict's understanding of religious pluralism and interreligious dialogue has evolved in remarkable fashion.[11]

7

Salvation in Secular Life

Let me return to my years at Fribourg.[1] After my ordination to the priesthood in 1954 and the conferral of my doctorate in 1956, I continued my studies in the monastery during the week and served every weekend in a parish at Neuchâtel. My contact with people outside of the monastic environment, some of them non-believers, made a great impression on me. I began to feel that people everywhere, be they believers or not, share the same existential drama: they want to be good but are handicapped by their selfishness; yet, at certain moments, they find the strength to be good (which is what they really want). People in search of the truth are misled by lies and ideologies, yet at certain moments they are allowed to see clearly. I felt that the existential struggle inscribed in human life is expressed in the biblical teaching of creation, sin, and grace. People are oriented towards the true and the good by their nature, which is created by God, yet they are prevented from doing what they want by the egotism or the pride that dwells within them; only when addressed by the divine summons are they able to see clearly and turn with love to their neighbour.

Reflections of this kind greatly disturbed me because the church's teaching at the time made a clear distinction between the "natural life" of people in the world and the "supernatural life" of believers, elevated by their faith and baptism in Jesus Christ. Christian life was a higher life sustained by the Spirit, not accessible to people outside the church. I have mentioned that, in my early years in the monastery, I was convinced that, without faith in Jesus Christ, there was no true life.

What made me question this teaching was also my study of the prejudices against the Jews. I realized that the persons who wrestled against anti-Semitism in the nineteenth and twentieth centuries were, for the most part, secular people committed to human rights and social equality, often members of socialist parties. The courageous Germans who resisted the Nazi regime were for the greater part nonbelievers, and the Christians among them did not have the support of their own church. In fact, the record of the two German churches in Hitler's Germany is not impressive. After the war, social scientists studied the Germans and Poles who risked their lives by hiding Jews, saving them from extermination: some of these brave persons were motivated by Christian values, some by secular values. The Holy Spirit blows where it wills.

In his *A Secular Age*, published in 2007, Charles Taylor argues that the immanent humanism devoid of any reference to transcendence, proposed by the Dutch philosophers Justus Lipsius and Hugo Grotius in the seventeenth century, was a creative humanistic response to the religious wars in Europe and the narrow limits of Christian charity.[2] Christians had no love for heretics, Jews, or pagans; their charity stopped at the borders of the church. The two Dutch thinkers were deists: they believed that God had given human beings intelligence, enabling them to think, learn, and listen to one another and, together, to formulate a set of norms that would allow all men and women to live together in peace and justice. Their arguments, Taylor shows, were not utilitarian. They held that, built into human reason, was a benevolent thrust that opposed the exclusion of any group of humans from universal care – a rational beneficence that was wider than the idea of Christian charity practised at that time. According to Charles Taylor, this immanent humanism was, for many thoughtful people, a dignified alternative to Christianity and thus contributed to the secularization of European society.

Already at the end of my stay in Fribourg in the late 1950s, I became convinced that the gift of God's grace prompting people to love their neighbour was as universal as the sin that breeds their self-centredness. This is what I wrote in the introduction to *Man Becoming*:

> At the end of the fifties, when these convictions became strong in me, I did not know how to relate them to orthodox Catholic doctrine. I even wondered if I could remain a Catholic. It was then that I began to read the works of Karl Rahner. This original thinker, this great theologian presented a theological anthropology which was in harmony with my own experience of life. It is possible, according to Rahner, to affirm the uniqueness of the Church and at the same time to hold that the mystery of new life is operative in every single human being. Jesus Christ has revealed what takes place in the heart of every person. The Church proclaims the mystery of redemption that is universal and constitutive of human history.[3]

The article in the *Summa* of St Thomas on the salvation offered to every human being, which scandalized me when I heard about it in a lecture in 1946, now became an important theological witness for me. As I mentioned above, this teaching represents an ancient tradition going back to the Eastern church fathers of the third and fourth centuries. They cited the biblical passage "The true Light enlightens every human who comes into the world" (John 1:9) as the pledge that God's eternal Word resounded in the whole of human history. This ancient interpretation had been mediated to St Thomas by John Damascene, an eighth-century Eastern theologian. God's offer of grace is as universal as sin. According to St Paul, "where sin has abounded, grace has abounded even more" (Rom. 5:20). The drama of human existence is the struggle between sin and grace.

While the church is the only community in which the redemptive mystery is confessed, proclaimed, and celebrated, this mystery is operative in the whole of humanity, in individual persons and in their communities. The church is not an oasis of salvation in a desert of perdition: salvation is offered throughout the world, mediated by religious traditions, humanistic cultures, and people's experience of solidarity. The first means of grace is human life itself.

That God's offer of new life is universal was confirmed by the Second Vatican Council in a passage already quoted above but worth repeating here:

> Since Christ died for all humans and since their ultimate vocation is in fact one and divine, we ought to believe that the Holy Spirit in a manner known only to God offers to every person the possibility of being associated with the paschal mystery (the death and resurrection of Jesus).[4]

8

My Book *Man Becoming*

After the Second Vatican Council, in the late 1960s, while teaching theology at St Michael's College in Toronto, I discovered the thought of the French philosopher Maurice Blondel. His writings at the end of the nineteenth century had initiated an entirely new way of thinking about God's presence in human history. Karl Rahner, whom I just mentioned, was affected by Blondel's philosophy. Blondel had protested against theologies that presented God as the Father in heaven, the omnipotent sovereign above history, the supreme Being external to human life, whose grace descended upon humans from above. In these theologies God is seen as extrinsic to human history, intervening at times to lift people up to a higher order. Blondel named these theologies "extrinsicist." For him, God was not an outsider to human life; rather, God was involved in people's efforts to become themselves and to constitute their world. The Gospel is not a message about a higher sphere: it addresses the challenge experienced by people in this world. Blondel made the provocative remark that if an angel were to come to his office with a message about a higher world, he would refuse to listen to it, for his calling as a human being (le métier d'homme) was to deal with life in *this* world.

In a detailed philosophical phenomenology, Blondel describes an internal dynamics that moves human beings to ever wider concerns until they reach the limits of their finitude and hear the call to surrender themselves to the Infinite. This internal dynamics is not that of the intellect seeking deeper truth; it is, according to Blondel, the dynamics of the will seeking ever greater self-realization through continued action. It is there, in their willing, that God is present to human beings, and it is in their actions that they say Yes to the divine presence.

Blondel's rejection of "extrinsicism" was shared two generations later by Karl Rahner, Henri de Lubac, and the so-called Transcendental Thomists: they, too, regarded God's self-donation as present in the lives of human beings, sustaining their entry into the fullness of their humanity. Blondel's original idea was that truth is present in action: the trusting surrender to God takes place in what people do. Blondel argued that, implicit in action, is a cognitive dimension, a tacit insight, ready to be made explicit knowledge. The French philosopher did not belittle the intellectual life; on the contrary, he held that, in reflecting on what we do, our intelligence is able to clarify the insight implicit in our actions.

Blondel's idea that human beings are internally impelled to encounter divine transcendence did not convince me. Not only did I find his phenomenology too abstract, but I also failed to be persuaded that implicit in people's lives is an orientation that leads them to pursue the question of God. In a recent study of Fernand Dumont and other theologians in Quebec, I discovered that many of them share Blondel's idea that the internal logic of human striving moves people towards an encounter with Transcendence.[1] Again, I do not share this position: I know too many people committed to justice and solidarity who do not have a religious bone in their body.

At the same time, I was greatly excited by Blondel's rejection of extrinsicism and his idea of the divine presence in human action. I decided to write *Man Becoming* to show that people encounter Transcendence in their lives not as the result of a dynamics internal to them but, rather, as a response to God's free and unmerited initiative. Standing in the Augustinian tradition, I emphasize the gratuity of God's self-donation. Had I written the book after my encounter with feminist theology, I would have chosen a different title; however, its theological proposal is that both men and women constitute themselves through "dialogue" and "communion" and, in so doing, are visited by God.

"Dialogue" here refers to listening and responding to the words addressed to us, which enables us to enter upon our humanity. This dialogue starts with the words spoken by our mother and other members of our family, to which we make an effort to respond. An ongoing conversation teaches us our language and offers us the ideas that allow us to interpret our experience and to entertain relationships with other people. Dialogue permits us to grow, expand our perception, and enter upon a development that never stops. I interpret the Good News to mean that, at crucial moments in this dialogue, we are addressed by God's Word, enabling us to see the truth about ourselves and our world and converting us to greater love.

In my theological proposal "communion" refers to what takes place among people who share the same values, trust one another, and support one another in their attempts to realize themselves. This starts in the family and later takes place in the groups or communities with which we identify. Communion generates other-love, transforms the participants, and enables them to extend their solidarity to people in need. This widening of the heart cannot be produced by will power. I interpret the Good News to mean that people in communion are visited by the Spirit. Through dialogue and communion, we learn to forget ourselves, serve the well-being of others, and promote the common good, thus entering more fully into our own humanity. This transformation is possible because dialogue and communion are sustained by the Word and the Holy Spirit. In other words, human self-making is grounded in the triune God.

Inspired by Blondel, yet using a different theological approach, *Man Becoming* fosters a new religious imagination. Instead of envisaging God as heavenly Father or supreme Being above the world, we learn to imagine God as the Ground that carries us, the Summons that empowers us, and the Light that illumines our way. Here we do not have to leave history to encounter the Absolute: God is personally present in history as Life, Light, and Love, as Origin, Word, and Spirit. Instead of the great Outsider who occasionally intervenes in human life, God is here envisaged as the great Insider sustaining us as we struggle to fulfill our human vocation. Needless to say, the claim that God is immanent in human history does not imply that God is either determined by history or imprisoned in it. The mode of divine immanence is transcendence.

Blondel was the first Catholic thinker who taught that divine revelation is not information about another world but, rather, an initiation into a new self-understanding and a new way of being and acting in the world. I call this the Blondelian shift.[2] Thanks to God's self-revelation in Jesus Christ we recognize ourselves as sinful and broken, yet as divinely summoned and empowered to trust and to love. While St Thomas tries to understand human life by reflecting on human nature, Blondel's thought is more existential: he tries to understand human life by reflecting upon people's struggles to uncover their human potential, widen their spiritual horizon, and realize themselves in the surrender to the Infinite. For Blondel, the human decision about God is not made in thought but in action, in people's daily efforts to become themselves and to enter upon their destiny.

This theology of God, often called "panentheism," differs from traditional theism. Panentheism puts greater emphasis on God's immanence. Here, God is never simply over against us; God is already present in our turning to God. Here, God is never simply a Thou to whom we pray since God is already present as the Grace that enables us to pray. While we used to make a clear distinction between the sacred and the profane, the Blondelian shift makes us aware that the secular – daily life – is the locus of God's self-communication. In *Man Becoming*, I argue that, in contemporary culture, many Christians discern God's presence in their daily experiences, which may include the voice of conscience, the openness to truth, the bond of solidarity, the joy of friendship, enrichment through dialogue, and/or commitment to social justice.

The emphasis on God's presence in human interactions did not make me forget the power of evil. In *Man Becoming*, I reflect on "the demonic" in personal life and human history.[3] A few years later, reflecting on the Holocaust, the topic of evil assumed greater importance for me. But already in the 1960s I failed to be persuaded by Pierre Teilhard de Chardin's evolutionary interpretation of the Christian message: the New Testament does not tell us how human history will end – in fulfilment or in catastrophe.

My theological proposal of human self-making through dialogue and communion was influenced by my experience of ecumenical dialogue and its power to transform the self-understanding of all partners. A yet stronger influence on my theological proposal was my participation in a psychotherapeutic movement called Communication Therapy (subsequently renamed Therafields), which was founded in Toronto in the early 1960s. It was started by a gifted psychoanalyst from Great Britain and was supported by a group of young men and women whom she had trained, many of whom were Catholics belonging to various religious orders. In addition to private sessions, it offered group therapy, the opportunity to live together in communities, and therapeutic approaches to work and artistic creation. Eventually, it involved as many as nine hundred participants.

I was greatly impressed by the experience shared by many that engagement in dialogue and communion allowed participants to come to greater self-knowledge, escape from their destructive impulses, discover new energies, and enter more deeply into their humanity. The therapeutic word often produces resistance, yet, if supported by a community of friends, people allow themselves to be challenged, take a critical look at themselves, and open themselves to the vital resources hidden in their lives. As a theologian in the Augustinian tradition, I recognized a redemptive dimension in the therapeutic process. To leave a destructive past behind and become capable of living freely and finding a purpose – to work, to love, to be concerned about others, and be patient in adversity – this appeared to me the fruit of God's redemptive immanence. To become psychologically well, to be delivered from self-pity, envy, narcissism and resentment, and to be rendered capable of loving others and acting with them to reconstruct society – this appeared to me as the work of the Spirit. I became convinced that the secular is not as secular as it looks. People's struggle to be well – to find the truth and do the good – is the fruit of God's immanence as Word and Spirit.

My friend Grant Goodbrand wrote a history of Therafields that presents an account of its ideas and its institutional development.[4] In his final chapter on the collapse of the movement in the early 1980s, he offers an explanation with which I disagree. He overlooks the psychic decline of the woman who founded the movement. He also fails to draw attention to the men and women who became flourishing personalities through their engagement in Therafields. When the movement closed its doors, several of the therapists started a new venture, the Toronto Centre for Training in Psychotherapy, which is still going strong. After my wife and I moved to Montreal, we used to return to Toronto for Christmas to join the festive party at Grant's house where twenty or so people, former members of Therafields, met to reaffirm their common friendship. I always marvel at these men and women: they are dedicated, intelligent, generous, and cheerful. Something very good has happened in their lives. A special friendship binds me to Grant and his wife Marion and to Philip and his wife Sharon.

In *Man Becoming* I was not yet aware of the political dimension of the Gospel. I did not see, as yet, that humans are called to assume responsibility for their world. How I made this important discovery is something I discuss further on.

9

God Is Light

In *Man Becoming* I embrace the idea that God is all good, the purest light "in whom there is no darkness" (1 John 1:5), and I argue that God may not be regarded as the author of evil. The artisans of evil are we ourselves. While God does not *will* evil, many ecclesiastical and theological texts propose that God *permits* evil to happen. Since God is omnipotent, the theologians argue, evil things cannot happen unless God has permitted them. I did not accept this idea when writing *Man Becoming*, nor did I accept it some years later when dealing with the question of whether Auschwitz had a place in divine providence.

Is it possible to believe in God after Auschwitz? Jews have asked this question in anguish, and so have many Christians. The effort to respond to it has produced an important debate among Jewish and Christians theologians.[1] A few traditionalist Jewish thinkers hold that the Holocaust was a divine punishment for the refusal of modern, assimilated Jews to obey the Law – an outrageous idea, according to most Jewish thinkers. Thoughtful conservative Jewish and Christian thinkers argue that, since God's providence is mysterious and incomprehensible to us, we have no explanation for why God has permitted torture and murder and why God did not intervene to stop the Holocaust. "We cannot peer into God's mysterious plan – we see only piecemeal, and we would be wrong to set ourselves up as judges of God and history." These words were uttered by Benedict XVI in his memorable address at Auschwitz on 28 May 2006.

Several theologians, both Jewish and Christian, are unwilling to concede that the Holocaust has a place in divine providence. Some even hint that they could not remain believers if they believed that God had permitted this massive horror to happen. Rethinking the idea of divine omnipotence, these theologians argue that God does not rule world from above like a heavenly king in control of his subjects. Late medieval Jewish kabbala had already relativized divine omnipotence. It proposed the idea that, in creating the world and humans within it, God had contracted the divine being to make room for the created order and restricted divine omnipotence to concede freedom to human beings. People are free to resist God's will, and the evil they do is in no sense part of God's providence. The idea of God's self-emptying, or *kenosis* (the Greek word for emptiness), is taken up by several contemporary Protestant and Catholic theologians, most famously by Jürgen Moltmann, who remembers that Jesus "emptied himself, taking the form of a slave, becoming as human beings are" (Phil. 2:7). Since Jesus is the image of the Father, we argue, it is not inappropriate to speak of *kenosis* in the Godhead. Quite independently, Simone Weil came to write these two sentences: "God's creative love that keeps us in existence is not only an overabundance of generosity, but also a renunciation and a sacrifice. Not only the Passion [of Jesus Christ], but Creation itself is renunciation and sacrifice on God's part."[2] If God has freely chosen, out of love, to put a limit on divine omnipotence, then not all events in human history are part of divine providence. We are thus allowed to conclude that Auschwitz is in no sense part of a divine plan. I find this kenotic theology persuasive. Divine providence, I argue in *Man Becoming*, manifests itself in the redemptive events of human history, primarily in the death and resurrection of Jesus Christ and universally in all graced acts of love, justice, peace, and other works of humans touched by God's grace. God guides human history through the Word addressed to people's conscience and the Spirit empowering them to act. God rescues us from many traps and prisons in which we are caught; and when unable to rescue us from them, God becomes our Comforter.

Because God is Light, I argue in the same book, God does not inflict cruel punishment and decree torture. Every encounter with God is redemptive. God's judgment of the sinful world is accompanied by the grace of conversion. What, then, are we to think of hell? In *Man Becoming* I argue at length that the hell of which Jesus speaks is not information about another world but, rather, the disclosure of the human potential for self-destruction. The sin that has wounded our human nature can make us prefer deafness to hearing, hatred to love, cruelty to compassion, and, at the end, self-destruction to the fullness of life. The evil we do is its own punishment: it cuts us off from the divine ground that sustains us and leads us to death and nothingness.

When I moved to Quebec in 1986 and studied the rapid secularization of its Catholic society, I found that many Quebecers had left the church because, as children, they had been taught that God was judge and punisher and so had lived in constant fear. While the creation of fear is a dimension of Catholic piety, it has sometimes become an overwhelming sentiment. The mediaeval sequence *Dies irae, dies illa* (that day is a day of wrath), at one time sung at the funeral mass, depicts the Lord as a threatening judge shaking the foundations of the earth and making people tremble in fear of eternal punishment. The prayers of the funeral mass inherited from Christian antiquity are quite different: they refer to the future in terms of *lux*, *pax*, and *requies* (light, peace, and rest). At the present time, theologians tend to emphasize God's total goodness. God is non-violent; God is Light without a shadow of darkness.

Hans Urs von Balthasar has thought about the doctrine of hell in an innovate manner.[3] He recognizes that, in his preaching, Jesus retained the images of the Scriptures that depict God as a strict judge rewarding and punishing people according to their deserts, yet that, after his Resurrection, the Apostles adopt a discourse intimating that the future of humanity is the risen Christ. In Acts 3:21, Peter announces "the universal restoration" in Jesus Christ; in 1 Cor. 15:28, Paul proclaims that, at the end, "God shall be all in all"; and John reports the word of Jesus, "When I am lifted up from the earth, I shall draw all people to myself" (John 12:33). In the third century, the Catholic Church condemned as heretical the doctrine of restoration, or *apocatastasis*, which predicts that, at the end, all human beings will be saved and that even the devil shall be forgiven. Avoiding the idea of restoration, von Balthasar proposes that hard-hearted humans committed to evil radically separate themselves from the divine ground and, at the end, will fall into nothingness – so God will be all in all.

Benedict XVI has been influenced by von Balthasar's theology. In his encyclical *Spe salvi* (2007), he shows that God is not violent, not the torturer of the wicked. This is what he says about hell:

> There can be people who have totally destroyed their desire for truth and readiness to love, people for whom everything has become a lie, people who have lived for hatred and have suppressed all love within themselves. This is a terrifying thought, but alarming profiles of this type can be seen in certain figures of our own history. In such people all would be beyond remedy and the destruction of good would be irrevocable: this is what we mean by the word *Hell.* (*Spe salvi*, no. 45)

Many theologians of the past, citing the verse "many are called, but few are chosen" (Matt. 22:14), believed that vast numbers of people would find themselves rejected and that a single mortal sin merited eternal punishment. Benedict XVI does not agree with this interpretation. Only the few, he argues, the total haters, will be rejected: they will, in fact, destroy themselves. To correct the message of *Dies irae, dies illa*, making believers tremble in fear before their divine Judge, Benedict writes: "Grace allows us to hope and to go trustfully to meet the judge whom we know as our advocate" (*Spe salvi*, no. 48).

Because *Man Becoming* was addressed to believers integrated into secular culture, I had to raise the issue of miracles. Blondel held that implicit in belief in miracles is an extrinsicist perception of God: God as the invisible Outsider who at times reaches into history to help people in need, even if this demands breaking the laws of nature. For Blondel, God was not an occasional visitor: God was the gracious Insider sustaining people in their daily existence. In *Man Becoming* I mention another difficulty raised by the idea of miracles. At one time, miraculous events strengthened people's faith; however, after the great horrors of the Second World War, accounts of miraculous healings make it more, not less, difficult for people to believe in God. For if God is the heavenly king who, at times, miraculously intervenes to heal a mortal illness, why, people will ask themselves, did this heavenly ruler not intervene at Auschwitz and Hiroshima? To an increasing number of believers, God as invisible sovereign ruling the world from above is no longer credible.

In *Man Becoming* I distinguish between miracles and marvels. Miracles are divine events inexplicable in the order of nature, while marvels are divine events in the order of persons. Examples of miracles are walking on water or turning water into wine, while examples of marvels are conversion from sin, hope overcoming despair, and other-love vanquishing egotism. Some events reported as miracles are actually marvels: God's touch may release the as yet unexplored restorative potential of human nature and summon forth an unexpected flourishing. However, reports of miracles in the strict sense I do not find credible. The Resurrection of Jesus is an event beyond history, not a miracle: it transcends earthly human existence, entering upon the sphere of the divine.

At the same time, the miracles of Jesus reported in the New Testament are precious to me: in feeding the hungry and healing the sick Jesus reveals God's will for the world, a world in which people have enough to eat and in which the sick are being cared for. Praying

"Your kingdom come" and "Your will be done on Earth" includes yearning for a world in which men, women, and children have food and shelter and live in peace. Jesus' miraculous healing of the sick also has an intimate meaning: we encounter the Saviour in faith as the healer of our brokenness.

10

Dialogue with Sociology

Studying sociology at the New School of Social Research in New York City from 1969 to 1971 became an intellectual adventure that affected my self-understanding, my outlook on the world, and my interpretation of the Gospel. After two months of studying at the New School I had published an article in the *Ecumenist* entitled "Personal Testimony to Sociology," in which I explain why I took a leave of absence from St Michael's College to study sociology. Reflecting on my experiences in the church, I wrote, had brought me to the threshold of sociological inquiry. I discovered the power of institutions to affect personal consciousness – positively or negatively:

> The renewal initiated by the Second Vatican Council has failed to produce the anticipated results because a certain heaviness of the institutions opposed it. Despite the good will of the officers, the institution has largely resisted the new spirituality. The Church's central bureaucracy was totally unable to open itself to the new spirit.
>
> The English theologian Charles Davis thought that the institutional Church was so unwilling to listen to the truth, so afraid of new ideas proposed by the believing community and so attached to its inherited structures that it remained indifferent to

the well-being of individual persons and no longer deserved the name of Church. Charles Davis, as is well remembered, left the Catholic Church. In my reply to him in *The Credibility of the Church Today* I argue that the Church's ills as described by the English theologian are manifestations of a more universal pathology, one from which all institutions suffer to a certain extent. Every institution is tempted to resist change and renewal; every institution is liable to forget the purpose for which it was set up and regard itself not as a means, but as an end. To the extent that this happens, the institution – be it an association, a university, a company, a State or a Church – becomes defensive in regard to a rational critique, tries to control the truth in its favour, fears new forms of life, and values its rules and principles more highly than the well-being of its members. "The Sabbath is made for man, not man for the Sabbath" Jesus said (Mk 2:27).

My theological experience in the Church has introduced me not only to pathological social trends, but also to social processes that heal some of these pathologies. The ecumenical movement of the 1950s and early 1960s and the institutional event of the Second Vatican Council convinced me that certain social processes are able to change people as well as their institutions. Processes such as dialogue, cooperation and conflict can have a transforming influence upon the people involved in them, helping them to see more clearly where they stand, making them critical in regard to themselves, initiating them to new forms of relationships, and making them more conscious of the ministerial role of their institutions. These processes make institutions more open to reality, enable them to trust the new that is being born in them, and lead them to genuine concern for their individual members.

I had seen with my own eyes that the collegial process at the Second Vatican Council affected the self-awareness of the bishops and made them rethink their understanding of what the

> Church is. Yet when the conciliar process came to an end and the popes returned to a monarchial understanding of the papacy, most of the bishops, now deprived of institutions of dialogue, were unable to persevere in the ecclesial consciousness that had emerged at Council.
>
> My intuition at that time was confirmed and clarified by my study of the sociology of institutions, initiated by the pessimistic Max Weber and subsequently developed by more hopeful sociologists convinced that dialogue across the hierarchical levels allows institutions to remain self-critical and open to new challenges.[1]

In the same article, written in 1969, I mention my surprise at how seriously religion is taken by the classical sociologists.

When I began my study of sociology I thought that the sociology of religion would be a comparatively small part of it. To my surprise, I discovered that, in the sociological tradition, religion had an altogether central place. Reacting against the individualism encouraged by the early Enlightenment, sociologists paid attention to the social bond and the common values that constitute society and recognized the cultural creativity of religion. The sacred was a central category for classical sociologists, even if they were positivists of one kind or another and had abandoned belief in God.

I had the privilege of studying the classical sociologists, in particular Tocqueville, Marx, Toennies, Durkheim, and Weber, who laid the foundation for subsequent developments in the field of sociology. These scholars agree that modern society, created by democratic institutions and industrial capitalism, had generated a profound cultural transformation. Destabilizing the traditional institutions of social solidarity, modernity has created a new individualism and an exclusive reliance on utilitarian reason. While sociologists followed different lines of thought, they all recognized the dark side of modernity. Tocqueville announced the possibility of a government-controlled cultural domination, Marx predicted the pauperization of the great majority, Toennies foresaw the decline of ethical values in public life, Durkheim warned of the personal anguish produced by individualism, and Weber announced the coming of "the iron cage," the scientifically administered society. These sociologists were thus critical of "liberals" – that is, of political thinkers who welcomed modernity, found no fault in it, and expected it to produce ongoing progress. Welcoming modernity must be done critically.

I read these sociological authors as great humanists, as people concerned about human well-being under the conditions produced by modern society. I paid attention to the ethical values they took for granted, even if they had not articulated them clearly themselves. When I returned to St Michael's College in 1971, I had the chance to teach courses on the sociology of religion and culture, which were cross-listed in the sociology department of the University of Toronto. In 1975, in *Religion and Alienation,* which is subtitled *A Theological Reading of Sociology*, I published my interpretation of these sociologists and the relevance of their thought for theologians.

Here I moved beyond *Man Becoming*. I continued to follow the Blondelian shift, understanding divine revelation as initiation into new consciousness and regarding God as the gracious Insider, summoning, converting, and sustaining humans in their totality. But I now discovered the role institutions play in determining personal consciousness. In the following pages, I offer five examples of the importance of this discovery for theological reflection.

Example 1

Sociology recognizes the interaction between society and consciousness. Like most theologians and philosophers, I used to think that culture and human self-understanding were produced by the ideas and values originating in people's minds. What I learned from sociology is that culture and human self-understanding are also affected by the social and economic institutions in which people live. Society and consciousness interact: the institutions to which we belong affect our thinking and feeling, and, in turn, the commitment to strongly held values and ideas is capable of transforming social, economic, and political institutions.

I had no sympathy for a deterministic understanding of the relationship between society and culture. I rejected the positivism of both the left and the right, which assumed that consciousness is completely determined by infrastructural factors, thus leaving no room for human freedom. Yet I also learned to reject the idealistic assumption of many liberals, theologians among them, that personal virtues like love and generosity alone will make society more just and more humane, thus making superfluous the collective struggle to transform institutions. Christian preaching often responds to social injustices by urging people to become more virtuous. The best of Catholic social teaching avoids this naïve idealism. In his encyclical of 1931, responding to the Great Depression, Pius XI writes that, to make society more just, we must engage in two struggles, "the reform of institutions and the conversion of morals."[2] Modern society calls for an ethic of citizenship that demands obedience to the law as well as critical thinking, commitment to social change, co-responsibility for the common good, and, under special circumstances, civil disobedience.

Example 2

Classical sociologists analyzed the transformation of culture and consciousness produced by the industrial and democratic revolutions, starting at the end of the eighteenth century. They recognized that the cultural impact of modernity was contradictory. Both capitalism and democracy opposed the aristocratic order – capitalism by objecting to the economic control of the king, democracy by objecting to his autocratic rule – yet they promoted different sets of values. Both call for freedom, but capitalism demands the freedom to buy and sell as one pleases and to increase personal wealth, while democracy calls for political co-responsibility and hence for freedom of thought and expression. Industrial capitalism promotes science and technology; yet it also fosters the market mentality marked by individualism, utilitarianism, and materialism. By contrast, the institution of democracy generates respect for citizens of all classes and concern for the common good of society.

To gain a better understanding of the social dynamics in which they lived, sociologists analyzed the difference between traditional and modern society. Though there are differences between Comte and Durkheim in France and Toennies and Weber in Germany, their comparison of traditional and modern society is almost identical. In traditional society people were deeply identified with their community, enjoyed a strong social bond, shared the same religion and the same values, and attached more importance to their collective identity than to their personal aspirations. By contrast, in modern society, the "I" emerged as more important than the "We." People began to understand themselves as individual actors: they followed their own ideas, chose the religion that spoke to them, embraced the values they found convincing, and, in so doing, weakened the social bond of society, producing a pluralistic culture. This transformation began in the industrial and democratized parts of Europe and North America; however, as modern institutions spread to other parts of Europe and to the world, their impact challenged traditional cultures and their religious ethos. I once wrote, I can't recall where, that the social and cultural world produced by modernity "altered the conditions of human existence, affected people's understanding of the true and the good, and changed their vision of who they were as persons and as collectivities."

While liberal thinkers praised the arrival of modernity as progress, possibly even its inevitability, sociologists clearly recognized the ambiguity of the emerging culture, induced in part by the contradiction between the social solidarity generated by democracy and the possessive individualism produced by capitalism. Weakened by this internal contradiction, modern society became increasingly controlled by the capitalist ethos, prompting people to make political decisions that promoted their personal advantage rather than the common good.

The churches and, in fact, all the world religions have been challenged by modernity. I wish to recall a famous essay by the American sociologist Robert Bellah. As editor of a collection of articles on the reaction of religion to modernity in Southeast Asia,[3] Bellah wrote its concluding article, in which he shows that the religious leaders in this area of the world reacted to modernity in one of two ways: they either clung rigidly to the past – he called this neo-traditionalism – or they returned to their origin, reread their sacred texts, and reacted creatively to the new historical situation. The second response produces religious currents that foster interreligious dialogue and cooperation in the service of the common good. However, Bellah foresaw in all religions the emergence of the first response, which produces currents that foster sectarian resistance to modern society. His predictions have been confirmed. Today, rigidly conservative currents, often referred to as fundamentalist, have a strong presence in all religious traditions, including Roman Catholicism.

Example 3

My study of the sociology of knowledge developed by Ernst Troeltsch and Karl Mannheim taught me that the meaning of a sentence (or any cultural expression) remains unclear until its relationship to its social situation has been clarified. To understand a sentence, two interpretive steps are necessary: (1) placing it in the conversation in which it was uttered and (2) locating the conversation in its historical context. Repeating the same sentence in a different conversation or in a different setting may change its meaning in a significant way. "We Shall Overcome," the theme song of the civil rights movement of the 1960s, meant that we, who are powerless, will persevere and eventually see justice done. If the police department had adopted "We Shall Overcome" as its theme song, it would have meant that we, who are powerful and have guns, will crush the discontented mob and protect the existing order.

That a sentence changes its meaning when it is repeated in another historical context raises difficult theological questions that have as yet not been fully explored. Scripture scholars realize that, in order to understand the literal meaning of a biblical text, one must situate it in its *Sitz im Leben*, the situation in which it was uttered or recorded. Its literal meaning is misunderstood if it is read as a contemporary text. Theologians insist that biblical texts – like all great literature – have a surplus of meaning, beyond their literal sense, capable of addressing believers in new ways as they move from one historical context to another. A biblical text continues to question us and to make us see what we have refused to look at. After the killing fields of the Second World War, the Christian churches heard the commandment of Jesus – "love your neighbour as yourself" – in a new way, summoning them to extend their solidarity to all human beings, whatever their origin, culture, or religion. The new reading of the ancient text radically changed the church's relationship to the world.

Theologians have hesitated to apply the same principle to the understanding of the church's doctrinal statements. We tended to understand them as abstract truths whose meaning was independent of the culture in which they were formulated. Yet to lay hold of their truth, we should interpret them by taking account of their *Sitz im Leben*, clarify what they meant at that time, and then ask ourselves what they mean in the present. John XXIII hinted that this was the task of theology when he introduced the distinction between "the deposit of faith" and the subsequent "doctrinal formulations."[4] His idea was taken up in the conciliar Decree on Ecumenism:

> If the influence of events or of the times has led to deficiencies of conduct, in Church discipline, or even in the formulation of doctrine (which must be carefully distinguished from the de-

> posit of faith), these should be appropriately be rectified at the proper moment.[5]

In *Gaudium et spes* we read:

> From the beginning of her history the Church has learned to express the message of Christ with the help of the ideas and terminology of various philosophers, and has tried to clarify it with their wisdom. Her purpose has been to adapt the Gospel to the grasp of all as well as to the needs of the learned ... Indeed this accommodated preaching of the revealed Word ought to remain the law of all evangelization. For thus the ability to express Christ's message in its own way is developed in each nation. (no. 44)

Undertaking this theological task requires an intellectual freedom that the ecclesiastical authorities have been reluctant to concede. Pope Francis is bolder: he tries to interpret the pastoral meaning of the Gospel contextually, taking into account the conditions of contemporary society.

Example 4

The study of sociology has helped theologians to recognize "social sin." In the past, we paid attention to original sin (the inherited fault that has produced the world of violence and oppression) and to personal sins (the consciously chosen violations of God's law or God's love). What sociologists have taught us is that social conditions have an effect on personal consciousness and can make people participate in evil without their being aware of it. In *Religion and Alienation*, I propose that there are four levels of social sin.[6] The first level is the social structure that damages human beings, such as the colonial subjugation of the Aboriginal peoples of Canada. The second is the ideology that legitimates this oppressive structure – the idea that Aboriginal peoples lack the intelligence to be in charge of their own affairs and that the whites, creator of a "superior" culture, must assume responsibility for them. The third level is the entry of this ideology into people's collective consciousness, something that renders them wholly unaware of the damaging structure and the human suffering it produces. Until recently, Canadians hardly ever thought of the First Nations, nor were they disturbed by the oppressive conditions inflicted upon them (unless they lived in parts of the country where Aboriginal peoples are strongly represented). The fourth level of social sin refers to acts that give the oppressive system a twist for the worse, such as the government's encouragement of an industry that pollutes the protected regions where most Aboriginal peoples live.

The example of social sin I provide in *Religion and Alienation* is world hunger as analyzed in a pastoral letter of the Canadian bishops.[7] The first level of this social sin is the market system that distributes food only to persons able to pay for it, even though all humans are in need of food; the second level is the cultural taboo against questioning the capitalist system; the third level is the First World's disregard for the hunger experienced by the major part of humanity; and the fourth level concerns the rules imposed upon poor countries – rules that oblige them to produce goods for export rather than food for their own people.

It follows from this analysis that the collective effort to overcome social sin begins with the raising of consciousness, with becoming aware of the previously overlooked suffering of so many people, and with delegitimizing the ideology that has led to such blindness.

Social sin is related to personal sins, yet this relation is not easy to analyze. In the apostolic letter *Reconciliatio et paenitentia* (1984), John Paul II offers insightful reflections on this issue:

> Whenever the church speaks of situations of sin or when she condemns as social sins certain situations or the collective be-

> havior of certain social groups, big or small, or even of whole nations and blocs of nations, she knows and she proclaims that such cases of social sin are the result of the accumulation and concentration of many personal sins. (no. 16)

What are these personal sins?

> It is a case of the personal sins of those who cause or support evil or who exploit it; of those who are in a position to avoid, eliminate or at least limit certain social evils but who fail to do so out of laziness, fear or the conspiracy of silence, through secret complicity or indifference; of those who take refuge in the supposed impossibility of changing the world and also of those who sidestep the effort and sacrifice required, producing specious reasons of higher order. The real responsibility, then, lies with individuals. (ibid.)

This remarkable analysis shows that none of us is innocent of the socials sins of our own society. In one way or another, we are all complicit in social evil, even if in varying degrees. I know of no other ecclesiastical text that so clearly recognizes the moral ambiguity of human existence.

Example 5

The study of sociology also reveals the ambiguity of religion. My attention to the anti-Jewish rhetoric of Christian preaching had already convinced me of the ambivalence of the Christian tradition. My study of sociological literature taught me to examine the ambiguity of all religious traditions in a systematic way. The radical Enlightenment critiques of religion failed to convince me since they were based on rationalistic presuppositions and ignored the spiritual dimension of human existence. At the same time, these critiques contain a grain of truth that helps us to uncover the dark side of religious traditions. Religion may, arrogantly, come to interpret its truth as its own achievement, generate contempt for outsiders, and bless the subjugation of women. Religion may become an ideology legitimating empire, domination, and wars; it may also infantilize people, foster their dependency on authority figures, and prevent them from becoming responsible adults. I am grateful to social scientists who recognized the ambivalence of religion: to Max Weber, who distinguished between priestly and prophetic religion; to Karl Mannheim, who distinguished between ideological and utopian religion; and to, Erich Fromm, who distinguished between pathogenic and therapeutic religion.[8]

When the English theologian Charles Davis left the Catholic Church in 1966 and produced a book indicting the fault and failures of the ecclesiastical government, I replied to him, offering a sociological analysis of large organizations to show that all of them, including the church, were vulnerable to systemic malfunctioning, to becoming indifferent to individual needs, and to being reluctant to tell the truth.[9] A perfect ecclesiastical bureaucracy free of faults and failures does not exist on this earth. When St Paul wanted the church to be "without spot or wrinkle" (Eph. 5:27), he had in mind small local communities.

11

The Impact of Latin American Liberation Theology

While studying sociology in New York City I turned to a more radical analysis of social evil. I did not learn this at the New School of Social Research; rather, I learned it through my friendship with Rosemary Radford Ruether and my study of Latin American liberation theology.

The American theologian Rosemary Ruether, a scholar of Christian origins, believed that the messianic promises contained in Scripture had empowered Christians throughout history to wrestle against empire and other forms of domination. She studied the struggles of radical Christians in the sixteenth and seventeenth centuries and, in perfect consistency, extended her solidarity to the victims of society in her own time. She produced a liberation theology, based on God's promises, that supported the historical struggles against the great social evils: colonial domination, capitalist empire, racism and anti-Semitism, the subjugation of women, the oppression of Aboriginals, and the damage of the natural environment. Her 1974 book, *Liberation Theology*, anticipates in brilliant fashion the theological movements of subsequent decades. I had faced the evil in history in relation to the Holocaust, yet my conversations with Rosemary Ruether, during which I at first resisted her analysis, opened my eyes to the oppressive, structured inequalities of society and made me hear, in the promises of Jesus, the liberation of men and women from the institutional powers of darkness.

Meeting Rosemary Ruether made me discover that I had been a hopeful liberal, trusting that present society could be reformed by the good will of the majority, making a structural transformation unnecessary. I remembered that, at the Second Vatican Council, I had been delighted with the social teaching of *Gaudium et spes*, which endorsed the high ideals of justice, freedom, and solidarity in the hope that the people persuaded by them would make their society more humane. My friend Paolo Ricca, a Waldensian pastor, whom I had met at a press conference in Rome, was not impressed by *Gaudium et spes*. He referred to it as "liberal stuff." At the time, I did not know what he meant: liberal, I thought, was a good thing. It was only during my studies in New York that I discovered what he had meant. He called the social teaching of Vatican II "liberal stuff" because it lacked a concrete analysis of the oppressive structures kept in place by the powerful of this world.

Rosemary Ruether's radical perspective was supported by developments in the post-conciliar Catholic Church – developments that had a profound influence on me. In 1968, the Latin American Bishops Conference met at Medellin to apply the pastoral message of the Second Vatican Council to the church on their continent. The bishops recognized that the council had looked upon the world from its rich centre, the North Atlantic countries, while they, situated in Latin America, looked at the same world from the impoverished margin. Impressed by the achievements of the industrialized and democratic societies of the North, the council had hoped that this development could be exported to the poor and authoritarian societies of the South. By contrast, the Latin American bishops, looking at their own continent, were deeply troubled by the exclusion and the misery inflicted upon the majority of the population. They felt obliged to name the injustices that made their people suffer and to offer an analysis of the institutions that had caused them. In the Medellin Conclusions, drawing upon Catholic social teaching, the bishops boldly denounced the political domination of the North, the invasion of liberal capitalism, and the stubborn will of the Latin American elites to defend the present society "marked by classism – where a few have much culture, wealth, power and prestige, while the majority has very little."[1] The bishops recommended the pastoral policy of "conscientization" – raising people's awareness of the forces and structures that produce their impoverishment.[2] Since the bishops believed that God's Word is judgment and new life, they now professed that Jesus Christ condemns these oppressive structures, embraces the poor in solidarity, and supports their struggle for a more just society.

In producing their statements, the bishops had been in conversation with theologians on their continent who had studied critical thought at European universities, and, more important, they were in close contact with Latin American movements of protest and reconstruction. Announced in the Medellin Conclusions are three principles subsequently explored in Catholic liberation theology: (1) the preferential option for the poor, according to which the bishops chose to look upon the world from the margin, in solidarity with the poor, fully conscious that what they saw differed greatly from what was seen by observers located at the centre; (2) the message of Christ as liberator, as someone condemning injustice and empowering the people to struggle for a more just society; and (3) the idea that Christian faith summons believers not only to love God and their neighbour but also to be in solidarity with the victims of society and to support their social struggle for liberation.

The Latin American bishops insisted that this struggle be nonviolent. They slightly qualified their position by citing a sentence from Paul VI's encyclical *Populorum progressio*, conceding that "a revolutionary uprising may be licit if there is manifest, long-standing tyranny" that is damaging to fundamental human rights and dangerously harming the common good.[3] The bishops designated such tyranny as "institutionlized violence": "If the powerful elites jealously retain their privileges and defend them through violence, the bishops argue, they are responsible to history for provoking explosive revolutions of despair."[4]

The Medellin Conclusions exerted great influence on the social teachings of Paul VI and certain episcopal conferences. In the apostolic letter *Octogesima adveniens* (1971), Paul VI lifted the taboo that Catholic social teaching had attached to socialism: he recognized that some forms of socialism are compatible with the Catholic tradition (no. 31) and admitted that Marxism was a movement subject to evolution (no. 320). The World Synod of Bishops held in Rome in the same year adopted the perspective of the Medellin Conclusions:

> In associations of persons and among peoples themselves there is arising a new awareness, shaking them out of fatalistic resignation and spurning them on to liberate themselves and be responsible for their own destiny. Listening to the cries of those who suffer violence and are oppressed by unjust systems and structures ... we have come to recognize the Church's vocation to be present at the heart of the world by proclaiming the Good News to the poor, freedom to the oppressed, and joy to the afflicted. The hopes and the forces that are moving the world in its very foundations are not foreign to the dynamism of the Gospel which, through the power of the Holy Spirit, frees humans from personal sin and its consequences in social life ... Action on behalf of justice and participation in the transformation of the world appear to us as a constitutive dimension ... of the Church's mission for the redemption of the human race and its liberation from every oppressive situation.[5]

According to the World Synod of Bishops, the Gospel is a power that transforms the heart and sustains the struggle for social justice. Embracing the same theology, the Canadian bishops produced several pastoral statements in the 1970s and early 1980s that analyzed the structural injustices in Canadian society and proclaimed the

Gospel as the divine summons calling believers to join the struggle for greater justice in Canada and the world.[6]

According to the conviction of vast numbers of Latin Americans, the 1970s constituted a special historical moment, a kairos, during which the objective conditions of society and the emerging political culture made the radical reconstruction of society a realistic possibility. Catholics who shared this conviction included bishops, priests, and lay men and women, many of whom constituted small communities in which they prayed, reflected, and acted in common to support radical social change. Theologians developed carefully worked out liberation theologies, some biblically based, beginning with the Medellin Conclusions, and others more radical, relying on some version of Third World Marxism. The intellectual achievements of the Latin American theologians stimulated Catholics in all parts of the world to ask what the liberationist approach to theology would lead to in their own society. It was the good fortune of North American Christians that Orbis Books, the publishing company of the Maryknoll Fathers, published in English translation the important works of the Latin American liberation theologians.

Liberation theology is founded upon "the preferential option for the poor." This faith-based option consists of a twofold commitment: (1) to look upon society, its culture, and its texts from the perspective of the poor and otherwise excluded, and (2) to give public witness of solidarity with their struggle for liberation. Theologians like to refer to this option as a *praxis* – that is, an action prompted by love that produces a new way of seeing the world and living in it, leading, in turn, to a new way of acting. The option for the poor is based on faith: it is sustained by solidarity with Jesus persecuted by the mighty and by the promises of liberation made in his preaching.

> The Spirit of the Lord is on me, for he has anointed me to bring the good news to the afflicted; he has sent me to proclaim liberty to captives, sight to the blind, to let the oppressed go free and proclaim a year of favour from the Lord. (Luke 4:18–19)

Christians are called to be in solidarity with all human beings and, hence, with the whole of society. The option for the poor is called "preferential" because an emancipatory movement begins with solidarity with the victims of society, supports their struggle for structural change, and then, after establishing greater justice, extends its solidarity to all members of society. Then the oppressor will become a brother or sister. For now, though, given the present injustices, solidarity is preferentially extended to the poor and excluded.

The change of perspective produced by the preferential option for the poor is so profound that it has been called "an epistemological break." For many Christians it has even produced a crisis of faith. I had occasion to explain the shock experienced by many Latin American Catholics in the Massey Lecture broadcast by the CBC in 1987, subsequently published as a small book, *Compassion and Solidarity.* Latin Americans belonging to the middle class were not aware of the troubling fact that the majority of the population lived in utter poverty. Their act of solidarity with the poor opened their eyes to what was going on in their society. When they asked themselves why they had been so blind in the past, they became aware that their consciousness had been formed by the ideology mediated by the dominant culture, including their religious education, an ideology that rendered the misery of the majority invisible.

Frei Betto, a Dominican brother in Brazil, tells us that, after his conversion to the perspective of the poor, he was deeply disturbed by the blinding nature of the ideology, including religious creeds, that he had been taught.[7] The God in whom he had believed and the salvation he desired had been so otherworldly that the social inequality and the consequent suffering of the majority appeared to him a minor issue. The rich and the poor, if they were believers, would be together in heaven. Frei Betto reports that, after his acceptance of the option for the poor, he could no longer believe in God, fearing that had become an atheist. An older brother of his Order counselled him to be patient in the silence of his heart: God would speak to him again, but this time God would be in solidarity with the poor and powerless. And this, Frei Betto thankfully confesses, is what happened.

Frei Betto's spiritual anguish has been shared by a vast number of Christians whose religious experience has opened their eyes to the destructive side of their world or, if I may use a Jungian term, to the repressed "shadow" of their society. In my Massey Lecture I describe this "dark night of the soul" as the uncertainty produced by two fears: (1) the fear that the God who tolerates these unjust structures cannot be trusted and (2) the fear that my inherited faith is an ideological construct reflecting my privileged position in society. Would I remain a person of faith if I shared the exclusion and wounds inflicted upon the poor and oppressed? Would I remain a believer if I sat in the train on the way to the death camps? Some passionate believers get stuck in the dark night of the soul: they lose their faith, unable to believe in God's goodness. In Canada, this happens to some Aboriginal people who are fully conscious of what the dominant society and its churches have done to them over the centuries. This also happens to many women shocked by the recognition of the subjugation imposed on them by their religion. Yet many Christians are rescued from the dark night by the message of the crucified and risen Christ: they come to believe that God accompanies them in their prison and enables them to be witnesses of hope and agents of love.

Cardinal Joseph Ratzinger, president of the Vatican Congregation of the Doctrine of Faith from 1981 to 2005, did not like liberation theology. He recognized that liberation theology introduces a new theological method by exploring the meaning of the Gospel in solidarity with the victims of society. It starts with an act of love, the will to listen to oppressed people articulating their predicament, followed by an understanding of divine revelation as God's compassionate offer of rescue, salvation, and new life. The cardinal recognized that liberation theology is contextual, adopts the perspective of the powerless, and denounces the unjust structures approved by the powerful, including the church's complicity with them. Because liberation theology questions the church's alliances with the masters of the world, the cardinal held that this approach to theology disrupts the unity of the church and undermines the authority of popes and bishops. Yet the church's alliances with the political powers and economic elites deserve to be analyzed. In 1984, an instruction published by the Vatican severely criticized Latin American liberation theologians,[8] yet between 1976 and 1983 the Vatican made no criticism of the Argentine bishops who supported Videla's murderous military dictatorship, which claimed to save the Catholic civilization from its enemies. Cardinal Ratzinger was correct when he feared that liberation theology would raise questions embarrassing to the ecclesiastical authorities.

In an instruction of 1984, Cardinal Ratzinger condemned liberation theology, offering as an additional reason the contention that it does not sufficiently criticize the Marxist categories upon which it depends. In a report written for his own use but that was subsequently published, the cardinal admits that "liberation theology involves a whole spectrum from radically Marxist positions ... to efforts made within the framework of a correct and ecclesial theology, stressing the responsibility which Christians necessarily bear for the poor and oppressed."[9] But then he adds that the instruction he plans to write will not deal with these diverse trends but, rather, will focus on liberation theology narrowly conceived and dependent on Marxist categories. The readers of the instruction, unaware of this narrow focus, inevitably think that it denounces all forms of liberation theology. The Catholic world was deceived. The shadow now fell on many innocent theologians, including Gustavo Gutierrez, the author of *A Theology of Liberation,* a work deeply rooted in Scripture and the Catholic tradition.

Pope Francis put a quick end to the ecclesiastical witch hunt of Latin American liberation theologians. With his election on 13 March 2013, the tone of the Vatican changed quite rapidly. The new pope wanted the church to be of service to the poor and to act in solidarity with them. Latin American liberation theology was now rehabilitated. Within a single week in early September 2013, the Vatican newspaper *L'Osservatore Romano* published an interview with the founder of liberation theology, Gustavo Gutierrez, an article by Gutierrez himself, and two articles praising his work – one of them by Archbishop Müller, the prefect of the Congregation for the Doctrine of the Faith.[10] Since then Gustavo Gutierrez has been invited to a private conversation with Pope Francis.

12

North America in the 1970s

In the 1960s, in struggling for the civil rights of Afro-Americans and opposing the lethal war in Vietnam, American Christians learned to think in critical terms, to challenge the government and the dominant culture. In the 1970s, many Christians in the North were inspired by Latin American liberation theology, even though its sociology of oppression could not be applied in unmediated fashion to developed industrial societies. In some historical situations, society is marked by a single form of oppression, such as a military occupation, an apartheid regime, or an economic system that produces misery for the great majority. In these cases, the commitment to justice gathers people in a single movement of resistance. Yet, in most societies, the unjust structures that damage people's lives are several and interdependent, generating movements of resistance on various levels. A sociology of injustice appropriate for North America will analyze the inequality-producing impact of capitalism while also taking into account the political domination exercised by the American Empire, the structured racism inherited from the institution of slavery, the conquest and humiliation of Aboriginal peoples, the inferior status imposed upon women, the devastation of the natural environment, and several other forms of injustice. What North American Christians have learned from Latin American liberation theology is, primarily, the ability to recognize that God's revelation in Jesus Christ has an emancipatory impact on society. We have learned to read the Bible from a new perspective – the perspective of the people who have been marginalized in various ways.

I recall reading a book by an American evangelical missionary working in Central America who, for many years, had preached that believers find in Jesus the salvation of their soul and life eternal. Eventually, the utter misery of his congregation began to trouble him. Looking for an answer, he decided to reread the Bible and to underline with a red pencil the texts referring in various terms to the poor and the oppressed. At the end, to his great amazement, he saw that major parts of the Bible were now in red. He then recognized that God loved the poor, demanded justice, and promised rescue. He changed his preaching: he still proclaimed that Jesus offered salvation from sin, but this time he included the structural sins that oppress, humiliate, and devastate the poor.

A Symposium on the Holocaust

In the 1970s, three major theological conferences dealt with justice issues with which I was deeply involved. I had taken part in these conferences as a speaker and, reflecting on them afterwards, wrote three long articles summarizing the results and significant debates that had taken place. In 1974, a three-day symposium, "Auschwitz: Beginning of a New Era?," was held at the Episcopalian Cathedral of St John the Divine in New York City. At the time of the Second Vatican Council, the Holocaust had not yet been recognized as a world-shattering event demanding theological reflection, even though its unspoken memory persuaded the bishops to change the church's teaching on the Jews.[1] Jewish thinkers themselves still tended to avert their eyes from the horror of Auschwitz. A friend of mine, the Jewish philosopher Emil Fackenheim, published *Paths to Jewish Belief* in 1960, in which he presented the Jewish faith to young members of the synagogue without mentioning the Holocaust. It was the Arab-Israeli war of 1967 that prompted him and many other Jewish thinkers to face the awfulness of the Holocaust and to interpret its meaning for Jewish existence. Fackenheim changed his entire theological orientation, as did a number of Christian theologians. In an issue of the review *Concilium*, entitled *The Holocaust as Interruption*, several theologians argue that this catastrophic crime has shattered the traditional categories of human self-understanding and that even reflection on God and salvation cannot be conducted without attention to this event. In the formula of Johann Baptist Metz, one can no longer do theology while turning one's back on Auschwitz.[2] Jewish and Christian believers were now obliged to rethink the meaning of divine providence, a topic to which I refer above.[3]

The symposium "Auschwitz: The Beginning of a new Era?," held in New York City, reflected the openness to pluralism characteristic of American theology. This was something quite different from the anguished reflections of European thinkers. In their presentations Jewish and Christian thinkers asked themselves whether, in the era after Auschwitz, the reconciliation of Judaism and Christianity has become a possibility. The Christian speakers advocated different ways of reforming Christian teaching, redefining the church's mission, and extending its solidarity to the synagogue, while the Jewish speakers expressed their readiness, despite the terrible past, to engage in dialogue with Christians and to cooperate with them in support of humanitarian causes.

Before writing the above paragraph, I took a second look at the proceedings of the symposium published in 1977.[4] All speakers agreed that the Holocaust must never be forgotten; it must be remembered as a historical event without which we cannot understand ourselves as Jews, as Christians, and as people of Western civilization. I found that, in may paper, I argued that, in reflecting on the Holocaust, the church recognizes that it has no mission to convert Jews to the Christian faith, a position confirmed by the Second Vatican Council when it recognized the abiding validity of God's covenant with the house of Israel. I also noticed that most of the

Jewish and Christian speakers were strong supporters of the State of Israel: only a few Jewish speakers were critical of the politics of Zionism. I later show that, after the Second Intifada in the year 2000, responding to Ariel Sharon's provocative visit to the Temple Mount, Christian theologians and a significant minority of Jewish thinkers re-examined their attitude towards the State of Israel.

I remember that, as we left the Episcopalian cathedral after the symposium, a group of gay activists stood outside with posters complaining that this conference on the Nazi genocide had not mentioned the brutal persecution of homosexuals. I told these men (there were no women in the group) that, if they had come to see me before the conference, I would have mentioned the humiliation and the torture of homosexuals in the Nazi concentration camps.

The symposium was disparaged by Gabriel Habib, an Arab Christian and a member of the Middle East Council of Churches. Invited as a speaker, he had refused to be present for reasons he provided in a long letter addressed to the organizing committee.[5] Habib objected to the narrow perspective of the symposium, which looked at the genocide of the Jews perpetrated by the German government without relating it to the history of the Western empires, their colonial conquests, and the exploitation and oppression inflicted upon peoples, including, in many cases, the elimination of whole populations. Modern racism is the product of empire, and it is aimed at oppressing people deemed inferior. Reacting to the Holocaust as a singular event, as was the case with the symposium, urges Christians to rethink their relationship to the Jews, but it does not urge them to oppose the politics of empire. What is needed, Habib suggests, is a colloquium on the Holocaust that includes thinkers of non-European origin who are ready to examine the death-dealing dimension of the dominant Western culture.

After the symposium, there was a vehement debate regarding whether or not Habiib's letter should be included in the Proceedings. I strongly favoured its inclusion. I did not realize, and no one mentioned at the time, that Habib's critical perspective was quite similar to the reflections of Max Horkheimer and Theodor Adorno in their *Dialectic of Enlightenment*, which was first published in 1946.[6] According to these two German Jewish philosophers, the founders of the Frankfurt School, the Holocaust was not a pathological regression to a past barbarian age: it was, rather, the manifestation of the sinister side of modernity – the reliance on techno-scientific reason to control people and, if need be, to eliminate them in the interests of a powerful minority. The domination of instrumental reason, eliminating ethical reason from public life, has produced death-dealing oppression in the colonization of Asia and Africa and, in the twentieth century, more virulently, in the dictatorships produced by German fascism and Russian communism. For Horkheimer and Adorno, this was the historical context of the Holocaust.[7]

The Detroit Conference on Liberation Theology

In 1975, the week-long Theology in the Americas conference, which was held in Detroit and rallied the Christian left from across the continent, revealed in dramatic fashion the complexity of oppressive structures and, hence, the multiplicity of liberation struggles. Among the invited speakers were liberation theologians from Latin America as well as black theologians and feminist theologians from the United States. Among the hundreds of participants were a few Canadians from Ontario and Quebec. In the public debate, the black theologians challenged the Latin Americans, asking them why they were all white. Were there not people of colour on their continent? The Latin Americans, in turn, challenged the black theologians, asking them why they did not denounce capitalism. Were black people in the United States not among the most exploited? Intervening in the debate were feminist theologians, saying: "a pox on both your houses, for both of you ignore the subjugation inflicted upon women." This spectacular conflict, uttered in friendship, made a deep impression on the participants, convincing them that the oppressive forces are interrelated and differentially structured in each society, thus calling for a contextual analysis. The Marxist Christians present in Detroit became aware that their social analysis was incomplete.

In my article summarizing the talks and debates at the conference, I mention that next to no attention was paid to the exclusion of Aboriginal peoples and to the marginalization of Mexican Americans in the United States. Representatives of these communities had been invited to participate, yet they were not given an opportunity to speak. Still, one Mexican American Catholic grabbed a microphone and, uninvited though he was, explained to the gathering that his people did not regard themselves as descendents of immigrants; rather, they saw themselves as a conquered people whose land, language, and culture had been subjected to the control of the United States in 1848. He argued that even the American Catholic Church, with a hierarchy largely of Irish origin, did not recognize the distinctive Mexican American tradition. When I was invited to speak of liberation theology in Canada, I explained that, in English-speaking Canada and Quebec, the faith and justice movement takes on different forms, responding to different historical conditions. In particular, Quebecers feel that their society is still marked by the remnant of colonialism. Yet, despite significant differences, Canadian Christians committed to emancipation make every effort to be in solidarity with one another. Solidarity, in fact, marked the entire conference: the common faith in God's redemptive activity in human history allowed us, despite our different locations, to pray and sing together and to recognize the common mission of the Christian left within the various churches.

Among the topics debated at the Detroit conference was the meaning of divine transcendence. For many Protestants, including black theologians, God was the heavenly king who guided and accompanied people in their daily lives, to whom they could turn in their prayers and who blessed their struggle for justice. This corresponds to the traditional theism widely held in various Protestant churches. By contrast, according to many Catholics, including Latin American theologians, God had chosen to be immanent in human history, converting the human heart, opening people's eyes to see the evil they do, and strengthening them to become servants of God's approaching reign. The recognition of God's life-giving and truth-revealing immanence is what, earlier, I refer to as the Blondelian shift.[8] In the context of liberation, turning to God in prayer presupposes solidarity with the victims of history. Pharaoh had no access to God unless he was willing to release the Israelites he had enslaved. The public interchange concerning God's presence helped many Christian activists who found it difficult to link their practical engagement to spirituality and prayer.

Recognizing the different levels of emancipatory struggles, many North Americans and Europeans preferred to reserve the term "liberation theology" for the new theology in Latin American and other parts of the Third World. In Germany, theologians of the left, in particular Johann Baptist Metz, Dorothee Soelle, and Jürgen Moltmann, produced what they called "political theology," and in Canada I used the expression "critical theology" to designate reflection on the emancipatory meaning of the Gospel. "Feminist theology," trusting in God's promises, promotes the rescue of women from patriarchal domination. Despite the different names, these theologies rely on the same, or at least very similar, methodological approaches. However, at the 1975 Detroit conference there was as yet no reference to the destruction of the natural environment.

A Conference on Political Theology in Canada

In 1977, a two-day conference entitled "Political Theology in the Canadian Context" was held at St Andrew's College in Saskatoon. It differed strikingly from the 1975 conference in Detroit. In Saskatoon, the principal debate dealt with the relation of Christian believers to the various forms of Canadian socialism. From the beginning, socialism in Canada was an echo of the pluralistic socialism of Great Britain, uniting different currents – the labour movement, Fabian socialism, Marxism, and Christian socialism. In 1933, Canadian socialism constituted itself as a federal political party, the Co-operative Commonwealth Federation (CCF), representing workers and farmers and supported by a wide network of Protestant Christians.[9] The political engagement of these people was blessed by an original Protestant theology that anticipated the methodical approach of Latin American liberation theology.[10] Apart from a few exceptions, Catholics had remained aloof from the CCF.

At the Saskatoon conference most of the Protestant and Catholic speakers held that, in Canada, injustice, exploitation, and exclusion were the result of the economics and the culture of unregulated capitalism. One presentation argued that many twentieth-century Protestant theologians, in particular Karl Barth, Paul Tillich, Helmut Gollwitzer, and Jürgen Moltmann, had been socialists; another presentation – this one given by me – documented Catholic social teaching's shift to the left after the 1968 Medellin Conference and the 1976 critique of the free market system in the pastoral statement of the Canadian bishops. The question passionately debated at the conference concerned what kind of socialism Christians should support. Was the New Democratic Party (NDP), which had succeeded the CCF in 1961, still advocating socialism? Some conference participants mentioned that they had supported the socialist Ginger Group within the NDP, called the Waffle, which had been excommunicated by the party in 1972. Should they now return to the NDP? Or should they join one of the smaller Marxist movements?

A lively argument about Marxist socialism took place between two theologians from outside of English-speaking Canada, Dorothee Soelle, the well-known German Protestant theologian, and Yves Vaillancourt, the founder of "les politisés chrétiens," a Catholic Marxist movement in Quebec.[11] Dorothee Soelle, an active member of Christians for Socialism in Europe, said that her organization strongly opposed authoritarian Marxism because it repressed human freedom and scientific Marxism because it dismissed the creativity of culture. She defended a kind of Marxist humanism, which had as yet not produced an appropriate political party. Dorothee, who later became a personal friend of mine, once said – possibly even at Saskatoon – that she was a socialist without a party and a Christian without a church. Speaking against her was Yves Vaillancourt, who argued that the democratic socialist parties of Europe have failed: they wanted to reform an irreformable system and, when in power, actually defended the capitalist economy. For the same reason he rejected the Canadian NDP and le Parti Québécois, the social-democratic sovereignist party of Quebec. Vaillancourt advocated instead revolutionary politics. He saw no reason for one to be afraid of scientific Marxism, which, according to him, provides a sociology of oppression and guides the political struggle, yet allows Christians to draw their vision of human destiny and their spiritual motivation from their faith in Jesus Christ.

These debates stirred up my interest in the history of socialism in Canada. I asked myself why Catholics in Canada had rejected the CCF in the 1930s, while Catholics in England had supported the Labour Party in the 1920s. I eventually wrote *Catholics and Canadian Socialism*,[12] in which I study not only the condemnation of the CFF by the bishops of Quebec and its impact on Catholics throughout Canada but also individual Catholics who, unconcerned about the bishops, supported the CCF and exercised leadership in it.

In my article on the 1975 Saskatoon conference,[13] which I have just reread, I record the observation, made by some participants, suggesting that the argument between proponents of reformist and radical politics overlooks an important point. There are, in fact, reformist activities that introduce innovative principles in society and that question the present order and prepare its future transformation. The speakers had in mind the cooperative movement, which fosters economic activity organized in democratic fashion, subverting capitalist principles. Many years later, as I explain further on, I discovered in the work of Karl Polanyi an analysis of the radical political implications of community economic development.

The specifically theological issue discussed at the Saskatoon conference concerned the reasons that the dominant piety in all churches tends to ensure that Christians will support the status quo. Dorothee Soelle made an important contribution to this debate. Understanding the theological sources of Christian political conservatism helps political theology to produce an alternative interpretation of the Christian message, one that makes believers yearn for and act on behalf of social justice.

It should be noted that the coming ecological crisis was not mentioned at the Saskatoon conference.

Five Dimensions of Christian Piety

In what follows I mention the five dimensions of Christian piety that are considered sources of Christian social conservatism, and, following each, I indicate the response of political theology. Some of these responses are short since I have already discussed them.

Dimension 1

Preoccupation with saving one's soul makes the social conditions in which people live, even if these conditions are gravely unjust, matters of minor importance. Longing for heaven may prompt Christians to shrug their shoulders when it comes to contemplating what happens in history. By contrast, political theology insists that the Gospel appoints believers to promote love, justice, and peace in the world and that, for this reason, faith in life eternal does not produce indifference to the historical conditions that cause human suffering. This is a point made by the Second Vatican Council.

Dimension 2

Imagining God as the Lord of history suggests to Christians that God rules the world from above and that all lords, on every level, impose their rule with divine authority. This belief has often made obedience the primary Christian virtue. Women theologians have pointed out that, if God is Lord, and therefore male, all males will come to think of themselves as lords over females. By contrast, political theology emphasizes God's immanence in human history and thus God's guidance of the world from below. Here God is the matrix of human life – that is, the foundation that sustains and empowers people to become responsible agents and to create the historical conditions of their lives. Earlier, I refer to the recognition of God as the divine Insider as the Blondelian shift. God as the ground of life – as *Lebensgrund*, as the German mystics used to say – is neither "he" nor "she" and thus does not legitimate a hierarchical relationship between men and women.

Dimension 3

Trust in divine providence has suggested to many believers that whatever happens in human history is part of a divine plan and must therefore be accepted in patience and humility. While God does not "will" evil deeds, theologians have argued that God "allows" these deeds to happen as part of a mysterious overall design, of which we are ignorant. As I mentioned previously, after the Holocaust, Jews and Christians asked themselves the anguished question of whether Auschwitz had a place in divine providence.[14] Replying to this, a number of Christian theologians argued that not all events of human history are part of God's providence: the evil deeds humans perform are contrary to God's will. Divine providence manifests itself in the resurrection of Jesus Christ and the redemptive events of human history – that is, the acts of love, justice, and peace, performed by graced men and women.

Dimension 4

A certain pious discourse in favour of unity and peace often disguises disturbing events in society, encourages people to avoid social conflicts, and fosters political conservatism. A striking example, which I mentioned in my writings many years ago, concerns the statements made by the Canadian churches in 1967 as part of the celebration of Canada's hundredth anniversary.[15] The Anglican and Protestant churches gave thanks to God for the first hundred years and prayed that unity and peace would continue to reign in Canada. By contrast, the Catholic bishops were unable to praise God for the first hundred years because the bishops of Quebec insisted that such praise would have political meaning, favouring federalism, an issue over which Quebec Catholics were divided and which the bishops were not authorized to resolve. Unable to use the pious discourse supporting unity and peace, the Canadian Catholic bishops were obliged to produce a thoughtful pastoral statement on the interplay of justice and injustice in Canada, asking God's blessing on the efforts of reform.

The Christian preference for unity and peace, and the lack of a spirituality of conflict, are surprising because Jesus, the Son of God, was a prophet and troublemaker, denouncing the religious establishment and proclaiming a reign of love and peace, at odds with the reign of Caesar. Political theology recognizes that Christians live in a situation of conflict, a conflict sustained by an appropriate spirituality and a commitment to love, justice, and peace.

Dimension 5

Belief in original sin has persuaded many Christians to think that, being sinners, they are unable to create a just and peace-loving society and that the efforts towards social reform are based on an illusion. They hold that divine grace promises to lift us into personal holiness, but no such promise has been made to society. The spiritual task of Christians, they think, is to put up with the unjust structures of society with humility and patience, hoping for ultimate liberation beyond death.

Some Christian theologians, Catholics among them, hold that the church should forget the doctrine of original sin. They argue that this doctrine is not contained in the Scriptures: it is simply St Augustine's interpretation of the biblical story of Adam's disobedience, which was subsequently adopted by the ecclesiastical magisterium. Augustine used the belief in original sin as the theological justification of infant baptism – a practice not recorded in the New Testament. Yet there was a deeper reason for Augustine's abiding sense of the world's sinfulness. Reflecting on the Roman Empire, first on its conquests and its colonial expansion and then on its decline (in his own day it was becoming increasingly ungovernable), he came to think of society as "the proud city" produced by the will to dominate and the desire for riches.

I share with Augustine the abiding consciousness of the world's sinfulness. Of course, I do not share his outrageous idea that babies who die without baptism carry the guilt of original sin and deserve eternal punishment. Nor do I agree with his absurd hypothesis that the guilt for this sin is passed on to the newly born by the sexual intercourse that begot them. Still, after the horrors of the twentieth century – the Holocaust and the other genocides; the atomic bomb; the hot and cold wars; the carpet bombing of civilian populations; the structured injustices that inflict domination, exploitation, and exclusion upon the masses; and the destruction of the natural environment – all this and the daily reading of the newspaper convince me of the world's sinfulness. Looking at the whole of human history, I recognize that evil has been with us from the beginning: we have created a world of competition, conflict, and violence, marked by a radically unjust distribution of wealth and power.

I hold that the story of Creation recorded in the Old Testament continues to shed light on the human condition. In the early biblical texts, the God who rescues Israel from the land of bondage is still seen as the God of legions, a warring god, more powerful than the gods of other nations. The story of Creation told in the book of Genesis was written centuries later. It was based on the message of the Hebrew prophets that the divine rescuer of Israel is in fact the God of the universe; it was also influenced by the encounter of the exiled Israelites with Babylon's religious literature. Still, when the Bible was put together the story of Creation, a late composition, was placed at the very beginning. I wish to mention two messages drawn from this divinely revealed myth. First, it announces that all human beings are descendants of Adam and Eve, a political message rejecting every tribal, ethnic, or nationalist theory that presents humanity as divided into peoples or races of unequal dignity. Genesis is God's Word against racism and all other forms of contempt and exclusion. Second, the story of Adam and Eve's disobedience and its consequences reveals that the historical conditions that make people suffer are caused by human sin. God is not the author of evil: we are. Creation was good, but we produced empires, wars, conquests, genocides, oppression, slavery, and famines.

The New Testament recognizes that the world's sinfulness wounds the heart of people everywhere. St Paul speaks of sin almost as a personal force that entered history through Adam's disobedience and now dwells in people's lives (cf. Rom. 5:12; Rom. 6:12) producing in them a deeply divided self. John the Evangelist speaks of the sin of the world (cf. John 1:29; 1 John 2:2), producing resistance to the truth and the hatred of God and neighbour. At the same time, Paul and John announce that Jesus takes away the sin of the world, that the Spirit renews us internally, and that where sin has abounded, divine grace abounds even more (cf. Rom. 5:20).

The sinful dimension of society is largely hidden by the dominant culture; it becomes visible when we look upon society from the perspective of its victims – the poor, the disadvantaged, the weak, the excluded. Liberation theology refers to this perspective as the preferential option for the poor. Looking at Quebec and Canada from the perspective of Aboriginal peoples, the unemployed, or other marginalized groups reveals structures of domination that the government and the cultural mainstream ignore. In more general terms, political theology recognizes that there is something profoundly wrong with humanity: we seem to be unable to organize our collective existence without competition, contempt for outsiders, and the shedding of blood. Every civilization, writes Walter Benjamin, is at the same time a barbarity.

Fortunately, the sin of the world is not the whole story. We see ourselves surrounded every day by goodness, generosity, friendship, and fidelity; we marvel at the beauty of heaven and earth; we rejoice in music and works of art created by gifted men and women; we cherish human wisdom and the insight of the sciences; we are grateful for the work done by innumerable persons that allows us to live and be well. We love the world because of the groundswell of truth, goodness, and beauty engendered by people who resist the dark powers.

The Old Testament predicted the arrival of a messianic figure, and the New Testament proclaimed Jesus as the Saviour of the World and the incarnate Word of God. Revealed in this Jesus is, first, the knowledge that God has embraced in love the whole of humanity and, second, that God has been graciously present in human history from the beginning. The Good News in this dark world is that men and women are summoned by the divine Word to become critically conscious of themselves and to be empowered by the Holy Spirit to love their neighbour and build a community of equals. Divine grace retrieves the potential of human nature, enabling us to strive for self-knowledge and the selfless love of others. St Thomas speaks of *gratia sanans et elevans*, grace as healing and elevating wounded human nature. God is the redemptive mystery that makes reconciled humanity possible.

13

Rethinking Sexual Ethics

Reporting the evolution of my theology obliges me to write a section on the norms of sexual ethics. Never having been fully convinced by the church's official teaching on this topic, I eventually arrived at a principled disagreement with it. I fully agree with the church's denunciation of the contemporary trend that separates sexuality from love and ends up turning sexual relations into commodities. Many years ago I was invited by the left-wing review *Canadian Dimension* to write an article on the Catholic critique of capitalism – an article that the editor entitled "The Left Hand of God" – in which I speak of the invasion of market values in the sphere of human relations and mention, in particular, the commodification of sexuality. When the article was published, I discovered to my surprise and amusement that the editor had taken out my reference to sex as a commodity without seeking my approval. I never experienced censorship by a Catholic review.

In 1976, invited by the student paper of the University of Toronto to write a short article on the Catholic Church's teaching on human sexuality, I decided to explain why I personally disagreed with it. Archbishop Philip Pocock of Toronto, who has always been good to me, now felt obliged to withdraw my permission to preach in the churches. He found himself in an uncomfortable position: he was blamed in Rome – quite wrongly – of being responsible for the Winnipeg Statement of the Canadian bishops,[1] which allowed Catholics to follow their conscience if they were not convinced by Paul VI's 1968 encyclical *Humanae vitae*, which forbids the use of artificial birth control. Because of my disagreement with the church's official teaching, I thought the honourable thing to do was to resign from the priesthood and leave the religious order. I was grateful to Father John Kelly, the president of St Michael's College, who asked me to remain in my position as professor and continue to teach theology and religious studies.

I first intended to seek the appropriate permission from the Vatican to retire from the active priesthood, yet, when I saw the official form containing the questions that I had to answer, I found myself unable to do so. Implicit in these questions was an admission that I had sinned, had been unfaithful, and now sought forgiveness. Since the Vatican authorities were unwilling to listen to my deep convictions, I decided to leave informally. I published a brief statement in the *Globe and Mail* saying that I was leaving the priesthood because of my disagreement with the church's sexual ethics but that I would continue to work for the church's renewal and carry on teaching theology at St Michael's College. I saw myself as a theologian working within the Catholic tradition.

As I look back over my life in the ecclesiastical institution, I am aware that I never met a priest who was mean or whose intentions were bad. Those who disagreed with my theological ideas were respectful. All the priests and bishops I met in the church tried to live up to their high ideals.

In the spring of 2011, Michael Higgins was asked by *Commonweal* to write an article on my life as a theologian. In preparation for this article, he asked me how I formulated my disagreement with the church's teaching in a 1976 student paper. Unfortunately, I have only a vague memory of my argument. I think I wrote that the official Catholic sexual ethics was unacceptable because it provided a set of fixed rules to be applied universally, without taking into account either cultural setting or the personal struggle for maturity.

Because of my work at the Second Vatican Council I was keenly aware that the cultural values of modern society had challenged the church's official teaching and obliged it to return to the Scriptures and to rethink its position. Listening to God's Word in the new historical context, the Second Vatican Council changed the church's teaching on religious liberty and redefined its relation to non-Catholic Christians, the Jewish community, and the followers of the great world religions. The council convinced me that, to remain faithful to the Gospel in a new historical situation, the Catholic magisterium had to be capable of changing its mind.

Wrestling with changing cultural ideals, the Anglican Church decided at the 1930 Lambeth Conference to recognize that, under certain conditions, birth control was ethically acceptable. In December of the same year, Pius XI replied to this in his encyclical *Casti connubii*, insisting that every act of sexual intercourse in married life must be open to conception and that the use of contraceptive devices is thus immoral, whatever the circumstances. This was the starting point of a new conflict between the Catholic Church and the churches of the Reformation – a conflict that, in recent decades, has assumed ever wider proportions.

According to the official Catholic teaching, the primary end of marriage is the procreation of children, to which conjugal love and sexual satisfaction are added as secondary and tertiary ends. A few Catholic philosophers in the 1930s, sensitive to the emerging personalist thought, designated the bond of love between husband and wife as the primary end of marriage, alongside the begetting of children, but these thinkers were censured by the Roman magisterium.[2] The official Catholic position became confused when, in 1951, Pius XII, in a speech given to an association of midwives, recognized that, under certain conditions, "the natural method" of birth control was ethically acceptable. In other words, a couple had the right to find the days of the month when the wife was infertile and then engage in sexual intercourse with the intention of avoiding conception. Pius XII offered no theological argument for this concession. His decision introduced a logical contradiction into the church's official teaching, forbidding *all* sexual acts in marriage that were not open to conception and, at the same time, allowing *some* sexual acts that intended to avoid conception.

In the 1960s, after the invention of the contraceptive pill, Catholics asked themselves if the pill, not being a material obstacle preventing conception, might be regarded as a natural means of birth control. Catholic philosophers and theologians began to publish books and articles on sexual ethics that were critical of the church's official teaching. I wrote an essay for the book *Contraception and Holiness*, edited by Bishop Thomas Roberts, in which I make a theological proposal, the broader meaning of which I only discovered later. I argue that the Gospel imperative with regard to sexual relations in married life is spousal love between equals, implying mutuality, respect for one another, tenderness on both sides, and the refusal to control the other. This is an ethical ideal that is absent in traditional Catholic teaching, which looks upon marriage in legal terms, granting to the husband "the right to his wife's body" (*jus in corpus*) and obliging the wife to pay "her marriage debt" (*redere debitum conjugale*). The new ethics of love and mutuality allows spouses to decide how many children they want and how to limit conception. By insisting on equality between the spouses, the new ethics actually offers a stricter moral norm than does the traditional teaching.

At the Second Vatican Council, the section on marriage in the schema *On the Church in the Modern World* provoked a lively discussion. The draft recognized spousal love and the procreation of children as the ends of marriage, without assigning priority to either of them, thus modifying the teaching of *Casti connubii*. This modification was challenged by conservative bishops; however, after an extended debate, it remained in the definitive text. If procreation were no longer the primary end of marriage, then the ethics of birth control would have to be rethought. When a few cardinals began the conciliar debate on this issue and suggested a new approach, the president of the council announced that Pope Paul VI had decided to remove this topic from the council's consideration. I have a clear memory of that day: many bishops and theologians were stunned by this announcement. The pope did not seem to trust the Second Vatican Council.

Paul VI now greatly enlarged the papal commission set up to study the ethics of birth control.[3] The commission eventually embraced seventy-five members, including bishops, theologians, medical doctors, and married couples. Its final report, handed to the pope in 1966, recommended that Catholics should be taught that married couples must make an ethically responsible decision as to the number of children they want and then feel free to choose the form of birth control that suits them. The report even included the draft of a papal encyclical presenting the new position to the Catholic world and showing the underlying continuity of the church's teaching. Six members of the commission disagreed with this report. The minority report they produced argued that the church, faithful to itself, cannot change its teaching on birth control. In his 1968 encyclical, *Humanae vitae*, Paul VI followed the minority report: without consulting the bishops worldwide, he declared artificial birth control, including the pill, as gravely sinful.

Catholics were not convinced by the papal teaching. Catholic women in particular felt that their moral experience had not been taken seriously. The Canadian bishops, meeting in Winnipeg, published a pastoral statement that accepted the papal teaching, but it also assured Catholics who failed to be convinced by this teaching that they were free to follow their conscience.[4] Empirical research of public opinion in the church has shown that the majority of Catholics in industrialized countries have not accepted the teaching of *Humanae vitae*. Today, believing Catholic couples make responsible decisions as to how many children they want and then choose the method of birth control that best suits them. Without knowing it, they are following the majority report of Paul VI's commission.

Among the pastoral consequences of *Humanae vitae* was the widespread loss of confidence in the sacrament of confession. Since priests must follow the church's official teaching, Catholics did not like to speak to them about their intimate life. They preferred to examine their conscience in private, repent of their sins, and pray for God's forgiveness. At the beginning of every mass, after the general confession of sins, the celebrant offers a prayer of absolution: "May almighty God have mercy upon you, forgive you your sins and bring you to life everlasting." Catholics used to overlook this prayer; now, having given up on private confession, they greatly appreciate this liturgical absolution. In some parishes the sacrament of forgiveness is celebrated collectively in a liturgy of repentance, offering absolution in God's name to all participants.

The belief that God's pardon is available in prayer has had a visible effect on parish life: everyone present at mass goes to communion. In the past, it is well remembered, many people remained in their seats, postponing communion until they had gone to confession. Today, they all stand up and move forward, which is beautiful to see.

The absence of agreement on the ethics of sexual love among the faithful, the papal commission, and the theologians reveals that the ecclesiastical magisterium must rethink its ethical teaching. Today the church addresses Catholics who have acquired a sense of personal autonomy from contemporary culture. The Anglican and Protestant churches have made a greater effort to combine fidelity to the Gospel with a personalist ethics. They have recognized that the biological dimension of sexuality is always cast in a particular cultural context and that sexual ethics is thus inevitably related to cultural factors. Catholic thinkers used to defend the idea of an unchanging human nature that can be defined in rational terms, providing ethical norms that are universally valid, thus being obligatory for persons in all historical contexts. Yet this idea of universality is today increasingly challenged by Catholic thinkers.

Even Cardinal Joseph Ratzinger challenged the traditional teaching. In his public dialogue with Jürgen Habermas in Munich in 2004,[5] the cardinal admitted that the time had come to abandon the idea held in the Catholic tradition that human nature can be known metaphysically and that, from this knowledge, one may derive universally valid ethical norms. He gave two reasons for saying that this is no longer convincing. First, we know now that human nature has evolved over two hundred thousand years, and, second, we have become more aware of the plurality of civilizations. Natural law, he said, had become a blunt instrument (*ein stumpfes Instrument*). The cardinal proposed to replace metaphysical reason by practical reason, that is to say, he proposed to foster a rational conversation, excluding no one, in order to devise ethical norms that enable people to live together in justice, peace, and mutual respect. In the dialogue of 2004, the cardinal accepted Habermas's approach to ethics. Yet the public statements of the cardinal – after 2005, as Benedict XVI – continues to defend traditional natural law theory.

That sexual ethics is embedded in particular cultures is well expressed by Michael Czerny, SJ, for many years a member of the African Jesuit AIDS Network (AJAN) that offered help to Africans in the present AIDS epidemic. Czerny thinks that people in the North do not understand how sexual relations are understood in Africa. He argues that the sexual norm accepted in the secular culture of the North is simply "mutual consent," the free agreement of two adults to engage in a sexual relation. By contrast, Czerny writes, "The idea we have in Africa is that there are other norms, and that these norms don't depend only on [the two people involved]: they also depend on our family, they depend on our community, they depend on our parish, they depend on our nation, and maybe even on our tribe."[6] This expresses well the idea that sexual ethics is embedded in a cultural context.

The Catholic social ethics we have inherited was embedded in a society very different from our own. The contrast between traditional society and modern culture has been extensively analyzed in the sociological literature that I examine in *Religion and Alienation*. In traditional society people were for the most part shaped by their community: they practised the same religion, shared the same values, and celebrated their collective identity, which was more precious to them than their personal freedom. In traditional society, people tended to look upon the hierarchical order as a given, to accept patiently the inherited social inequalities, and to believe in the justness of obedience to their superiors and the norms of their society. By contrast, in the culture produced by democracy and industrialization, people tend to define themselves first of all as persons, to embrace the religion and the values that seem right to them, and to choose the bonds that link them to the various communities with which they interact. Charles Taylor refers to this as the emergence of "the buffered self." In modern society, people tend to hold that all persons are equal, to resent inherited social inequalities, and to believe that, in some circumstances, disobedience is right.

Sociologists did not praise modern society as moral progress: on the contrary, they brought to light its moral ambiguity.[7] They recognized that modernity undermined traditional social cohesion and fostered, instead, the freedom of the individual, a problematic cultural development. Sociologists lamented that the emphasis on personal freedom brought forth a new individualism, a selfish desire for material success, and indifference to the common good. Yet they also recognized that assigning priority to personal freedom can have creative effects, making people explore their potentialities, discover new values, imagine a more just society, struggle to abolish slavery, and decide to extend their solidarity to people despised by society. Emphasis on personal freedom can also favour respect for people who are different, enabling us to see them as free agents, not obliged to correspond to our expectations. Modern society is ambiguous: it fosters values that are in fact contradictory.

Because modern culture does not provide a set of consistent values, people have to wrestle to clarify their own moral values and be true to their deepest convictions. Charles Taylor refers to this as "the search for authenticity." But if each one follows his or her own ethical journey, does this lead to relativism and produce confusion or even chaos in society? Taylor replies to this question. He argues, as did Wilhelm Dilthey at the beginning of the twentieth century, that people who take ethics seriously do their thinking within a particular tradition: people of faith do this within their religious community, and secular people clarify their ethical values by engaging in dialogue with a philosophical tradition. People do not invent values; they discover them. Taylor shows that ethical traditions are few, that they overlap in various ways, and that they do not constitute a pluralism that undermines the cohesion of society. What damages the well-being of society is not the pluralism of ethical convictions but, rather, the market mentality bent on stopping people from taking ethics seriously and making them embrace a narrow unreflective utilitarianism.

Even the Christian message is interpreted differently in traditional society than it is in modern society. A good illustration is the dramatic manner in which the Catholic Church has changed its teaching on religious liberty. The papacy had condemned the rights of "man" and, in particular, the freedom of religion in resistance to the liberal state set up at the end of the eighteenth century. Yet the absence of unanimity in modern society has obliged people to find their own spiritual way, support freedom of conscience, and respect ethical pluralism. Rereading the Scriptures, theologians found biblical teaching – above all the high dignity of the human person – that supported human rights. Yet the struggle to change the church's official teaching went on for decades. Only after a lively debate at the Second Vatican Council did the ecclesial magisterium recognize human rights and the freedom of religion.

The above reflections raise the question of relativism, a topic I discuss below.[8] At this point, I want to return to the cultural embeddedness of sexual ethics, a topic so well addressed by Michael Czerny. There is no doubt that the sexual ethics embedded in traditional society will be different from the sexual ethics, even Christian sexual ethics, practised in contemporary society.

In traditional society marriages were, for the most part, arranged so as to create a bond between two families, even if the free consent of the bride and the groom were honoured. Marriages were meant to produce children and to share responsibility for the extended family. Marriages were rarely unions of two people in love: they were defined in legal terms, which assigned to each partner his and her respective duties. The family was a school of virtue that prepared the young for their life in society. Because society was patriarchal, so, too, were the families. The husband was the master: in addition to the care and protection he owed to his wife and children, he had the authority to give them orders and, if they disobeyed, to chastise them. Because sexuality was seen as oriented towards procreation, sexual relations outside of the marriage bond were strictly forbidden. In traditional society, sexual ethics was articulated in clearly defined rules, with no attention to the subjective factor – that is, the growth and enrichment of the persons involved.

Let me add two points to this brief description of traditional sexual ethics in the West. First, from the teaching of the ancient church fathers, traditional Christian culture had inherited a suspicion of sexual pleasure, inappropriate especially for women. My admiration for St Augustine does not prevent me from lamenting the lasting influence of his bizarre idea that Adam's originating sin was passed on from one generation to the next by sexual intercourse. Second, before the discovery of the female ovum in the first part of the nineteenth century, people thought that the male seed carried human beings in miniature (*homunculi*) and that the female womb was simply the vessel for the male seed and made no contribution to the procreative process. The spilling of male seed was thus regarded with dismay as an act close to murder. This twofold inheritance affected the sexual ethics of traditional Catholic society.

Marriage in modern society is different from marriage in traditional society. In modern times, the nuclear family, constituted by husband, wife, and children, acquires more importance than the extended family. Marriages are not planned by parents: they are chosen by their sons and daughters who love one another, believe in equality, and think they can create a happy home together. Because they do not want their union to be *un égoisme à deux*, they plan to have children and/or to become responsible actors in society. Here the family is still a school of virtue, preparing the children for life in modern society, teaching them human rights, gender equality, respect for religious pluralism, and concern for the natural environment.

For married couples in modern culture the sexual embrace is the celebration of their love. Having responsibly chosen how many children they want, they limit conception in a manner approved by both partners.

Let me return to Michael Czerny's remark that modern, secular society recognizes common consent, or mutuality, as the single moral norm of sexual practices. He is rightly troubled by this. While mutuality is a great moral achievement, unknown in patriarchal cultures, it is not, in matters sexual, a sufficient criterion for Christians and humanists.

Mutuality is a moral principle that makes ethical demands on married life that were not recognized in traditional societies. The principle of mutuality excludes sexual relations between persons of unequal status, between doctors and their patients, teachers and their students, ministers of religion and their parishioners, and, of course, between adults and children or youth. Mutuality excludes manipulation, oppression, devious behaviour, and the seeking of rewards. Yet it is not the only ethical principle guiding sexual relations.

Because the church's official sexual ethics is a reflection of a culture different from their own, Catholic theologians have proposed a set of norms for a contemporary Catholic sexual ethics. In addition to mutuality, I wish to propose two other principles: loving concern for the good of the other and critical attention to the relationship's impact on the soul.

To be ethical, sexual relations must include concern for the good of the partner: the search for personal happiness is not enough. Needed is tender love for the partner and the readiness to support him or her in the effort to live well and to flourish. Under certain conditions this tender concern may be expressed outside of the marriage bond. What counts is that sexual relations express the desire of the partners to become intimately united, to support one another in their life's project, and to share their fears and hopes. This ethical criterion excludes sexual relations prompted by a purely self-regarding interest, a search for pleasure indifferent to the partner's well-being.

Of course, there are many situations in which people unable to find love, living as strangers in a strange world, engage in sexual relations of which they are not proud. These situations abound in contemporary society. To protect their humanity while doing what they regard as in some way wrong, these people at least have to be considerate and respectful of their partner(s). Domination and exploitation are always sinful. Christians must have compassion for lonely people – isolated by their work, their poverty, their location, or other circumstances – who seek sexual satisfaction in moments of tenderness, even if they feel that in doing so they are somehow morally defective.

Attention must always be paid to the effect of these relations on the two partners. Do they foster self-realization? Do they make them more mature, more generous, more spiritual, more ready to embrace their human vocation? Or do these relations produce excessive dependency, making the partners more selfish, fostering indifference with regard to their work, their spiritual growth, or their social engagement? A Catholic sexual ethics demands that the partners take a critical look at themselves and evaluate the impact of their sexual relations on their lives.

Sexual ethics, Michael Czerny reminds us, is embedded in a particular culture. I suggest that a Catholic and humanistic sexual ethics for contemporary Western culture proposes three principles: (1) mutuality between the partners, (2) loving concern for the good of the other, and (3) critical attention to the relation's impact on the soul. The ideal realization of this relation takes place in married life.

Several Catholic theologians have proposed a new Catholic sexual ethics for present-day Western society, even though they knew they would be censored by the magisterium.[9] Among them is a man for whom I have great respect, Stephan Pfürtner, who had the courage to publicly criticize the Nazi government on ethical grounds. He was arrested and imprisoned in 1941. After his release he saved the lives of three Jewish women by hiding them in his parents' home. I became acquainted with Stephan Pfürtner in the 1950s when we were both students of theology at the University of Fribourg in Switzerland. Over a decade later, then a professor of theological ethics at the same university, Pfürtner published his *Kirche und Sexualität*,[10] a proposal for a new Catholic sexual ethics. In this book he shows that the church's official teaching suffers from a *Sexualfeindlichkeit* (hostility towards sexuality) inherited from ancient Hellenistic currents and some early church fathers. This teaching, he argues, recognizes the need of sexuality for the propagation of the human race but refers to sexual desires in largely negative terms, belittling the human striving for sexual happiness. Wishing to correct this negative approach, Pfürtner proposes that, within the bounds of love, truth, and justice, every person has the right to sexual happiness. His book was condemned by the Vatican; he lost his professorship; he was rejected by his religious order; and he then left the Catholic Church, continuing his theological research within a wider ecumenical orbit. Yet no one could take from him the honour of having been a witness of Catholic ethics in a dangerous time – a time when most German bishops and priests, the official teachers of Catholic ethics, had nothing to say.

14

The Issue of Homosexual Love

In 1973, I gave a public lecture on ecclesiology in Los Angeles, in which I proposed that the structure of the church should be such that the religious insights of Catholics on the ground could influence the teaching and pastoral policies of the ecclesiastical authorities. When I returned to my office in Toronto, I received a letter from a person in Los Angeles, whose name I don't remember, who told me he had founded Dignity, an association of Catholic homosexuals, men and women, committed to expressing their sexuality in a manner consonant with the Gospel. Having heard my lecture, he now sent me the faith statement of Dignity, asking me to evaluate it in theological terms. This would help these Catholics, he wrote, to communicate their religious experience to the church at large. After some hesitation, I wrote a positive evaluation of their faith statement, which was later published in *Commonweal* (15 February 1974). I believe I was the first Catholic theologian who publicly defended the ethical status of homosexual love.

In my article I provide two arguments. In the first I show that human nature is always embodied in a particular culture and that what appears to us as "natural" is, in part, a cultural product. Thus the hierarchical relationship between men and women appears "natural" in traditional society, which is unaware of its patriarchal inheritance. The definition of human nature tends to reflect the self-understanding of the cultural elite. To say that homosexual love is "unnatural" is to make a cultural statement. Today, in a culture open to diversity, scientists have come to look at homosexual orientation as "a natural variant" – like being left-handed.

My second argument is derived from my study of the anti-Jewish rhetoric of Christian preaching and the cultural hostility to Jews that it has created. The church's anti-homosexual rhetoric has produced a culture that despises and persecutes homosexuals, devises cruel punishments for homosexual acts, and fosters self-doubt and self-hatred in homosexual men and women. Recognizing the destructive cultural power exerted by the discourses of contempt, the church is urged by Christ's great commandment – to love one's neighbour as oneself – to review its teaching with regard to "outsiders": women, Jews, followers of the world religions, Aboriginal peoples, and, yes, gays and lesbians.

The biblical authors and the theologians of the church were unaware that, in all societies, some persons experience homosexuality as their natural orientation. They condemned homosexual acts, thinking they were committed by heterosexual men and women who were acting against their nature, searching for pleasure without responsibility.

In our day, reflecting on the teaching of Jesus and trusting their spiritual experiences, the men and women associated with Dignity are convinced that homosexual love is a gift of God, just as is heterosexual love, and that the moral criteria guiding these human powers are in fact quite similar. Since the 1970s, Christian gays and lesbians, reflecting on what the Gospel means in their lives, have produced a spiritual literature that deserves to be taken seriously. Without taking this literature into account, writes John Coleman,[1] no one should engage in an ethical evaluation of homosexual love. Since the magisterium has until now paid no attention to the Christian experience of homosexual men and women, a remark made by Pope

Francis could be a turning point. Speaking on the plane returning from Brazil on 28 July 2013, Francis said: "If a person is gay and seeks the Lord and has good will, who am I to judge that person?"

The Anglican Church and several Protestant churches have listened to the Christian witness of homosexuals and, from the 1990s on, expressed their respect for their gay and lesbian members, recognizing their right to become candidates for the ordained ministry. The United Church of Canada has decided to bless same-sex marriages. Why, one may ask, do gay couples want to get married? Why is a purely civil union, which has the legal and juridical consequences of marriage, not sufficient for them? I actually once wrote (I don't remember where) that the civil union of a gay couple cannot become a marriage in the Catholic sense because marriage is a sacrament, effectively symbolizing the divinely sustained reconciliation between men and women, the two halves of humanity. Still, a good number of gays and lesbians desire to get married because they have a Christian understanding of marriage as a union rooted in God's promise, symbolizing their fidelity and binding them as they grow old and take care of one another.

In an article published a few years ago I dealt with a question I have been asked several times.[2] Should a gay Catholic remain in the Catholic Church, where he or she is despised and forbidden to choose a partner for life? Why should she or he not join the United Church of Canada, where homosexuality is seen as a natural variant and the love for a same-sex partner receives God's blessing? This is a question for which I have no easy answer.

15

Moving to Montreal

In Ontario, university professors were obliged to retire at the age of sixty-five. This law, eventually withdrawn in 2005, was inconvenient for me in the 1980s. I would have had to retire in 1988, a step for which I was not prepared financially. While a priest, my paycheque at St Michael's College went directly to the Augustinian Order: only when I left the priesthood in 1974 did I receive a professor's salary. In these short years I had not saved enough to afford retirement. I was therefore grateful when I received an invitation to take up a position in the Faculty of Religious Studies at McGill University in Montreal. My wife and I moved to Montreal in 1986, and this turned out to be an amazing adventure.

McGill is an anglophone university, and since it is possible to live in the western part of Montreal and speak only English, professors at McGill do not easily find entry into the French-speaking society. My situation was different. Because I had written articles for *Concilium*, a review published in several languages, including French, I was not unknown in Quebec's theological community. I had already taught a semester at McGill in 1977 and an entire academic year in 1981 at the francophone Université de Montréal à Québec (UQAM). When I moved permanently to Montreal in 1986, I was invited by Albert Beaudry, the editor of the francophone review *Relations*, to join its editorial committee. *Relations* is published by le Centre justice et foi and is supported by the Jesuits. Its orientation reflects the shift to the left taken by the Society of Jesus at its General Council of 1975, at which it redefined its mission as the promotion of faith and the justice demanded by faith.[1]

I considered my work at the editorial committee of *Relations* a great privilege. It allowed me to observe and participate in the political and cultural debates carried on in Quebec society. I was an outsider invited to become an insider. Embracing the social concerns of les Québécois had an effect on my perception of the world and my work as a theologian. According to Bernard Lonergan, whenever the horizon of what we see before us is enlarged, understanding the world demands an intellectual conversion, a rethinking of previously held presuppositions and ideas.

Even though this book is not an autobiography in that it does not tell the story of my personal life, I wish to mention the good friends I left behind in Toronto, in particular Marion Malone and her husband Grant Goodbrand, and Sharon McIsaac and her husband Philip McKenna. They were part of a circle of young men and women associated with the Therafields movement mentioned above. For many years, my wife Shirley and I would return to Toronto to celebrate Christmas with this circle of friends. I found new friends in Montreal: let me mention Andrée, Colleen, Élisabeth, Margie, André, Doug, John, Normand, and Réjean. My close association with le Centre justice et foi kept me alert, attentive to the developments in church and society.

When invited in 2009 to give a lecture on how moving to Quebec had affected my theology – a lecture subsequently published in the *Toronto Journal of Theology*[2] – I spoke of the Catholic left in Montreal and my involvement in it. The Catholic left is promoted by several centres and organizations. Le Centre justice et foi engages in social analysis to promote a prophetic faith and a critical culture: it does this through its review *Relations*; les soirées *Relations*, which involve panel discussions of critical issues pertaining to church and society; and the team "Vivre ensemble," which puts out a newsletter concerned with justice for refugees and immigrants. There are two centres of contextual theology in Montreal, an academic one at l'Université de Montréal and another, La théologie contextuelle, giving voice to Christians engaged in social movements. L'Autre Parole is an association of Catholic women committed to gender equality and social justice, and it promotes a vision of Catholicism liberated from its patriarchal inheritance. In an attempt to explore the prophetic dimension of the Gospel, Le Centre St-Pierre carries on popular education and dialogue with those who have been marginalized. L'Entraide missionnaire examines the problematic relationship between the global North and the global South in order to understand the meaning of the Gospel and to foster the church's mission in a world cruelly divided between rich and poor. I also wish to mention Les journées sociales, a weekend of study and reflection that takes place every two years and that is attended by Christian activists from all parts of Quebec. The head office of Development and Peace, located in Montreal, also made an important contribution to raising the consciousness of church-going Catholics. Strong support for this faith and justice movement is given by a great number of women belonging to various religious orders and congregations. The Catholic left, as I indicate in my lecture, became my spiritual home.

We hear the Gospel as a prophetic message, as God's judgment on the sinful world and God's promise of liberation and new life. Since we want Quebec to thrive as a just and compassionate society, we examine it from the perspective of the poor, the unemployed, the exploited, and the marginalized. We promote Quebec's cultural identity, keenly aware that the francophone society constitutes a small minority on the English-speaking North American continent. We are also in solidarity with critical Christians in the global South, and we denounce neoliberal capitalism both as an economic system and as a culture. We remember the bold pastoral statements made by the Canadian Catholic bishops in the 1970s and early 1980s, endorsing the preferential option for the poor and applying the principles of liberation theology to the Canadian situation.[3] These statements, largely forgotten by the bishops of today, have retained their relevance. We are now delighted by Pope Francis and give thanks to God.

The witness of the men and women involved in this faith and justice movement supports me in my work. These people teach me what the option for the poor means in concrete terms in Quebec and in Quebec's relation to Aboriginal peoples, to Canada, and to the world at large. With them I share the sorrow over the suffering inflicted upon the powerless in this world, and with them I am saddened by the conservative current in today's church, which renders people indifferent to the suffering of others. Pope Francis himself has lamented today's "globalisation of indifference."[4] While the members of the Catholic left may not be in agreement on all issues, they are firmly united in a common effort to explore what the option for the poor means in Quebec. Thanks to this movement, my work as a practical theologian is not abstract: it is grounded in the experiences of committed Christians, it listens to their intuitions, and it learns from their concrete involvement in society.

At this point, I wish to make a few remarks about the difference between the Catholicism of Quebec and that of English-speaking Canada. While the Catholic Church is doctrinally and structurally the same everywhere, Catholicism has a different appearance in each historical community. Very little research has been conducted on comparative Catholicism. A characteristic of Catholicism in Quebec is that it was the religion of the great majority and, at one time, was an integral part of this province's national identity. It was a *Volkskirche*. By contrast, in English-speaking Canada, Catholicism was the religion of a minority, many of whom were, at one time, exposed to prejudice and discrimination. Catholicism in Quebec had a determining impact on the public culture, while Catholicism in English-speaking Canada was necessarily defensive and had little direct influence on the public culture.

These two forms of Catholicism also reacted differently to the Second Vatican Council. In Quebec, starting in 1960, the conciliar renewal of the church was accompanied by the Quiet Revolution, which produced a cultural transformation that eventually led to the secularization of Quebec society. The bishops experienced the Quiet Revolution as a rupture. Since they now represented only a minority in Quebec, they lost their power to influence the government and control the public culture. They were now in charge of a Catholic community that wanted to be consulted, that demanded greater freedom, and that wished to play a responsible role in the church. Many bishops, themselves affected by the Quiet Revolution, welcomed this reformist trend. In fact, they set up a commission to study the aspirations of the Catholic community. Needless to say, the renewal of the Second Vatican Council also had a strong impact on Catholicism in English-speaking Canada, yet there it did not produce a rupture; rather, its influence was gradual, continuity was preserved, and the role of the bishops did not change.

Today historians of Quebec debate to what extent the Quiet Revolution was a radical transformation of society and to what extent it was simply a cultural evolution whose results were similar to the impact of liberal ideas on other Western societies. For the Parent Commission (1963–64)[5] and the Dumont Commission (1968–71),[6] the cultural upheaval of the Quiet Revolution was undoubtedly a significant turning point. Published in several volumes beginning in 1971, the Dumont Report concludes that Quebec Catholicism had entered a new phase, characterized by the freedom and responsibility of the laity, both men and women, and their ongoing dialogue with their priests and bishops. It refers to this renewal as "rupture and fidelity" – startling innovation and, at the same time, a deeper embrace of the Catholic tradition. The Dumont Report recommended the creation of institutions on the parochial, diocesan, and national levels to facilitate intra-ecclesial dialogue. The bishops were asked to acknowledge the internal pluralism in the church and to respect dissenting Catholics faithful to their personal conscience. According to the report, the new democratic ethos is reconcilable with the church's sacramental papal-episcopal structure.

Even if the Quebec bishops were unable to accept many of these recommendations, they encouraged the creativity of the laity, took their aspirations seriously, tolerated pluralism within the church, and, while they upheld the official Catholic teaching, they respected dissident voices. While, following the rapid secularization of society beginning in the early 1970s, the bishops represented only a minority of the people, they nonetheless remained pastorally concerned with the whole of society. They affirmed their solidarity with the new Quebec. They continued to address national and social justice issues, thus participating in the public debate that constitutes modern democratic society. On the first of May, the bishops publish a pastoral statement, critical of society's structured injustices and in solidarity with workers, the unemployed, and the poor. These progressive pastoral statements greatly encouraged the Catholic left. The bishops also respected the pluralism of Quebec society – the vivre ensemble of believers of various traditions and unbelievers. Recognizing the frustration of women in the church and listening to their aspirations, the bishops made repeated proposals for institutional change at the Vatican – yet to no avail.[7]

The Dumont Report also set the tone for the development of theology in Quebec. The cultural transformation of Quebec and its rapid secularization summon theologians to become creative and to articulate the Gospel in a new way. They do this in great freedom. They respect the ecclesiastical magisterium, yet they also think that raising theological questions with regard to the official teaching is a task theology cannot avoid. They understand themselves as mediators promoting dialogue on every level of the church. I was so impressed by the theological vitality in the Church of Quebec that I decided to write *Truth and Relevance: Catholic Theology in French Quebec since the Quiet Revolution*.

16

Quebec Nationalism and Human Rights

Living and working in Quebec, I found myself surrounded by nationalists. People often think of nationalism as an aggressive ideology that glorifies the nation and produces hostility towards outsiders. Yet nationalism has many faces. In Toronto, I was familiar with Canadian nationalism advocated by the Committee for an Independent Canada, a group of intellectuals and politicians who wished to protect Canada from economic and cultural domination exercised by the large republic south of the border. Douglas Hall, a good friend of mine, refers to this as "nationalism at the edge of empire." Yet in Canada this nationalism was a minor movement. In Quebec, by contrast, nationalism is a pervasive political culture, embraced in various ways by federalists and sovereignists. Federalists promote Quebec as a nation within Canada, and sovereignists want Quebec to thrive as a sovereign nation adjacent to Canada.

Quebecers and Canadians define their identity with reference to quite different sets of historical memories. Quebecers remember that their ancestors came from France over three hundred years ago; that their society was later ceded to the British Crown; that they struggled to preserve their language and their culture; and that, when they became a province of the Canadian federation in 1867, they were assigned a subordinate place – a condition challenged by the Quiet Revolution. These memories have produced a culture of resistance.

Federalist and sovereignist Quebecers are in agreement that their small French-speaking nation, with its particular cultural inheritance, has to defend itself against the cultural power of the English language in North America. The cultural power of a language refers to the societal impact exercised by the major institutions that operate in that language. In North America (and not only in North America), the language of technology, industry, commerce, administration, communication, the sciences, and even entertainment is English. In this situation, the multiculturalism formally adopted by the Canadian government in 1985 presented no threat to the English language. By contrast, the government of Quebec rejected multiculturalism, replacing it with an intercultural policy that welcomes the cultural customs brought by immigrants and, at the same time, protects the French language and Quebec's cultural memory. In the North American context, the French language requires the support of the law. Already in 1974 and later again in 1977, the Quebec government made French the official language of the province.

Nationalism raises important ethical and theological questions. Being well acquainted with German nationalism, I am spontaneously suspicious of nationalist movements. Moreover, Christianity is a universalist faith that has no preference for any one nation. Theologians in Quebec have dealt with these issues. Because the nationalism of my friends raised many questions for me, I made a study of this topic, eventually writing a book entitled *Nationalism, Religion, and Ethics*.[1] In it I deal with four religious thinkers – Mahatma Gandhi, Martin Buber, Paul Tillich, and Jacques Grand'Maison – who offer criteria for distinguishing between ethically acceptable and ethically unacceptable forms of nationalism.

The teaching of the bishops of Quebec on nationalism is impressive. In 1979, prior to the first referendum on sovereignty, the bishops published a pastoral letter that recognized the right of Quebecers to political self-determination in keeping with international law.[2] The bishops insisted that it was not their task to tell Quebecers how to vote in the referendum. Their task was, rather, to offer ethical reflections on nationalism in the light of the Gospel. They argued in their letter that a nationalist movement is ethical only if it observes four conditions: first, it must aim to create a more just and more open society (what is rejected here are forms of nationalism that are non-democratic or that are driven by a national bourgeoisie indifferent to the concerns of workers and peasants); second, it must protect the human rights of minorities (what is rejected here is ethnic discrimination); third, it must aim at maintaining peaceful relations with adjacent societies (what is rejected here is an aggressive nationalism guided by an expansionist dream); and fourth, the nation must never be allowed to become the highest good – this would be idolatry.

Since Catholic social teaching contains hardly any ethical reflections on nationalism, the letter of the Quebec bishops made an important contribution to Catholic thought. The bishops actually relied upon the book *Religion et nationalisme*,[3] written by Jacques Grand'Maison, a prominent social theologian in Quebec. Addressing himself to Quebecers, Grand'Maison emphasizes that nations are dynamic communities capable of redefining themselves creatively in response to new historical circumstances, such as the arrival of newcomers or the emancipation of previously marginalized groups. A rigid clinging to an identity defined in the past, Grand' Maison argues, has socially destructive consequences. A nationalist movement is ethically acceptable only if it is ready to respond creatively to new historical challenges. In his book, which was published in 1970, Grand'Maison argues that the nationalism of the Parti Québécois, committed to social democracy and human rights, is in keeping with Catholic social thought and deserves the support of believing Catholics.

In my opinion, the mainstream of the nationalist movement in Quebec, initiated by the Quiet Revolution, passes the four tests proposed by the bishops and lives up to the norms spelled out by Grand'Maison. In particular, the Quebec government under Liberal and Parti Québécois leadership has welcomed the new cultural pluralism. It has expressed its intercultural policy in several public statements, favouring Quebec's francophone culture and, at the same time, guaranteeing the rights of the established Anglo-Québécois community, the human rights of the cultural communities, and equal citizenship for all Quebecers whatever their ethnic origin. This was confirmed in Quebec's Charter of Human Rights and Freedoms, which was published in 1975, five years before the Canadian Charter.

At the same time, within this broad consensus, there exists an ongoing debate between Quebecers who emphasize Quebec's new pluralism and Quebecers whose main concern is Quebec's cultural identity. The debate becomes passionate when it deals with the response of secular society to the presence of the new religions in the public sphere. Because of a lingering resentment against the Catholic Church, many Quebecers are displeased to see visible religious symbols in public institutions. The Bouchard-Taylor Commission, appointed by the government in 2007 to resolve these debates, had recommended freedom of religion in the widest sense and, at the same time, insisted on *la laïcité* of the state. It counselled that men and women in high positions of authority in government should abstain from wearing visible signs of their religious faith but that government employees on lower levels, especially in schools and hospitals, should have the freedom to wear such signs, including the Islamic veil. The Bouchard-Taylor Report favoured "la laïcité ouverte," the secular character of the state and its respect for the religions of its citizens. Since the Liberal government did not react to the Bouchard-Taylor Report, the heated debate continued. In 2013, the Parti Québécois government decided to submit to the national assembly a charter of Quebec values, proposing a stricter laïcité, demanding that all government employees, especially in schools and hospitals, abstain from wearing visible religious signs. This proposal again created a vehement public debate, which ceased very suddenly in April 2014 when the Parti Québéois lost the provincial election.

The new Liberal government is likely to endorse the proposals of the Bouchard-Taylor Report.

The Catholic bishops favour the "open laïcité" recommended by Bouchard-Taylor. Le Centre justice et foi has been actively involved in the public debate defending the more generous understanding of religious pluralism. What worries us in particular is that the strict laïcité proposed by the Parti Québécois government limits the freedom of Muslim women and makes Muslims feel that they cannot become Quebecers in the full sense. While we opposed the Parti Québécois government's proposal, we thought that the negative reaction of newspapers in English-speaking Canada – which accused the Quebec government of racism and xenophobia – was uncomprehending and unjust. Racism does exist in Quebec, as it does in the rest of Canada, and it deserves to be denounced in both societies. What the anglophone critics overlooked is that the theoretical basis of the proposed Charter was a people's right of cultural self-determination, a human right recognized by the United Nations on the condition that the rights of individuals are not curtailed.[4] The tension existing between the right of self-determination and personal human rights calls for a delicate balance, a compromise achieved through mutual respect and dialogue.

Faith and justice Catholics, in particular, are concerned with the inclusion of newcomers. Julien Harvey, the founder of le Centre justice et foi, himself an ardent nationalist, always insisted that justice was a higher value than nation. Because of this, he founded Vivre ensemble, a team at le Centre with which I am closely involved, to promote justice for immigrants and refugees. We also try to reflect theologically on pluralism and cultural identity. We regret that the public debate tends to confuse people by suggesting that they have to choose between (1) openness to pluralism and (2) concern for Quebec's identity; we insist, rather, that the two must go together. With many thoughtful Quebecers, Julien Harvey argued that collective identities have a dynamic character, enabling a people to respond creatively to new historical conditions. This happened to Quebecers in the Quiet Revolution: they were able to redefine their identity. And this is happening at present as they open themselves to the integration of new immigrants.

A similar unhappy debate occurs when Quebecers are made to choose between "ethnic nationalism," which takes pride in society's past history, and "civic nationalism," which celebrates the common citizenship of the present. Again, this is not a choice between two opposites. Societies that enjoy equal citizenship remember their historical origin and especially their long struggle to constitute themselves as a democracy. Civic nationalism is not devoid of historical memories. In fact, the memory of past struggles for freedom and justice remains a source of political engagement for reform in the present. Newcomers in a society enter upon the history of a people – a history in which, in due time, they will participate economically, culturally, and politically.

Ethical reflections on nationalism are relevant in many parts of the world. Because of my theological interest in nationalist movements I was invited to speak at the Centre of Theology and Public Policy at the University of Edinburgh, which deals in critical and sympathetic fashion with the present left-leaning nationalist movement in Scotland.

17

Learning from Karl Polanyi

Moving to Montreal also led me to discover the critical social thought of Karl Polanyi (1886–1964), whose original analysis of modern society is of relevance today. I remember listening to him in the early 1960s, when he addressed an ecumenical gathering organized by the Christian Student Movement at Macdonald College at Ste Anne de Bellevue, Quebec (I do not now recall what he said). Now I have learned that he was a Hungarian scholar, born in Vienna, committed to social justice in theory and practice, with great sympathy for the social thought of the British left, its pluralism, and its ethical concern. When he moved to Britain in the 1930s, he joined the public debate in that country and chose to cooperate with thinkers of the Christian left.[1] Eventually, Polanyi moved to Canada. Because his thought is original and remains influential, his daughter, Kari Polanyi Levitt, professor at McGill, and Margie Mendell, professor at Concordia, both of whom are economists, decided in 1987 to found the Karl Polanyi Institute of Political Economy, a research centre at Montreal's Concordia University. The institute is also a forum for lectures, panel discussions, and dialogues that apply Polanyi's critical thought in an attempt to better understand the globalized liberal economy and culture. Invited to become a member of the institute, I started to explore Polanyi's thought.

Studying his classic, *The Great Transformation*,[2] first published in 1942, I soon discovered that Polanyi was an economic historian and social scientist whose critical analysis of the unregulated market system differed from Marxism in that he paid serious attention to cultural and ethical factors. Polanyi shows, first, that critical scientific research must be guided by an emancipatory commitment – against the "objectivity" claimed by positivists of the left and the right – and, second, that oppression and liberation are processes that involve cultural factors and, hence, may not be accounted for by purely material considerations. As I read Polanyi, I regretted that Latin American liberation theologians had not engaged in dialogue with him rather than with Marx. In 2014, after the publication of Pope Francis's exhortation *Evangelii gaudium*, Leonardo Boff, prominent Latin American liberation theologian, suggested that the critical social thought of Francis had been influenced by Karl Polanyi.[3]

I wish to mention two of Karl Polanyi's ideas that have been important in my own reflections. First, he recognized that the organization of labour has a cultural impact on workers. In traditional societies, it was through their labour that workers occupied their respected place in their community and strengthened the bond between its members. What made these people work was not the profit motive but, rather, the will to keep their standing in the community. In industrial societies, whether capitalist or communist, Polanyi argues, the organization of labour "disembeds" workers from their community: their work removes them from their village or town and ceases to be of service to their community. Obliged to follow the instructions of the head office, workers are turned into obedient instruments of production: no one listens to their ideas, which they have derived from their work experience. Removed from their community, they quickly become isolated individuals whose work is motivated simply by the will to survive. Having lost the social solidarity they had inherited, they are not ready to participate in a political movement to transform society. Polanyi believes that, before a political movement to create social democracy can be successful, the organization of labour must be changed, thus "re- embedding" workers in the community, making them co-responsible for their labour, and having their work serve the community to which they belong. What is urgently needed, Polanyi argues, is the democratization of industrial production. The participatory organization of labour fosters social solidarity and prompts workers to become active citizens, ready for a political struggle for an equitable distribution of wealth and a more just society.

Karl Polanyi's idea of "re-embedding" labour within society offers a theoretical foundation for community development and the social economy. In Quebec, we refer to these phenomena as *le mouvement communautaire* and *l'économie solidaire*. Here work and action generate social solidarity. Community development and the social economy have cultural consequences: they rescue people from individualism, turn them into responsible actors, and make them long for a society that is just and participatory. Action from the bottom up may eventually produce a culture of solidarity, capable of supporting a political movement to create a more just and more humane society.

Action from the bottom up has become an important movement in Quebec. I wish to mention, in particular, the social economy constituted by a wide network of enterprises that produces goods and services for society and provides paid employment, yet operates according to democratic principles, at odds with capitalist practice.[4] Because cooperatives have a long history in Quebec, and because the provincial government supports them, the social economy represents a significant sector of the economy. According to an estimate in 2006, it includes six thousand enterprises, provides between 7 and 8 percent of the gross national product, and employs 120,000 people.[5] While the social economy is unable to transform society as a whole, it transforms the lives of a vast number of people. It fosters a culture of critical thinking and innovative practices that may lay the foundation for a new political movement.

Let me mention in passing that the impact of the organization of labour on the humanity of workers was recognized by Pope John Paul II. In his 1981 encyclical on labour, he argues that, if industrial workers are treated as tools or as "objects of production," they will be humiliated and prevented from assuming their full humanity: only if they are treated as responsible agents or "subjects of production" will they be able to achieve self-realization.[6] The Polish pope was keenly aware that nationalizing industries does not by itself make society more just and more humane. What counts is the movement of workers to transform the industrial process, thus giving them joint responsibility, making them subjects of production and agents of social solidarity.

The second of Polanyi's ideas that is of particular importance to me is that liberal capitalism – or the unregulated market system, as he liked to call it – has a harmful effect on society as a whole. Land, work, and money are treated as commodities bought and sold on the market, even though they have not been produced by human labour. Polanyi calls them "fictitious commodities." If land goes to the highest bidder, then poor people in the country will lose their property and become unable to grow the food they need; if work and employment are ruled exclusively by the market, then vast numbers of people will find themselves unemployed; if money is treated as commodity, then the rich and powerful, who have control of the market, can manouevre weak nations into poverty. Polanyi's sensitivity to the human consequences of the unregulated market system has an affinity to Catholic social teaching, which is critical of liberal capitalism or any other economic system that is unrestricted by ethical norms. In his 29 October 2014 address to popular movements, Pope Francis's vocabulary is close to that of Karl Polanyi's: Francis laments that land, housing, and work have become commodities subject to the market, depriving poor people of the necessities of life – "their sacred rights," as he calls them.[7]

In 2005, Novalis decided to republish *Religion and Alienation*, a book I had written thirty years earlier. This gave me the chance to add a chapter on the critical social thought with which I had become acquainted since 1975. In the new edition, I refer in particular to the thought of Karl Polanyi and to the critical theory of the Frankfurt School. I also admit that I have come to recognize the sinister side of modernity, which I had overlooked when first writing this book.

18

Learning from the Frankfurt School

The sinister side of modernity was explored in an original manner in the early 1920s by the Frankfurt School of Social Research, founded by Max Horkheimer and Theodor Adorno, philosophers well known for their cultural pessimism. After 1933 (the year of the Nazi seizure of power), this pessimism was recognized as prophetic. The Frankfurt School combined two famous critiques of modernity: (1) the Marxist critique of class oppression and (2) the Weberian critique of the cultural domination of instrumental, or techno-scientific reason. The founders of the Frankfurt School were deeply disappointed by political Marxism. First, during the First World War, the Marxist-inspired parties of the European countries had supported the military policy of their respective governments, and, second, the Marxist-inspired Russian Revolution had produced a political dictatorship. According to the Frankfurt School, the Marxist analysis that people are imprisoned by economic conditions is incomplete. This is because it does not recognize that people are also prisoners of cultural presuppositions that affect their thoughts and actions.

The Frankfurt School saw the Enlightenment as a cultural revolution of great promise. It expected human reason to rescue society from its injustices and internal contradictions. Enlightenment reason had two dimensions: (1) *substantive* reason, dealing with the ethical vocation of humanity, with the ideas of freedom, equality, and solidarity, and (2) *instrumental* reason, dealing with science and technology. In the nineteenth century, Horkheimer and Adorno argue, the dominant culture of industrial society turned its back on substantive reason and looked upon techno-scientific reason as the only valid approach to truth. The cultural domination of instrumental reason, they argue, resulted in the ideological prison in which modern society finds itself – a prison devoid of ethical norms, disrespectful of personal conscience, and reducing human needs to purely material requirements while trusting that technology will solve all social problems. Here, society is largely seen as a complex machine. This culture will allow a powerful minority, for its own benefit, to manipulate and oppress people by exploiting their labour and controlling them through rigid bureaucracies. According to the Frankfurt School, a reversal has occurred: present-day Enlightenment has become the greatest obstacle to the humanization of society.

At the same time, the Frankfurt School did not repudiate modernity altogether, as did Heidegger and the existentialist philosophers after him. Horkheimer and Adorno upheld the modern institution of human rights against communist practice and emerging fascism. They resisted what the Enlightenment had become: a culture dominated by techno-scientific rationality, deprived of ethical reason. They called their negation of the Enlightenment "dialectical" because this negation (the first step) is followed by the retrieval of ethical reason from past philosophical traditions (the second step). Horkheimer and Adorno referred to their method of negation and retrieval as Critical Theory. They did not repudiate science and technology; rather, they simply limited them to make room for ethical reason at the cultural centre. While they had great respect for the rational ethics of Kant, they doubted that the culture to which they belonged had the inner resources to recover ethical values and put them into practice. This is why they were pessimistic. It did not occur to them that religious traditions were bearers of social values that might be retrieved to aid in a humane reconstruction of society.

After Hitler's rise to power, Horkheimer and Adorno took refuge in the United States. After the war, reflecting with dismay on the Holocaust, they proposed the bold thesis that this horrendous crime should not be seen as a regression of a civilized nation to primitive barbarism but, rather, as a revelation of the sinister side of modernity – the willingness to use techno-scientific reason to control and, if need be, eliminate human beings to fulfill the wishes of a powerful minority. The atomic bomb, they thought, was another instance of this sinister side. In recent decades, I sadly observe, many governments have sought to expand their power through political and military polices that employ ever more sophisticated technologies to inflict misery and death upon masses of people through starvation, bombings, killings, and wars.

With a good number of theologians, I have great sympathy for Critical Theory. Since I found Horkheimer's and Adorno's writings very difficult to read, I studied books and articles that interpreted their thought. I was inspired by the writings of Johann Baptist Metz. I also listened to my friend Rudi Siebert, professor of religion at Western Michigan University, a creative follower of the Frankfurt School, who has used the methods of Critical Theory to understanding the complex role of religion in human history.[1]

Critical Theory, as I have suggested, consists of negation and retrieval. To understand ideas, cultural movements, or historical events, one must begin with negation, discerning and repudiating their destructive implications, and then, after this, one must rescue the truth contained in them and explore its contemporary relevance. As we have seen, Critical Theory approaches modernity through dialectical negation: first clarifying and denouncing its sinister side, and then retrieving its positive inheritance, especially phenomena related to social solidarity and human rights. The Frankfurt School rejected liberal political theory but retrieved the liberal concern for personal freedom. Its negation of classical Marxism was also dialectical in that it rescued Marxism's critique of capitalism and its utopic vision of an alternative society.

The Frankfurt philosophers were opposed to non-dialectical negations: they called for the end of "innocent critiques." A critique of theories or movements is "innocent," first, if it does not rescue the grain of truth contained in them and, second, if it does not ask what its social consequences will be should it become an integral part of the dominant culture. Horkheimer and Adorno believed that Marx's critique of liberalism was "innocent" because (1) he failed to retrieve the liberal commitment to human rights and (2) because he did not ask himself what society would be like when a government-steered command economy replaced the market. Marx did not foresee the bureaucratic control that would be exercised by communist society. Conversely, liberalism's critique of Marxism is also "innocent" because it neither rescues the grain of truth in Marxist theory nor questions the impact of the unregulated market on the distribution of wealth.

Dialectical negation has its place in theology. In antiquity, the church exhibited a dialectical openness to the Platonic tradition and, in the Middle Ages, to Aristotelian philosophy. Yet, challenged by the Enlightenment, the popes negated modern philosophy non-dialectically, forbidding theologians to engage in critical dialogue with the philosophers of their time. Prior to the Second Vatican Council, the Catholic Church had rejected Protestant traditions non-dialectically, refusing to learn from their insights into the Gospel. Since the council, theologians and even popes have exhibited dialectical openness to secular thought and the plurality of religious traditions. A good example of this is Benedict XVI's dialogue with the Frankfurt School. In his encyclical *Spe salvi* (2007), he wrestles with the question of whether, after the Holocaust and the other massive evils of the twentieth century, it is still possible to believe in a good God. Here are two paragraphs from his encyclical:

> The atheism of the nineteenth and twentieth centuries is – in its origins and aims – a type of moralism: a protest against the injustices of the world and world history. A world marked by so

much injustice, innocent suffering and cynicism of power cannot be the work of a good God. A God with responsibility for such a world would not be a just God, much less a good God. It is for the sake of morality that this God has to be contested. Since there is no God to create justice, it seems man himself is now called to establish justice. If in the face of this world's suffering, protest against God is understandable, the claim that humanity can and must do what no God actually does or is able to do is presumptuous and false ...

No one and nothing can answer for centuries of suffering. No one and nothing can guarantee that the cynicism of power – whatever beguiling ideological mask it adopts – will cease to dominate the world. This is why the great thinkers of the Frankfurt School, Max Horkheimer and Theodor W. Adorno, were equally critical of atheism and theism. Horkheimer radically excluded the possibility of ever finding a this-worldly substitute for God, while at the same time he rejected the image of a good and just God. In an extreme radicalization of the Old Testament prohibition of images, he speaks of a "longing for the totally Other" that remains inaccessible – a cry of yearning directed at world history. Adorno also firmly upheld this total rejection of images, which meant the exclusion of any "image" of a loving God. On the other hand, he constantly emphasized the "negative" dialectic and asserted that justice – true justice – would require a world "where not only present suffering would be wiped out, but also that which is irrevocably past would be undone." This would mean, however – to express it with positive and hence, for him, inadequate symbols – that there can be no justice without a resurrection of the dead.

It is not surprising that the founders of the Frankfurt School failed to recognize the inequalities and injustices produced by the institution of patriarchy. Feminism became a strong cultural current only after the Second World War. When my conversations with Rosemary

Ruether, which took place at the end of the 1960s, convinced me to join the Catholic left, she herself was not yet a feminist theologian. It was only a few years later that she adopted a feminist perspective and then produced an original feminist theology that fully integrated her socialist critique of society and empire. While her work influenced vast number of women and men in all the Churches, it was not received by the Catholic magisterium.

Despite this lacuna, post-conciliar Catholic social teaching deserves careful attention. Thanks to a critical dialogue with secular thinkers, including the Frankfurt School, Catholic social teaching has become an original resource of critical social thought. The popes did not invent their social teaching; they relied on the critical reflections of Catholic social thinkers who had developed their ideas in dialogue with concerned intellectuals and with attention to the experiences of social movements. Catholic social teaching is not a closed system, nor is it an ideology. It does not provide a set of answers; rather, it offers moral values, analytical tools, and a social vision that Catholics may apply to acquire a critical understanding of their society and to discover what commitment to justice means in their situation. In European countries that have a Christian Democratic Party, left-wing Catholics are suspicious of the church's social teaching because it is used by Christian Democracy to legitimate its social policies. Yet in North America, where Christian political parties do not exist and intellectual traditions critical of modernity have no strong cultural presence, Catholic social teaching provides critical ideas, transcendent values, and utopian images that are singularly relevant. Unfortunately, most Catholics, even if academically trained, ignore this rich resource of critical thought.

I regret that I have never written a book to show that Catholic social teaching adds a balance and a depth to the good ideas of other social philosophies, refusing to make a one-sided choice between the person and society, between rootedness and openness to the future, between material and cultural factors in the reform of society, between attention to political and to economic oppression, between centralization and respect for subsidiarity, between commitment to justice and the practice of charity – and I could continue.[2] Because Catholic social teaching is not a system of thought, but a tradition of critical social thinking, it can be read in different ways, depending upon how one perceives the problems of society. A reformist reading of this body of teaching provides support for social democracy or democratic socialism, while a radical reading produces images of a society that has not yet been invented but whose realization lies within the realm of the possible. The latter reading is adopted by Catholics committed to liberation theology and/or to the World Social Forum, whose motto is: "Another world is possible."

19

In Dark Times

The Paulist Press, which, in most generous fashion, had published the *Ecumenist* since its foundation in 1962, decided for financial reasons to stop doing so in the spring of 1990. I have already mentioned how important this small review has been for me. At first, its main concern was the promotion of Christian unity; later, it added to this concern the emancipator dimension of the Christian message and published articles on what the church's option for the poor means in North America. Since I was the sole editor, I was able to publish my own articles dealing with borderline questions that troubled Catholics of my generation and, at times, expressing their and my frustration with the church. In my article "Good-Bye to the *Ecumenist*," which appeared in the last issue of the review,[1] I suggested that the end of this journal symbolized the end of a historical era and the entry into dark times.

I wish to cite in a slightly edited form several paragraphs from this article. However, let me first add that the *Ecumenist* did not disappear: it was published as a review of theology, culture, and society by Sheed and Ward from 1993 to 1996 and by Novalis beginning in 1999 and continuing today. I am very grateful to these publishers.

In "Good-Bye to the *Ecumenist*" I remember the hopes we had in the 1960s and the 1970s, both in the churches and in the societies of the North and the South. And I wrote the following paragraphs.

This period, I believe, is over. The Gulf War was for me the publicly approved massacre that sealed in blood the new politico-economic orientation, begun over a decade ago, that sought to enhance the material well-being of a privileged minority and assign to the margin the rest of the globe's population. At present, it seems to many analysts, there exists no realistic hope that society is about to change for the better: not in North America, not in the Third World and not on the international level.

The United States and Canada have turned their back on Keynesian-inspired welfare capitalism and foster instead neo-liberal, monetarist policies that promote the economy by relying exclusively on the mechanism of the free market. This social project calls for privatization, deregulation, cutting welfare programs, increasing the price of public services, lowering the wages of public employees, fighting the unions, creating conditions, such as tax breaks, favorable for domestic or foreign investment, etc. Even socialist or social democratic governments of countries are forced to follow the neo-liberal trend. The new adjustment policies have had devastating effects on the people in the Third World. Even in the North, for growing crowds unemployment have become a chronic condition: the jobs available are temporary or part-time and welfare support decreases. Working people live in constant insecurity. Young people have little hope. Even middle class people live in fear that the forces of marginalization will also engulf them. Under such pressures society tends to become angry and less tolerant, with harmful consequences for the visible minorities.

On the international level, the collapse of the Eastern European communist regimes and the arrival of democratic freedoms has been a source of great joy, ending the Cold War and creating an opportunity for a new global solidarity. But this is not what happened. Capitalist empire, no longer checked by a balance of power, has decided to create conditions that would guarantee its rule over the globe. The new regimen regulates the flow of money all over the world, controls oil and other natural resources, reins in the unruly by military force, and protects the interests of the developed nations, especially of their powerful elites. But there is one challenge, the approaching ecological disaster, that cannot be controlled for long.

In my judgment the present is a time of mourning. The 1960s were experienced by the Churches as a "kairos," a special time when radical social change toward greater justice was an historical possibility ... In my judgment, this kairos has been over for some time. We now live in the wilderness – an expression used by Douglas Hall. The dark times have also affected the Churches: they have become more conservative and withdrawn. In the Catholic Church anew emphasis on Catholic identity is making the hierarchy more self-involved, reluctant to seek cooperation in favour of the common good with other Churches, other religious traditions and secular movements. Fear is becoming the Church's counselor.

Living in the desert, mourning and lamentations have their place, the Scriptures tell us. Still, Christians are divinely summoned to live in hope, even as they sojourn in the wilderness. The prayer "Thy kingdom come, thy will be done on earth as it is in heaven," has one meaning when uttered during a kairos and quite another when said in the wilderness. During a kairos we long to see the emergence of God's justice with our own eyes, while in the wilderness we believe that God's work among us is one of preparation. God dwells in our hearts as we resist the present culture of indifference and yearn for the coming of a new day when the victims of society shall be released.

Christians for whom faith and justice have become intertwined will want to keep their networks, centers and institutions alive. They will continue to search for opportunities to involve themselves in action. Catholics will use the radical critique of liberal capitalism offered in John Paul II's social encyclicals as the starting point for the social analysis of the present situation. And they

> will be ready, if they hear the call, to enter upon a new spirituality, a new, possibly painful experience of God, where the peace that passes all understanding becomes a blessed restlessness.

These paragraphs make two important points: (1) we have entered a phase of history marked by an increase in violence and injustice, and (2) social engagement in this situation becomes principally resistance, creative resistance, in society and in the church.

Since the year 1990, the world situation has greatly deteriorated. We are now in the midst of several crises. First, neoliberal economics leaves the production and distribution of goods to the market and increasingly transforms all human goods into commodities to be bought and sold. Unregulated capitalism widens the gap between rich and poor countries and between rich and poor people in all countries. Vast numbers of people are condemned to live in body- and soul-destroying misery. "Such an economy kills," writes Pope Francis.[2]

Second, the colonization of the world by European empires has left its mark even upon the present, leaving many former colonies in unredeemed poverty, still economically dependent upon Western powers. As this humiliation continues, small groups in these parts turn to violent protests and engage in terror attacks that, in turn, provoke military interventions by foreign powers. The world of today is full of small wars, the weapons for which have been produced by the wealthy societies of the West. The policies of the Western democracies are marked by many contradictions. We say that we favour peace, but we derive great profit from the sale of arms. We denounce radical political Islam, but we do not challenge Saudi Arabia, the financial promoter of Wahhabism – the rigid, intolerant version of Islam that is, honestly or dishonestly, invoked by radicals. Our governments do not analyze the role of Saudi Arabia in the spread of intransigent Islam because this monarchy, despite its violations of human rights, is our ally, the purveyor of the oil on which we are dependent. Thus we live in a world of increasing violence.

Third, we are presently facing the limits of natural resources. The style of living created in the West, based on ever-expanding consumption, cannot become universal: there are not sufficient material goods to sustain it. The elites in most countries, North and South, are attached to material luxury and, hence, opposed to policies that would reduce their privileges, which means that the great majority will ever be excluded. Since the consumption-oriented lifestyle cannot be universalized and is, in fact, an obstacle to a just distribution of wealth, it is morally problematic or, more frankly, downright sinful. Many poor countries of the South do not denounce this situation because the tourism sponsored by the wealthy North has become an important source of their revenue.

Fourth, there is the ecological crisis: the pollution of rivers, the shrinking of arable land, and, above all, the rising temperature of the atmosphere, the latter having consequences that seriously threaten human life. Global warming is the result of carbon dioxide emission produced by human activities that have a greenhouse effect – that is, heating the air. This emission could be reduced or even stopped, but the nations of the world, despite many efforts and promises, have not taken the necessary steps. Canada under the Harper government refused to recognize the urgency of the situation. This has changed under the current Trudeau government, and the people who voted for him hope that Canada will now do what it can to address the grave problems produced by climate change.

It appears to me that these four predicaments – the lethal nature of neoliberal economics, the increase in violence, the limits of natural resources, and the pollution engendering global warming – constitute a civilizational crisis. The dominant culture of present-day Western society, with its global impact, lacks the wisdom and the will to overcome these major threats to human well-being. An economic system that serves the needs of people without exclusion, within the limits imposed by nature, has not yet been invented. What we need to overcome the current omnipresent violence is a more just distribution of wealth and power in the world – something for which Western society and the elites in other continents are not ready. The limits of nature and the threats to our ecology demand that we replace the present culture of consumption based on industrial growth with a culture of self-limitation, modest means, and dedicated service – an ethical endeavour for which the present civilization may not have the moral resources.

Christians committed to faith and justice discuss among themselves and with their secular friends how to react and what to do in the dark world of the present. At this time, no social thinker has a clear idea of how to transform the capitalist economy or of how a just global society might look. Social democratic political parties may be able to correct a few social injustices, but they are incapable of leading global society out of the present crisis. The word that constantly recurs in these conversations is "resistance."

I often find myself invited to speak on the topic of resistance. What can Christians do at this time to express their fidelity to the Gospel and their commitment to social justice? Christians will want to develop a spirituality and habits of prayer, mindful of God's solidarity with the poor and oppressed. I have often proposed four practical engagements:[3]

1 *Promoting a critical culture.* Since the dominant culture renders the unjust institutions of society invisible, it is important to provide categories of interpretation and to foster a discourse that allows people to discuss the damage to human life produced by their society. The Latin American bishops referred to this as "the raising of consciousness" and wanted priests and church workers to assume this critical task in their community. In Canada, a critical culture is fostered by people committed to an ethic of solidarity, be they thinkers, teachers, artists, or simply citizens conscious of their social responsibility.

2 *Supporting social movements*. In the second part of the twentieth century, as communist societies showed their internal contradictions and Western socialist political parties revealed their impotence, we witnessed the birth of new social movements, each in support of a particular cause, such as human rights, equality for women, international peace, global economic justice, the protection of nature, security for refugees, justice for immigrants, respect for homosexuals, and/or opposition to the arms trade. Social democratic parties promise to reform unjust social and economic institutions, yet when they are in power they are unable or unwilling to challenge the establishment upheld by powerful elites. Following their conscience, Christians participate in the new social movements, including the Word Social Forum founded in the twenty-first century. Pope Francis expressed his solidarity with the popular movements of the South in his speech of 28 October 2014, which was addressed to the meeting of their representatives held in Rome.[4]

3 *Spreading the vision of the United Nations*. While Christians are aware of the institutional problems of the United Nations and the power of the Security Council to prohibit democratic decision making, they share its vision of a cooperative world society and support its creation of international law aimed at producing greater global justice and protecting the poor regions of the South from the economic domination of the North. The UN resists the dominant economic theory based on a competitive vision of society. The popes have supported the United Nations from the very beginning and, on various occasions, have addressed the General Assembly. The speeches of the Vatican's Permanent Observer at the UN are sources of practical wisdom, and a series of Catholic NGOs accredited at the UN try to communicate the ideals, the thinking, and the policies of this world organization to a wider Catholic public.

4 *Participating in community development and the social economy*. In my explanation of some of Karl Polanyi's ideas, I mentioned his estimation that grassroots movements, such as community development and the social economy, generate a culture of solidarity and critical awareness of the authoritarian structure of the capitalist economy. In Quebec, l'économie solidaire involves more than 100,000 men and women living productive lives who see their activity as resistance to the societal mainstream. The social economy has been encouraged by the Canadian bishops: they see it as providing "alternative models of economic development," something different from capitalist and socialist production.[5] In Quebec, the social economy has been criticized by a number of radical social thinkers and some feminists as a form of self-exploitation of the poor, rendering them unwilling to challenge the dominant system. This is a criticism that has produced a useful public debate regarding what steps the social economy needs to avoid.[6]

In dark times, remaining passive leads to depression. There is always something we can do to support change. Christians act to keep alive the gift of hope. In the resistance described above, God is graciously present in today's world. Further on, I say a few words about the role of prayer in the resistance to self-destruction and in support of the victims of society. At the hospital where I receive my dialysis three times a week, I look with admiration at the work done by the nurses. If nurses, therapists, and physicians think of the care they give their patients as symbolic gestures aimed at healing humanity, their work acquires rich social meaning – like the stories of Jesus' miraculous healings. All acts of goodness and selfless love are sacramental signs of a redeemed world, rescued from its sin and self-destruction.

20

Theology after the Second Intifada

After the Holocaust, Christian churches were prompted by their historical guilt for the contempt they have shown to Jews and Judaism to support the State of Israel and to refrain from criticizing its treatment of the Palestinians. After the Second World War, yet a second historical guilt, their approval of the colonial conquests of the European empires, moved the churches to offer moral support to the anti-colonial struggles of peoples in Asia and Africa, eventually including the Palestinian people. The churches then affirmed their twofold solidarity, with the Jewish State and with Palestinian society, pleading for non-violent action and a negotiated compromise respectful of the aspirations and the dignity of the two nations. Because passionate defenders of the Jewish State quickly denounced critiques of Israel as expressions of anti-Semitism, few theologians were willing to examine the oppression of the Palestinians and to demand justice in their name. An exception to this may be found in Rosemary Ruether and her husband Herman Ruether. In 1989, they wrote *The Wrath of Jonah*,[1] in which they present the history of the two nations with fairness and sympathy and then proceed to analyze in detail the oppression inflicted by Israel upon the Palestinians in the Occupied Territories and within the Jewish State itself. In the same year, Naïm Ateek, an Anglican priest in Jerusalem, founded the pastoral centre Sabeel for the promotion of a Palestinian theology of liberation. In the year 2000, following the outbreak of the second Intifada provoked by Ariel Sharon's visit to the Temple Mount, a significant change occurred among Christian theologians and even in some churches: they were now ready to denounce the continuing Israeli occupation of Palestine, the illegal settlements of Israelis on Palestinian lands, and the institutional discrimination against the Palestinians living in Israel.

In 2009, the various Christian churches in Israel/Palestine published the *Kairos Palestine Declaration*, addressed to the politicians of the region and, more especially, to the churches in the West, asking them for gestures of solidarity.[2] Several churches in the United States and Canada responded to this declaration by calling for an end of the Occupation. The United Church of Canada sent an investigative committee to the Middle East and, on the basis of its findings and the testimonies of critical Israelis, produced a twenty-six-page report describing the harm done by the Occupation, the humiliation it inflicts upon the Palestinians, and the several ways in which it violates International Law.[3] Examining the declaration at the time, I found it factual and moderate, opposed to the boycott of all goods produced in Israel, and avoiding the radical stance adopted by the World Council of Churches. Among the people consulted were socially engaged Jewish Israelis.

That the mood in the Christian churches changed after the second Intifada in 2000 is, in part, due to the attention paid to the Jewish authors who live in Israel and who oppose the politics of their government. These Jewish voices greatly surprised me at the time. I had always been in touch with Jewish critics of the State of Israel through the Canadian Jewish review *Outlook*, a left-wing journal that believes in the universality of ethical norms and applies them to Israel as to any other society, refusing to regard Israel as a special case. In the year 2000, looking for critical Jewish voices on the internet, I found eleven human rights and social justice organizations in Israel and four in the United States, most of them secular, all of which justified their critical stance in terms of biblical ethics. The Israeli organizations offered detailed descriptions of the oppressive conditions imposed on the Palestinians; they also reported the efforts they made to influence public opinion in Israel and to urge the government to reform its policies. I was so impressed by this documentation that I downloaded a substantial collection of relevant texts (about 160 pages), wrote an introduction and a conclusion, and put together a book that, I thought, would make a contribution to the public debate in North America. Yet I was unable to find a publisher. Several of them rejected the manuscript, finding it too radical. They suggested that it adopted a tone unfriendly to the State of Israel, an attitude not appreciated in North America. They were unimpressed by my insistence that these reports were all written by Jewish Israelis. I sent my manuscript to a German friend, the theologian Norbert Mette, who must have shown it to a Catholic publisher. I soon received a letter from Bonifacius Verlag, asking me if I would be willing to have my book published in German translation, working with a co-editor who would add comments and explanations for the German readership. I agreed, and the book was published,[4] not in North America, which was its intended audience, but in Germany.

I believe that the distant cause of the seemingly irresolvable conflict between Israel and the Palestinians is Hitler's genocidal anti-Semitism and the Final Solution engineered by him. Before Hitler's ascent to power in 1933, Zionism was a small movement in the worldwide Jewish community. The Jewish middle classes in the West firmly believed in assimilation: they loved their country, they were patriots, they did not think of the Jewish people in political terms, and the idea of settling in Palestine did not appeal to them. Some Jewish intellectuals even accused the Zionist movement of racist nationalism: in the 1920s, Lion Feuchtwanger called it *eine jüdische Hitlerei*. If the assimilated Jews were religious, they embraced Reform Judaism, which opened the door for their full participation in modern society. Jewish socialists in the East and the West were committed to the reform or the reconstruction of their society, and, this being the case, few among them were attracted to Zionism. Orthodox Jews had religious hesitations with regard to Zionism: the promised return to Jerusalem, they believed, would be a religious event, an act of God, not the result of a secular movement supported by political power. If there had been no Hitler and no Auschwitz, Zionism would have remained a small movement, and the few thousand arrivals who wanted to create a Jewish cultural community in Palestine would have found a space there without gravely disturbing the local population. But because of Nazi anti-Semitism and the Holocaust, the self-understanding of Jews changed: looking upon their historical situation in the Diaspora as precarious, they now supported the aim of the Zionist movement – the creation of a Jewish homeland in Palestine, a safe haven for Jews experiencing persecution in their country. Now Zionism attracted vast numbers of Jews to Palestine. The mass migration, supported by the international Jewish community, led to the creation of the Jewish State and, inevitably, to the conflict with the Palestinian population.

Because of the military occupation of Palestine and the legislation that discriminates against Palestinian citizens of Israel, the Jewish literature critical of Zionism has been flouring for some time now. There are authors, like Peter Beinart,[5] who want to retrieve the democratic Zionism of the past; there are authors, such as Shlomo Sand,[6] who favour a post-Zionist Israel (i.e., a democratic society, pluralistic and egalitarian); and there are authors who think that Zionism is no longer an expression of Jewish values and who are looking forward to the flourishing of Jewish ethical culture in the Diaspora. This latter case is made in brilliant fashion by Judith Butler, the internationally respected American Jewish philosopher, in *Parting Ways*.[7] I have interpreted her book as a work in theology.[8] While she does not talk about God, she does tell her readers that she learned her Jewish values as a young girl in a Reform synagogue and that she currently belongs to such a synagogue in California. Jews have been most creative, she argues, when they have been in contact with other cultures:

this happened in antiquity in Babylon and in Egypt, in the Middle Ages in Spain, and in modern times in several Western societies. That Moses himself is presented as an Egyptian she regards as significant. She holds that, despite the Holocaust (in which some of her ancestors perished), the Diaspora continues to be the place where Jews will thrive, develop a Jewish ethical culture, and co-create with other citizen the society to which they belong. The State of Israel, she insists, does not define the Jewish identity. In line with classical Reform Judaism, she holds that this identity is created by the biblical call to justice and to truth, the summons to help people in need and to reduce human suffering.

These thoughts of a great philosopher may well be the sign that a transformation of Jewish self-understanding is on the way. According to Dov Waxman's *Trouble in the Tribe*,[9] the American Jewish community, at one time united by its loyalty to the State of Israel, is presently deeply divided by contrasting attitudes towards the Israeli government. Waxman cites the Jewish critics and the Jewish groups in the United States that denounce Israel's military occupation of Palestine and the illegal settlements on Palestinians lands. In the past, Christian groups, such as the World Council of Churches and the United Church of Canada, which denounced the Israeli government's oppression of the Palestinian people, found themselves accused by ardent Zionists of anti-Semitism – an accusation that the Jewish denouncers cited by Waxman have rendered quite meaningless.

21

Dialogue with Islam

After the massive terrorist attack in New York City on 11 September 2001, prejudice against Muslims and contempt for their religion greatly increased in the United States and, possibly less virulently, in Canada. The anti-terrorist legislation in the two countries, which extended powers to the police and the courts, was deemed by competent layers to be at odds with the charters of human rights. In a lecture I gave at St Jerome's College in Waterloo in 2006,[1] I lamented that fact that Bill C-36, adopted by the Canadian government in 2001 and allowing the arrest and preventive detention of persons on unconfirmed suspicion,[2] made Muslims/Arabs feel insecure on the streets and assigned prejudice a legitimate place in Canadian culture. Bill C-36 was replaced in June 2015 by Bill S-7, the Zero Tolerance for Barbaric Cultural Practices Act, which was accused by its opponents of creating suspicion and fear of people of foreign origin.

In the same lecture, I quoted a remark made in October 2001 by Archbishop Rafael Martino, at that time the Vatican's Permanent Observer at the United Nations:

> Though poverty is not by itself the cause of terrorism, we cannot successfully combat terrorism, if we do not address the worsening disparities between the rich and the poor. We must recognize that global disparity is fundamentally incompatible

> with global security ... Any serious crime reduction effort cannot be confined only to intensified police work. Any serious campaign against terrorism needs to address the social, economic and political conditions that nurture the emergence of terrorism.

Governments do not seem to be ready for Archbishop Martino.

I was grateful to the Canadian Catholic bishops who, in a public statement of October 2001, denounced anti-Muslim prejudice: they "deeply deplored the crimes of hate towards mosques and towards Arab people, whether Muslim or Christian," and "reaffirmed the respect that Catholics hold towards Islam and its adherents." Muslims in Canada are deeply troubled when they read about radical Islamists who commit violent acts and then, at the same time, have to face the Canadian public's almost total incomprehension of Islam.

The Vivre ensemble team of le Centre justice et foi pays close attention to the difficulties and problems experienced by refugees and immigrants in Quebec. We are aware that, in Montreal, the percentage of unemployment among Arabs/Muslims is higher than that among other minorities, including the Haitian community. Prejudice has economic consequences. More than that, prejudice makes people of immigrant background feel that they are second-class citizens. In Quebec, a certain resentment against the Catholic Church is often projected upon pious Muslims who wear distinctive religious garb on the streets, especially women wearing a veil. I am greatly troubled by this spread of suspicion and hostility. As a young theologian I wrestled against anti-Semitism in church and society; now, decades later, in my eighties and nineties, I find myself called to wrestle against anti-Muslim prejudice and the lack of respect for Islam.

I decided to study Islamic thought. The association Présence musulmane, formed in Montreal in 2003, held public meetings at regular intervals, at which Muslim men and women listened to invited speakers and then discussed among themselves how to remain faithful believers in Islam and, at the same time, become responsible citizens of Quebec. I attended these meetings regularly. On one occasion I met and listened to the guest speaker, Tariq Ramadan, a gifted religious thinker, author, and lecturer, whose entire work deals with the practise of Islam in the pluralistic societies of the West. Greatly impressed by his wisdom and his scholarship, I began a careful study of his books and the evolution of his theology.

I soon discovered that Tariq Ramadan belongs to the renewal movement in Islam, *al-nadah*, initiated at the end of the nineteenth century. The history of this movement, written by Ramadan himself,[3] starts with its founder, Jamal al-Afghani (1838–97), the colourful intellectual leader who travelled through the Muslim world promoting the revitalization of Islam in the face of changed historical conditions. While al-Afghani denounced the increasing colonization of Muslim lands by Western empires, he was not, in principle, anti-Western. He wanted Muslims to study Western science and to learn from Western education and administration. The principal cause of the weakness of Muslim societies, he argued, was not the imposition of colonialism; rather, what was at fault was the stagnation of Islam, its conservative spirit, its indifference to social inequalities, and its suspicion of the modern sciences. He complained that ritual practices and popular superstitions had obscured the original message of Islam, which summons believers to become culturally creative and to produce a society pleasing to God.

The Islamic renewal movement *al-nadah* became an important current in the Muslim world, fostered by religious thinkers in various Muslim countries; it also influenced Muslim intellectuals in countries in which Muslims lived as minorities, such as India, South Africa, France, and the United States. These thinkers are often referred to as "modernists." Ramadan is a brilliant representative of the modernist movement. Also of great interest to me are the writings of Fethullah Gülen, a Turkish sage and educator whose reading of the Quran allows believing Muslims to feel at home in Turkey's secular society and to become creative citizens inspired by their faith.[4] In Canada, this movement is represented by Zijad Delic, the author of *Canadian Islam: Belonging and Loyalty*. These theological thinkers interpret the Quran according to principles recognized by the classical tradition and thus see themselves as fully orthodox. Still, they are criticized by conservative Islamic teachers in Muslim societies and are rejected by the rigid Wahhabist version of Islam promoted by Saudi Arabia. These modernist thinkers are also challenged by Muslim intellectuals who believe that, in order to make Islam relevant to present-day society, more is required than the retrieval of orthodoxy: what is needed, they argue, is a critical reading of the Quran, following the principles of scientific exegesis. These more radical intellectuals have produced an extensive literature that, in one way or another, calls for the rational rethinking of Islam.[5] It is my impression that these rational critics are professors and researchers who lack the pastoral concern of the modernist thinkers and their respect for the religious experiences of ordinary believers.

The theological writings of Ramadan and his modernist colleagues make fascinating reading for Catholic theologians. The effort of these Islamic thinkers is similar to that of the Catholic theologians in the first half of the twentieth century who tried to reconcile Catholicism with the humanistic values of modern society. They were repeatedly censured by Roman authorities until, finally, their ideas were endorsed by the Second Vatican Council. To respond creatively to modern society, Ramadan rereads the Quran to find insights that allow him to transcend the traditional teaching and to interpret divine revelation as a message relevant to the contemporary situation. His methodology has an affinity with the theological thinking that has led to the renewal of Catholicism. Reading Ramadan's work as a believer in the same God has given me an understanding of his thought that differs from that of his secular readers.

I was shocked to discover that books and articles published in France denounce Ramadan as an untrustworthy and deceitful Muslim preacher. Reading this hostile literature, I noticed that its authors had not studied Ramadan's published work; rather, they based their accusations on newspaper reports and interviews broadcast on radio or television. I wrote *The Theology of Tariq Ramadan* as a defence of this brilliant thinker.[6] While the book was reviewed positively in Canada and the United States, the French translation was not reviewed in any francophone publication (with the exception of *Relations*, with which I am associated).[7] In France, the prejudice against Ramadan is omnipresent.

My respect for Islam does not prevent me from publicly criticizing the spread of Wahhabism, the intolerant version of Islam named after Abd al-Wahhab, an eighteen-century Sunni Muslim reformer. Repudiating the practice of Islam accepted in the Ottoman Empire, al-Wahhab adopted a literalistic reading of the Quran and advocated a return to the early Islam practised by the Prophet and his companions, rejecting the very idea of development. Muslims who disagreed with him – the vast majority – he denounced as heretics or unbelievers. The small sect he founded in Arabia was embraced by the aristocratic family of Saud, which expanded its reign in the nineteenth century and, in 1932, founded the Kingdom of Saudi Arabia, continuing its commitment to this archaic, intransigent version of Islam. In fact, Saudi Arabia sees it as its mission to promote Wahhabism among Muslims the world over. It uses the enormous wealth based in its oil resources to send Wahhabist imams to Muslim communities in other counties, pay their salaries, and finance the construction of mosques. The success of the Wahhabi mission has been documented by Muslim scholar Abou El Fadl in his *The Great Theft: Wrestling Islam from the Extremists*,[8] which shows how the humane Islam practised by the majority is presently under attack. Intolerant religion is a danger in pluralistic societies. Yet, because Saudi Arabia is an ally of the United States and the West in general, which are dependent on its oil resources, the export of its intransigent religion is not publicly criticized. While Wahhabism does not advocate violence, its intolerant version of Islam has been a breeding ground for political Islamist extremism.

The important issue with which all religious traditions have to wrestle is how their followers can live as responsible citizens in a pluralistic society, uphold their faith as the singular truth, and, at the same time, have respect for the religion of others.

22

Pluralism Yes, Relativism No

In the year 2000, the Congregation for the Doctrine of the Faith published the instruction *Dominus Jesus*, signed by Cardinal Ratzinger, who was prefect at the time. According to this instruction, religious pluralism exists not in principle but only in fact: in principle exists only in Roman Catholicism. Cardinal Ratzinger was haunted by the danger of relativism. He had been critical of the interreligious assembly at Assisi convened in 1986 by John Paul II and of interreligious dialogue in general, even though it had been recommended by the Second Vatican Council. He feared that meetings of this kind encourage relativism and indifference to truth. In his homily preached at the mass prior to the papal conclave of 2005, he famously denounced "the dictatorship of relativism" operative in contemporary society. In his book on truth and tolerance, he claims that relativism has become the religion of modern "man," "the religion that stands at the heart of modern secular civilization in the way Christianity defined the heart of Christendom."[1] In this situation, he held, the church is not called to engage in dialogue with the world but, rather, to resist its influence. He warned that interreligious dialogue undermines the church's mission to proclaim the name of Jesus. In *Dominus Jesus*, Cardinal Ratzinger urged Catholics engaged in interreligious dialogue not to forget that the ultimate purpose of this dialogue is the conversion of their partners to the Catholic truth.

As Benedict XVI, Joseph Ratzinger gradually changed his mind about religious pluralism and interreligious dialogue. He was affected by his travels to Turkey, Jerusalem, Great Britain, and countries in Africa. I have documented this evolution in my writings.[2] Addressing a pluralistic gathering in Benin on 19 November 2011, the pope praised interreligious cooperation in Africa, encouraged the stability of mixed marriages, and urged the people to overcome prejudice against cultures and religions other than their own. He then added:

> I would like to use the image of a hand. There are five fingers on it and each one is quite different. Each one is also essential and their unity makes a hand. A good understanding between cultures, consideration for each other which is not condescending, and the respect of the rights of each one are a vital duty. This must be taught to all the faithful of the various religions.

This is a bold affirmation, the theology of which has as yet not been worked out.

There is a general agreement among religious people that interreligious dialogue does not imply that all religions are equally true. Every religion holds that it embodies a divine truth to which it is committed and which it is incapable of giving up. To foster mutual understanding and cooperative action among different religions, it is necessary that each religion finds in its own theological inheritance reasons for respecting the others.

According to the Second Vatican Council, the Catholic Church has a twofold mission: (1) to proclaim the Gospel that the world may believe and (2) to be engage in dialogue with the world and its religions to promote mutual understanding, social peace, and cooperation in support of the common good. The first calling aims at enhancing the *bonum ecclesiae,* while the second calling promotes the *bonum humanitatis*, the common good of the human family. This wider understanding of the church's mission raises theological and pastoral questions for which the magisterium and the theological community have not yet found a definitive answer. By what criteria does a diocese or a parish decide whether to aim at the conversion of its neighbours or to engage in dialogue and cooperation with them? Should Catholics support Catholic schools as a service rendered to the *bonum ecclesiae* or should they foster the public school system as a service to the *bonum commune* of their society? These are topics that preoccupy theologians.

I have argued that the church has no mission to convert to Catholicism men and women who are deeply rooted in another religious or humanistic tradition.[3] With them the church is called to engage in dialogue, trusting that such conversations will persuade all participants to lay hold of the most authentic values of their own tradition, such as humility, gratitude, peacefulness, concern for the neighbour in need, and the yearning for social justice. Interreligious dialogue summons forth renewal in all the traditions participating in it. That is why Christians believe that present in such dialogue is the Holy Spirit.

The church proclaims the name of Jesus, I have argued, to people who are searching, whose conscience is confused, who believe in idols, who are doing evil things, who have been hurt by religious intransigence, or who find themselves caught in destructive ideologies. I am grateful to the Second Vatican Council for retrieving the ancient "Logos Christology" to proclaim that the divine Word sounds and the Holy Spirit works throughout the whole of human history. This theology enables us to have a positive perception of religious pluralism. Yet this is just the first step. I am convinced that a more generous understanding of religious pluralism will emerge in the church, one that recognizes economies of enlightenment and salvation that are independent of the Christian tradition. One attempt at this has been the theology of *kenosis* that I mentioned earlier.[4] If God kenotically restricted divine omnipotence to grant a space for human freedom, and if Jesus, the Son of God, emptied himself to become like other human beings, then the church – it is argued –

should also become kenotic, emptying itself to become like the other religious communities, joining them in dialogue and cooperation. Such a kenotic ecclesiology would make the church recognize itself as surrounded by sister religious communities – a more generous perception of the plurality of religion.

In my opinion, the last word on the Catholic understanding of religious pluralism has not been spoken. I see emerging in Catholic thought and practice the recognition that the plurality of religions is God's gracious gift, in which we rejoice and for which we are grateful. In such a setting the transformative dimension of interreligious dialogue would be greatly enhanced. Here the religions would not simply put their best foot forward and explain to one another what they believe; here they would be willing to confess their failures, reveal their dark side, and describe what they are doing to renew themselves and become more faithful to their divine mission. Interreligious dialogue would here become an exercise of renewal involving all the participants, a Spirit-guided process that enlarges the common ground between them and increases their relevance to the contemporary world.

A good example of this kind of interreligious dialogue is the World Conference of Religions for Peace, which was founded in 1970 at a time when many feared a nuclear interchange between the United States and the Soviet Union. The World Conference holds an international assembly every four or five years and influences public opinion through local chapters set up in cities across the globe. In the declaration of 1976 published by the international assembly held at Leuven,[5] the representatives of the world religions confess that, in the past, their traditions have often blessed wars and supported unjust rulers but that their authentic values support peace and justice. As members of the World Conference they now commit themselves to the renewal of their religious traditions, making them a social force in support of peace and justice. Troubled by the violence committed in the name of religion, these religious leaders willingly confront the Enlightenment critique of religions and face, in all honesty, the sinister side of their traditions. But they don't give up hope; rather, they hold to the belief that they are divinely called to promote peace and justice.

More difficult and equally important is the philosophical problem of cultural pluralism. One year before his elevation to the papacy, Cardinal Joseph Ratzinger, in a public dialogue with Jürgen Habermas, made the surprising admission that traditional Catholic natural law theology has lost its validity.[6] We used to think, he said, that we had a metaphysical grasp on human nature and could find inscribed in it moral laws of universal validity. He gave two reasons that make it clear that this is no longer convincing: (1) the theory of evolution shows that humanity has passed through different stages over tens of thousands of years, and (2) the encounter with the plurality of civilizations prohibits a universally valid understanding of natural law. On this occasion, the cardinal admitted that we are in need of a non-metaphysical ethical theory, such as Habermas's reference to practical reason, which is guided by the confidence that humans of good will, in dialogue with one another, are able to come to a rational agreement on how to institute their social relations so that all will be well, that all will be treated justly, and that no one will be left out. The cardinal added that we have to overcome the Eurocentric perception of the world, engage in dialogue with other civilizations, and, together with them, try to formulate rational principles that make possible the construction of a world that is peaceful and just. Yet in his magisterial pronouncements, I note, Cardinal Ratzinger/Benedict XVI has continued to support the metaphysical natural law theory.

At this time we are obliged to admit that the many different cultures each have their own sets of values and their own moral precepts. Are we then obliged to be ethical relativists? Must we give up on the idea that humanity can become reconciled within a set of common moral norms? Both Professor Habermas and Cardinal Ratzinger expressed the hope that, through dialogue and cooperation, the peoples that make up the human family will be able to arrive at a set of moral norms that is binding on all of them. Hidden in the potentialities of the humanity of men and women is the power to overcome the unsettling ethical discord characteristic of today's world.

In this context I wish to mention the philosophy of pluralism proposed by Johannes Gottfried Herder (1744–1803). Herder argued passionately against the universalist claims made by French and English Enlightenment philosophers. According to him, humanity has been constituted as an ensemble of different cultures, each with its language, its truth, its laws, its customs, and its ethical practices. All of these cultures, Herder insisted, deserve respect. No nation can claim to be superior to others. In the nineteenth century, German romantic thinkers mistakenly referred to the thought of Gottfried Herder when they claimed an exceptional value for German culture and assigned a privileged mission to the German people. Herder had actually denied that there were privileged nations. He was a classical humanist committed to the ethical ideal of humanitas (*Humanität*), the moral and aesthetic flourishing of human life that occurs in different forms in the various cultures that constitute the human family. His respect for cultural pluralism led him to severely condemn the colonial conquest of European empires because these empires humiliated and damaged the cultures of the local populations. He wrote:

> What, finally, are we to say of the civilization and culture that the Spaniards, the Portuguese, the English and the Dutch have brought to the East and the West Indies and among the Negroes of Africa? Are not these countries crying out for revenge now that they find themselves plunged for an indefinite period of time into mounting disaster? If there were such a thing as a European collective spirit ... it could not but feel ashamed of the crimes committed by us, having insulted mankind in a manner such as scarcely any other group of nations had done.[7]

Herder dropped out of the Christian Church because of its alliance with kings and emperors and its approval of their colonial conquests.

Despite Herder's recognition of the diversity of cultures, customs, and ethical norms, he was not a relativist. He believed that in each culture people were trying to achieve *Humanität*, a human flourishing; a life of dignity, generosity, and creativity; an endeavour sustained by their own cultural inheritance yet also open to the influence of surrounding cultures. Herder held that the value to which people aspire within different cultures renders possible cross-cultural dialogue and mutual respect. He was a pluralist, not a relativist. This is how Steven Lukes presents Herder's idea of pluralism.

> He had a progressive view of history as the realization of "reason" and "humanity." He thought that the mental worlds of other cultures were always accessible through a kind of empathetic understanding. He thought that the infinite cultural variety he discerned was "striving for a unity that lies in all, that advances all," whose name was "understanding, fairness, goodness, feeling of humanity," and which was expressed in all human cultures by numerous different versions of the Golden Rule.[8]

In my own reflections on a non-relativistic understanding of cultural pluralism I have insisted that the cultural traditions of societies, including their religions, are dynamic historical realities, enlivened by internal debate among their members, by the response to changing material conditions, and by an ongoing contact with other cultural environments: "The vitality of cultural traditions allows them to respond creatively to historical challenges by rethinking their ideas and reforming their customs and practices. Cultural traditions that suppress internal debate and refuse external dialogue become atrophied. Their fate is insecure."[9] I have argued that all cultural traditions are challenged by modernity and have to wrestle with the tension between capitalism and modernity, between the individualism fostered by the market system and the concern for the common good fostered by the institution of democracy. In all cultural traditions, including religions, there are (1) currents that resist modernity and cling to the past, unaware that doing so fossilizes their inheritance; (2) currents that embrace the market civilization, unaware that doing so threatens to dissolve their inheritance; and (3) currents that are open to the challenge of modernity and find in their inheritance resources for affirming, in their own terms, responsible citizenship and social solidarity. The charters and covenants of the United Nations are remarkable documents expressing values and convictions shared by many nations of the world, each one being legitimated with arguments drawn from each culture's own tradition. The experience of intercultural and interreligious exchanges and activities suggests that human traditions with different sets of truths and values are sustained by the same underlying principles: it is these principles that guide them in rethinking their truths and values in response to the common challenge of modernity.

Ethical relativism has political consequences. Since it denies that the family of nations can be united by a common quest for shared truths and values, it follows that the world can be united only by the power imposed upon nations by political or economic empire – a frightening thought, legitimating dictatorship.

23

Listening to Fernand Dumont

I have mentioned more than once that my integration into Quebec society has been an intellectual and cultural adventure. My association with le Centre justice et foi and its review *Relations*, along with my daily reading of *le Devoir*, allowed me to follow the public debates in Quebec over political, social, and cultural issues. Quebec intellectuals are in constant conversation with one another.[1] I am impressed by the creativity of this small nation: its critical thought, its reflections on its future, its literature, its films and plays, its university life, and its public debates over national and international issues. The great lacuna is its indifference to religion. While the Catholic Church has shrunk and practising Catholics have become a minority, I am impressed by the creativity within this minority, which is producing original theological thought and undertaking bold pastoral experiments. To make this ecclesial development known to my friends in English-speaking Canada I wrote the book *Truth and Relevance*,[2] which addresses Catholic theology in Quebec since the Quiet Revolution.

In preparing this book I discovered an original thinker, Fernand Dumont (1927–1997), a sociologist, a philosopher, in fact, an original thinker, an author who straddled several disciplines, theology included. I was especially impressed by his book *L'institution de la théologie*, a work difficult to read and hence not widely received. I thought that, just as John Henry Newman's 1845 *Essay on the Development of Christian Doctrine* had helped a reluctant church to recognize the evolution of its teaching, so Fernand Dumont's *L'institution de la théologie* could help today's reluctant church respond creatively to the secularization of culture in the societies of the West. I decided to write a long essay on this book, eventually published as *Fernand Dumont: A Sociologist Turns to Theology*.[3]

At this point, I wish to present two of Dumont's theological proposals that address issues of great interest to Catholics at the present time: (1) the moral autonomy of believers and (2) the definition of their Catholic identity.

Moral Autonomy of Believers

Like St Augustine, Dumont puts great emphasis on personal conscience. Like Augustine, he recognizes that God's Word addresses us not only through the external voice of Scripture and the church's preaching but also through the internal voice of conscience. Augustine argued that we are able to believe the church's message because it corresponds to God's self-utterance in our heart. St Thomas and the Scholastics had a more rational view of conscience. Thomas argued that we are morally obliged to follow our conscience, even if it should be erroneous, because universal moral principles can be applied to a concrete situation only by the person living within it. The Protestant Reformers returned to a more biblical understanding of conscience as the spiritual ear within us that listens to God's voice. Cardinal Newman reintroduced this notion in the Catholic tradition, and the Second Vatican Council, following Newman, taught: "Conscience is the most secret core and sanctuary of a man. There he is alone with God, whose voice echoes in his depths. In a wonderful manner conscience reveals that law which is fulfilled by love of God and neighbor" (*Gaudium et spes*, 16).

In the past, Catholics were brought up, as children, to embrace the Catholic faith and to accept in their heart the teaching of the church.

When they, as adults, experienced a conflict between their personal conscience and the church's teaching, they felt obliged to obey the latter because disagreeing with the magisterium and following their personal conscience would have made them feel guilty. Dumont argues that, for two reasons, this has now changed.

First, Catholics realize that the church's official teaching evolves, as it did at the Second Vatican Council. They recognize that, in a new culture, the church listens anew to God's Word in the Scriptures and hears a message that replies to the questions raised by this culture. This doctrinal evolution, Dumont holds, begins when believers have new religious experiences. It then finds expression in the writings of theologians and, finally, affects the church's magisterium. There are thus historical situations in which dissent from official teaching is a significant moment in the development of doctrine.

Second, since Catholics now live in a pluralistic society, surrounded by followers of other religions and people who are non-believers, their Catholic faith is no longer supported by the culture in which they live. They become Catholic and remain Catholic because they choose to do so. Faith is a divine gift, yet it becomes available to us in the present culture through our free choice, through fidelity to our own conscience, through a confident affirmation of our own religious experience. Catholics do not give up this confidence in their own conscience as they continue their life in the church. They listen carefully to the magisterium and try to make its teaching their own; however, if they are unable to do this, if their Catholic conscience utters a different message, they listen anew to the Scriptures, engage in dialogue with the believing community, and then follow their conscience as it is formed during this process. Dumont refers to this as "the moral autonomy" enjoyed by Catholics in today's society.

Since Cardinal Gerhard Müller, the present prefect of the Congregation of the Doctrine of the Faith, continues to speak as though the decisions of his congregation settle all questions of faith and morals in the church, I sent him a letter in December 2014, in which

I explained that the relation of Catholics to the magisterium had undergone a significant change: if their conscience remains unconvinced, they feel free to dissent.

In *Amazing Church* I mentioned how shocked I was in the late 1950s when a young woman working for Pax Romana said to me that, in condemning the principle of religious liberty, the popes were wrong.[4] I was scandalized by her indictment. She argued that the human conscience wrestling with sacred texts and seeking obedience to the divine voice deserves the respect of society and the church. A few years later, her position was adopted by the Second Vatican Council.

Definition of Catholic Identity

Dumont offers an innovative interpretation of what it means to be a Catholic and be identified with the Catholic tradition. He starts his inquiry with sociological reflections.[5] Being part of a collectivity, he argues, occurs in a variety of ways, and these can be usefully divided into three types. First, we are part of a community by *belonging* if we know its members personally, engage in conversation with them, and decide together how the community should live and act. Membership by belonging occurs in villages, congregations, base communities, co-operative ventures, and many other small groups. Because people here decide together how to define themselves and how to engage in action, they make few fixed rules.

Second, we are part of a collectivity by *integration* if our membership assigns us a place in the institution, defines our rights and duties, and obliges us to obey the rules made by the governing authorities. In this manner we belong to a university, a government ministry, an industrial or commercial corporation, and/or many other large institutions. To function efficiently, institutions of this kind need a directorship that defines the rules that regulate the activity of their members. It is possible to interpret the church as an institution in which believers become members by integration. Dumont argues that, in order to reform the clergy, control the members, and centralize the ruling authority, the Catholic Church has greatly emphasized its organizational character. It has produced extensive legislation, insisted on doctrinal conformity, and made itself into a giant bureaucracy in which believers are assigned their place and their duties.

Dumont proposes a third way of being part of a collectivity such as a nation or a country. He does not refer to this as *belonging* because the members remain largely unknown to us, nor does he refer to it as *integration* since nations and countries are not organizations. According to Dumont, we belong to a nation by *référence* – a word that I freely translate as "symbolic identification." To be part of a collectivity by *référence* means sharing its memory and having hope for its future. The shared memory may be the nation's foundation, important events in its history, its cultural achievements, or the brilliant personalities that have affected its self-understanding in the past and the present. While we recognize the injustices committed by our nation, we trust in its cultural and spiritual resources for doing good and becoming more just, thus retaining hope for a better future. Even if people disapprove of the present government and disagree with its social philosophy, they continue to identify with their nation and remain ready to serve it. The Order of Canada, which I had the honour of receiving in 1995, has as its motto *Desiderantes meliorem patriam* (persons who want their country to be better).

The great Protestant theologian Paul Tillich, fleeing from Germany in 1933 to escape arrest by the Nazi government, was accused of betraying his country by the theologian Emanuel Hirsch, a former friend, now a Nazi supporter. Tillich replied to him that the person who truly loves his country wants it to be just. In other words, he held that he loved Germany more than did Hirsch.

Dumont argues that Catholics belong to the church by *référence*, by symbolic identification, sharing a common memory and a common hope. Catholics remember the events of God's revelation, first in the history of the people of Israel and later, definitively, in the redemptive life of Jesus Christ; they remember the early Christian community, the practice of baptism, the Eucharistic liturgy, and many other important events in the church's life, including the saints that impress them and the medieval cathedrals that inspire their admiration. The great events of the past assume symbolic meaning for them: they define who they are as a believing community. Despite the bad memories – the church's hostility to outsiders, its anti-Jewish rhetoric, its past approval of slavery and torture, the Inquisition, and its alliances with colonial empires and political dictators – Catholics believe that the resources for compassion and social justice in the Church's tradition, especially the Scriptures and the sacraments, allow them to have hope for a more holy future. If the ecclesiastical government disappoints them, and even if they disagree with its official teaching, they wholeheartedly belong to the church by *référence,* by symbolic identification.

What follows from this is that the Christian witness of the church is more important than its doctrines. Witnesses are acts of faith, gestures that incarnate the Gospel, actions that embody revealed truth. While all Catholics are summoned to give witness of their faith, Dumont argues, popes and bishops must do so in a special way. Their prophetic ministry and their public witness of compassion and justice reinforce *la référence* for the believing community and strengthens its faith. Dumont holds that the preoccupation of church authorities with orthodoxy and theological unanimity is lacking in pastoral wisdom, for what nourishes the Catholic community are public actions that embody the Christian message. John XXIII, called good Pope John, made the church more credible to vast numbers of people. Pope Francis seems to share Dumont's point of view: "Pastoral ministry in a missionary style is not obsessed with the disjointed transmission of a multitude of doctrines to be insistently imposed."[6] What must be communicated in word and action, he writes, is the central message of the Gospel as it applies to the given historical situation.

24

The Arrival of Pope Francis

The election of Pope Francis in March 2013 revealed itself very quickly as an extraordinary event, a total surprise, a miracle in the biblical sense, and as a turning point in the church's self-understanding and its mission in the world. I was overjoyed. Francis revived the spirit of the Second Vatican Council, and, in several statements made in the same year, he even moved beyond the conciliar teaching. In the fall of 2013, when I was working on the manuscript for this book, I was fascinated by two of his remarks.

First, following a radical reading of the church's social teaching and the inspiration of liberation theology, Francis announced his preferential option for the poor and repudiated as idolatrous today's globalized capitalist economy. This is what he told the workers assembled at Cagliari in Sardinia on 22 September 2013.

> God did not want an idol to be at the centre of the world, but man, men and women, whose work would keep the world going. Yet in the present system devoid of ethics, at the centre of which is an idol, the world has become an idolater of the "god-money." Money is in command! Money lays down the law! It orders all things that are useful to it ... And what happens? To defend this idol people crowd to the centre and those on the margins are put down, the elderly fall away, because

> there is no room for them in this world! Some call this habit "hidden euthanasia," not caring for them, not taking them into account ... And the young who do not find jobs collapse and their dignity with them. Do you realize that in a world where youth – two generations of young people – have no work that this world has no future?

The Latin American Pope here follows the teaching of the Medellin Latin American Bishops Conference of 1968 rather than that of the Second Vatican Council, which ended in 1965.

The second of Francis's remarks comes in the long interview he gave to a group of Jesuit editors and that was published in September 2013 in Jesuit reviews throughout the world.[1] Here Francis says that Catholics continue to wrestle with the truth, having their doubts and searching for faithful responses to the questions raised by the present – a state of mind, I might add, that has never before been respected by the magisterium.

> If a Catholic has the answers to all the questions – that is the proof that God is not with him ... The great leaders of the people of God, like Moses, have always left room for doubt ... We must be humble ... If the Catholic is a legalist or restorationist, if he wants everything clear and safe, then he will find nothing ... Tradition and memory of the past must help us to have the courage to open up new areas to God. Those who today always look for disciplinarian solutions, those who long for an exaggerated doctrinal "security," those who stubbornly try to recover a past that no longer exists – these Catholics have a static and inward-directed view of things. In this way, faith becomes an ideology among other ideologies ... Exegetes and theologians help the Church to mature in her own judgment. Even the other sciences and their development help the Church in its growth in understanding. There are ecclesiastical rules and precepts that were once effective, but now they have lost value or

> meaning. The view of the Church's teaching as a monolith to defend without nuance or different understandings is wrong.

This humility before truth is not yet present in the documents of the Second Vatican Council. Francis argues that the church's proclamation of God's Word is expressed in terms drawn from its cultural location and hence may not be clung to as an absolute. To proclaim the Christian message in a new cultural setting calls for theological creativity, making it relevant – that is to say, making it respond to people's anxieties and urgent questions.

Writing the following paragraphs in February 2016, I confess that Pope Francis's evangelical zeal and audacious teaching have moved me and touched my heart. That a new perception of the Gospel developed by theologians over the last decades (some of whom were censured by the Roman magisterium) should be adopted and further explored by the bishop of Rome, the church's universal teacher, I regard as a major spiritual event, a redemptive happening, a leap in the church's history. That I, through my work and publications, have been allowed to participate in this paradigm shift fills me with gratitude.

The two themes mentioned above, the theological critique of unregulated capitalism and the contextual character of Christian teaching, are greatly developed by Francis in his subsequent writings and speeches. While previous popes, attentive to conditions in Europe, condemned the exploitation of workers and the alienating labour imposed on them by liberal or unregulated capitalism, Francis, the Argentine Pope, confronting the misery in Latin America, denounces above all the exclusion of people from work and from the services offered by society. This exclusion not only makes people suffer: it actually destroys them. Francis shocked the world when he wrote in his exhortation *Evangelii gaudium*: "Just as 'Thou shalt not kill' safeguards the value of human life ... so we now have to say 'thou shalt not' to an economy of exclusion and inequality, for such an economy kills."[2] Francis denounces the globalization of the unregulated market system oriented towards the maximization of profit, unrestrained by any ethical norms, as an idolatry, the worship of the Golden Calf, which, like all idols, demands human sacrifices.

Addressing the representatives of popular movements, gathered in Rome at his invitation, Francis explained the mechanisms that produce the exclusion of the masses. He argued that land, food, housing, and work, having been turned into commodities subject to the logic of the market, become available to the highest bidder and are consequently lost to the poor and powerless.[3] Thus excluded, these people are deprived of their "sacred rights." In *Evangelii gaudium* Francis writes:

> In this context we can understand Jesus' command to his disciples, "You yourselves give them something to eat" (Mk. 6:37): it means working to eliminate the structural causes of poverty and promote the integral development of the poor, as well as small daily acts of solidarity in meeting the real needs they encounter.[4]

Francis's analysis of the above-mentioned "fictitious commodities" and their misery-creating impact made some commentators wonder whether the pope had been influenced by the thought of Karl Polanyi. I gave a paper at the International Karl Polanyi Conference in November 2015 in which I analyzed the surprising affinity between the critical thought of Francis and that of Polanyi, without suggesting that the former had read the latter's work.[5] This affinity is also apparent in the recommendation both of them make regarding what is to be done in the present. Since the present economic order is protected by the mighty, the economic and political powers, and since violent revolution produces even greater suffering, Polanyi and Francis urge people to become actively engaged on the ground, promoting community economic development and other collective self-help projects that improve their material conditions, cultivate their humanity, and render a service to the local community. For Polanyi, the social economy "re-embeds" workers in the community to which they belong; and for Francis, popular movements working on the ground create an economy that "puts the human person at the centre." If the person is not at the centre of an economy, Francis adds, "then another thing will be at its centre, and the person will be at the service of this other thing."[6] Both social thinkers hold that the forms of economic development invented by people on the ground may eventually generate models of economic organization destined to replace present-day capitalism.

The exhortation *Evangelii gaudium* also deals with the contextual character of Christian preaching. To present the Gospel as a set of truths to be believed and a set of commandments to be obeyed, Francis argues, reflects a bureaucratic idea of the church, or clericalism. The Good News that the church must proclaim is God's love revealed in Jesus Christ, permitting the faithful to encounter the Lord, be converted by him, and reorient their lives promoting love, justice, and peace in the world. "The heart of the message is always the same: the God who revealed his immense love in the crucified Jesus Christ."[7] But, in each place, this message must be made relevant. Francis writes: "Jesus can break through the dull categories with which we would enclose him; he constantly amazes us by his divine creativity."[8] Francis speaks of "the eternal newness of the Gospel." The church must step out into the community to which it belongs: it must listen to people's problems, bear their burden in solidarity, listen to their spiritual aspirations, and then announce the Good News as God's reply to their anguish, giving them hope.

In a talk to a theological congress, Francis said: "The Gospel continues to be incarnated in every corner of the world, in an ever new way ... In India and in Canada people are not Christians in the same way they are in Rome."[9] According to Francis, the Church of Rome promotes and protects the truth and unity of the church universal, but it does not impose uniformity nor does it possess a monopoly on truth: the Roman magisterium is in dialogue with the particular churches, respects their efforts to incarnate the Gospel in their societies, and, in this living way, fosters the unity in truth in the church universal.

Evangelii gaudium calls for a new evangelization, new because it takes into account the problems and hopes of contemporary society. Listing the church's doctrines and putting an emphasis on orthodoxy does not constitute a sound pastoral approach. Francis does not want preachers to be "obsessed with the transmission of a multitude of doctrines":[10] "There are times," he writes, "when the faithful, in listening to completely orthodox language, take away something alien to the authentic Gospel of Jesus Christ."[11] What worries the pope is that Catholics may think of faith as consent to a series of doctrines instead of a believing encounter with Jesus Christ.

The new evangelization is a complex endeavour: (1) it announces to Catholic parishes and communities that the Gospel sends them out into the world, giving witness to their faith in the commitment to love, justice, and peace; (2) it proclaims the name of Jesus Christ to the world living in spiritual ignorance and captured in sin; (3) it fosters dialogue and cooperation with other Christian churches and, on a different level, with the great world religions, eschewing any effort of proselytism; and (4) recognizing that today's society is pluralistic, "a society of encounter," as Francis calls it, the new evangelization calls upon the Catholic community to engage in dialogue with the secular citizens, respect their personal convictions, and be willing to learn from their true insights. This dialogue allows the church to discern the work of the Spirit in the world and to participate with others in God's redemptive action, making society more just, more humane, more authentically human.

Francis's new evangelization has a remarkable affinity to the pastoral proposals of Fernand Dumont. The Quebec theologian rejected a conceptual understanding of faith and criticized the multiplication of doctrines by the Vatican; he saw faith as a religious experience, a believing encounter with God's Word. What enlivens us and gives us hope, Dumont argued, is not orthodoxy but the Good News – more precisely, the Good News made relevant to people in their cultural context. The Dumont Commission sought to promote a Catholicism appropriate for the new Quebec. Respecting *la laïcité* and the ethical pluralism of his society, Dumont wanted the church to engage in dialogue with thoughtful secular people, to discern the element of truth they perceive, to articulate the values it held in common with them, and to cooperate with them, fostering social solidarity and a humane culture.

On a visit to Toronto in November 2015 I happened to meet Mary Jo Leddy, philosopher and activist in solidarity with refugees, a wise woman, actually a former student of mine. With a happy expression on her face, she told me that she had never thought that in her own lifetime she would have a pope with whom she was on the same wave-length. The arrival of an evangelical pope, both of us thought, was wholly unanticipated, an immense surprise, a precious gift of the Spirit to the church. We were reminded that "the unexpected" is a theological category: God's action in the world is often a surprise, an unexpected mercy, an unforeseen breakthrough, an unpredictable turn of events.

25

Towards a Pluralistic Catholicism

In November 2013, Francis called upon the bishops of the universal church to consult the Catholic people "as widely as possible" in preparation for a synod on the family, to be held in Rome in October 2014. Catholics were to fill out a questionnaire to make known their convictions about issues related to the family, procreation, and sexual life. A consultation of this kind was a first in the history of the Catholic Church. Francis wanted family life to become more joyful, more loving and more respectful of all its members; he also intended to affirm the erotic love between husband and wife as a divine gift. Since the pope desired the church to be more inclusive, the synod was to discuss whether divorced and remarried Catholics and other couples living in non-canonical unions could become living members of the church and participate in the Eucharist. The respect he had expressed for homosexuals committed to following the Gospel suggests that he also wanted the synod to examine whether these men and women could be fully integrated into the life of the church.

The majority of bishops of Canada and the United States did not consult the community of the faithful. They were probably disoriented by the boldness of the pope's proposal. According to Francis, the church is not a democracy wherein questions are resolved by the voice of the majority, nor is it a monarchy wherein a single man has the power to give definitive replies to all questions. The church is not fashioned according to a secular model of society. Francis sees the church as the community of believers, in which the Spirit is at work, in which all voices deserve a hearing, and in which the sacramentally appointed authorities are helped to discern which are the most authentic voices, even if in a minority.

An altogether original pastoral theology was formulated in a few paragraphs of the Preliminary Report of the Synod on the Family presented on 18 October 2014[1] – paragraphs that are left out of the Final Report of 31 October. The Preliminary Report begins by recalling the Second Vatican Council's paradoxical affirmation that the Catholic Church is the one, true Church and, at the same time, that the other Christian churches, thanks to baptism, Scripture, and other divine gifts, save and sanctify their members, thus making these churches part of the ecclesial mystery. The Preliminary Report then applies this paradox to the sacrament of marriage: while the Catholic marriage, sacramental and insoluble, is a unique divine institution, the Catholic Church also respects the good things that happen in other marital unions, civil and non-canonical, stable or fragile, such as selfless love, mutual support, tender care of the children, the practice of common prayer, and service to the community – all signs of God's gracious presence. The Preliminary Report presents several paragraphs under three headings: "Discernment of Values Present in Families Wounded or Caught in Irregular Situations," "Announcing the Gospel of the Family in Different Contexts," and "The Positive Values of Civil Unions and Cohabitation." Three paragraphs come under the heading "Welcoming Homosexual Persons." While Catholic marriage is the unique divine institution, other unions, even if imperfect and precarious, may embody love and devotion and, as such, merit inclusion in the church's pastoral care.

In traditional theology, marriage was theoretical and deductive: it started with the idea of the perfect marriage and deduced from this what was lacking in other unions, without ever looking at what was happening in them. The theology of marriage proposed in the Preliminary Report is empirical and inductive: it pays attention to what goes on in the union of husband and wife and appreciates their union if it is sustained by love and devotion. This inductive theology reminds me of the ancient antiphon sung during Holy Week, *Ubi caritas et armor, Deus ibi est* (Where charity and love are practised, God is there). Yet these above-mentioned paragraphs do not appear in the synod's Final Report of 31 October 2014.

The second Synod on the Family took place in Rome in October 2015, the Final Report of which adopted a more conservative tone. It appears that the innovative approach encouraged by Pope Francis had not convinced the majority of bishops. Francis announced that he would publish an important pastoral document to explain what he had learned from the two synods and to explicate his own message to the faithful on issues related to family life. He actually published the exhortation *Amoris laetitia* on 19 April 2016. Since he had discovered that the majority of bishops, especially those coming from Africa, were not in favour of the new pastoral approach based on compassion and solidarity, the pope decided not to impose it on them. He therefore refused to resolve two urgent pastoral questions: (1) whether divorced and remarried couples can be admitted to holy communion and (2) whether homosexual parishioners, living singly or as a couple, can be fully integrated into the parish. What he did instead was to introduce a new style of pastoral ministry, more sensitive to people's aspirations, more attentive to their problems, and more flexible, recognizing that, in some situations, following the rules does not lead to salvation. He writes: "I wish to make it clear that not all discussions of doctrinal, moral or pastoral issues need to be settled by interventions of the magisterium." He continues:

> Unity of teaching and practice is certainly necessary in the Church, but this does not preclude various ways of interpreting some aspects of that teaching or drawing certain consequences from it. This will always be the case as the Spirit guides us towards the

> entire truth (cf. John 16:13), until he leads us fully into the mystery of Christ and enables us to see all things as he does. Each country or region, moreover, can seek solutions better suited to its culture and sensitive to its traditions and local needs.[2]

The invitation to a pastoral pluralism within the church recalls the plurality of churches in the early centuries, each one faithful to its own tradition and each one loyal to the pope. Pastoral pluralism was already recommended by the Second Vatican Council when it urged the bishops to proclaim the truth of the Gospel adapted to the culture of their region, thus making it relevant to the people who live there.

> The church learned early in its history to express the Christian message in the concepts and languages of different peoples and tried to clarify it in the light of the wisdom of their philosophers: it was an attempt to adapt the gospel to the understanding of all and the requirements of the learned, insofar as this could be done. Indeed, this kind of adaptation and preaching of the revealed word must ever be the law of all evangelization. In this way it is possible *to create in every country the possibility of expressing the message of Christ in suitable terms* and to foster vital contact and exchange between the church and different cultures.[3]

In the preceding quote I italicize the phrase that assigns to the church in every country the responsibility of interpreting the Gospel so that the people can understand and follow it. This sentence was taken very seriously in Quebec during the Quiet Revolution, when Catholics were rethinking and adapting their Catholicism to make it respond to the needs of their new society. This is how the Dumont Commission understood its task (see above). Pope Francis's call to pluralism has gone farther. He suggested that the ordination of women to the diaconate might be accepted by the church in some countries but not in others.[4] I would not be surprised if episcopal conferences in the Northern countries decided to admit divorced and remarried couples to holy communion and recommended the integration of gays and lesbians into the life of the church.

PART 2

Questions and Answers

I started to write Part 1 of this book, "My Theological Pathway," in the year 2009. After the first 120 pages I had to turn to a different task, the preparation of a graduate course on Catholic theology in French Quebec since the Quiet Revolution. I gave this course at Concordia University in the Department of Theological Studies in the summer of 2011 and then published my lectures as a book entitled *Truth and Relevance*.[1] Since I was greatly impressed by the original theology of Fernand Dumont, Quebec's brilliant social philosopher, unfortunately unknown in the English-speaking world, I decided to write a small book on his masterful *L'institution de la théologie*,[2] a work that could have a beneficial impact on today's church. When the study of history in the nineteenth century rendered unbelievable the church's claim that its teaching had been identical throughout its history, John Henry Newman's *An Essay on the Development of Christian Doctrine* (1845) introduced the idea of doctrinal evolution, which allowed the church to admit that its teaching had changed, while remaining faithful to its original truth. In our day, as the church's credibility is threatened by the secularization of culture, Fernand Dumont's *L'institution de la théologie* introduces ideas that could help the church to demonstrate the relevance and fecundity of the Gospel in the context of modern society.

In the fall of 2013, I returned to "My Theological Pathway," expanding certain parts and adding about forty pages. Since we now had a new pope whose theological orientation differed considerably from Benedict XVI's, I inserted references to Francis in my text. Because of several other engagements, I started Part 2 of the present book in the spring of 2014 but was again interrupted by various commitments. I returned to it in the fall of 2014 and completed it in the spring of 2015. Preparing it for publication with McGill-Queen's University Press, I am still adding reflections and endnotes in the summer of 2016.

Part 2 takes an entirely different form from Part 1: I call it "Questions and Answers." A good friend of mine, Philip McKenna, a Toronto-based philosopher and psychotherapist, asks me questions about my ideas, my experiences, and my personal life, obliging me to clarify the experiential grounding of my intellectual journey and to make known the joys and the sorrows that have sustained me in my theological inquiry.

26

Looking Back over Your Life

Philip McKenna: *Looking back over your life, how do you evaluate it, now that you are over ninety years old? Have you achieved what you set out to do? Did your intellectual engagement have the impact that you desired? Are you disappointed or do you feel reassured?*

I am grateful that I have been allowed to participate in the theological movement that enabled the Catholic Church at the Second Vatican Council to open itself to the world – more concretely, I am grateful to have joined the ecumenical movement, to recognize the Protestant churches as part of the mystery of the church, to honour contemporary Judaism as the living heritage of God's ancient covenant, to respect the world religions and engage in dialogue with them, and to seek cooperation with people outside the church, be they religious or secular, promoting social justice, human rights, and the protection of the environment. I have been allowed to play a modest part in this extraordinary historical event.

I am grateful for so many spiritual events in my life. In "My Theological Pathway" I mention the impact of Augustine's *Confessions* on my religious existence. I am also grateful that I was impressed by liberation theology and the preferential option for the poor and became a thinker of the Catholic left, critical of economic, political, and cultural empire and longing for a just, egalitarian, and humane society. I am grateful that, despite Cardinal Ratzinger/Benedict XVI's opposition, liberation theology has had an impact on the church's official social teaching. The election of Pope Francis in March of 2013 gave me great joy. Francis hears in the Gospel the call of the church to be in solidarity with the poor and excluded, and to denounce as sinful the global invasion of neoliberal capitalism. "This economy kills," he writes.[1] I am grateful that he offers a clear analysis of the crises that threaten the civilization of the West and that affect all parts of the world. While only a minority of Catholics listen to him and make the option for the poor, the worldwide liberationist movement, despite its minority status, strengthens my faith, allows me to be hopeful, and gives me great joy. Creative renewal starts in the margins of society: this is where Jesus stood and, before him, the prophets in Ancient Israel and Socrates in Ancient Greece. In the dark times of the early twenty-first century, it is the movements of resistance and reconstruction on the ground that give me hope.

The term *missio Dei* is used in recent Protestant theology to express the mission God the Father has assigned to his incarnate Son, and the Spirit in which they share, to rescue the world from its self-destructive orientation, reconciling divided humanity in grace, unity, and love – a mission in which the church participates and in which each Christian and, in fact, each human being has a share. I like the term *missio Dei* because it suggests, first, that our activities inspired by faith are sustained by a power that transcends us and, second, that secular people and the followers of other religions are also offered the power to become healers, stand for justice, and foster reconciliation – so that God's will be done on Earth.

27

Your Hopeful Reading of the Catholic Church

Philip: *You habitually offer a hopeful reading of the Catholic Church's teaching. You did this especially in your book* Amazing Church, *yet you are well aware that several of your acquaintances and friends, especially thoughtful women, have withdrawn from the church, frustrated by the refusal of the institution to engage in dialogue with the believing community and to practise solidarity with the powerless and voiceless, women in particular.*

I agree that the ethics of governance in the present democratic age demands that a society, any society, institute forums wherein the rulers and the ruled engage in dialogue. This is a point made in the Dumont Report on the future of the church in Quebec.[1] Still, democratic participation does not guarantee the adoption of progressive policies. If the people who elected Stephen Harper as Canadian prime minister exercised power in the church, they would promote pastoral policies indifferent to the poor and powerless and hostile to critical thinking. If we want the church to be prophetic, to denounce social evil and call for an alternative to the present society, what is needed is not democracy but popes and bishops who listen to the prophetic movements in the church, including feminist voices, and engage in dialogue with secular critical thinkers and currents.

Pope Francis's indictment of today's unregulated capitalism as evil, life-destroying, and idolatrous is not likely to please the majority of Canadian Catholics, including a good many priests and bishops. Ecclesiastical democracy would not support his teaching. What is needed are popes and bishops who listen to the prophetic voices in the believing community, discerning the Spirit speaking in the church. I have hope for the church because the unexpected happens.

At the same time, I have great respect for several friends and acquaintances of mine who have decided to leave the Catholic Church. They are offended by the hierarchy's refusal to engage in dialogue and disagree with certain ecclesiastic teachings. Following their critically examined personal conscience, they leave the Catholic Church for spiritual reasons. A few join other Christian churches, while others remain religious and practise a spirituality of their own. Deeply disturbed by the suffering in the world – military violence, genocides, oppression, and persecution – some Catholics find it impossible to believe in Almighty God and drift into atheism.

Quite different is the unbelief and indifference that invade the minds of many Catholics affected by today's secular culture. These Catholics recognize nothing beyond the finite world; they are not puzzled by the mystery behind the universe and do not hear a divine summons in their conscience. Some unbelieving former Catholics become pragmatists, accepting the world as it is, while others, retaining the utopian yearning of the Gospel, participate in movements for an alternative society – just, compassionate, and humane. There are also Catholics whose upbringing has made Catholicism a burden to them, an obstacle to their self-discovery and a source of irrational guilt: they now drop their faith in search of personal freedom. I have the impression that in Quebec the negative memory of Catholicism has become part of the public culture.

28

Your Sinful Existence

Philip: *In "My Theological Pathway" you do not mention your personal failures and shortcomings. Since you identify yourself with the Augustinian tradition, I dare to ask you whether you see yourself as a sinner.*

Yes, I do. I don't live up to my ideals. I am aware of the egotism that dwells in me and marks, faintly or strongly, everything I think and do. Even in my prayers I am more concerned with myself than with God and God's coming reign. I mistrust myself: under compelling circumstances I may come to betray what I believe in and do evil. I also lack spontaneous sympathy for all the persons I meet, even though universal solidarity, beginning with the poor and excluded, has come to define the orientation of my theology. My friend Normand finds all persons he meets interesting, respects them, listens to them, and communicates something unspoken to them that gives them strength. He even speaks to the homeless on the streets. I am unable to do this. A certain middle-class arrogance is a barrier that I disguise with a smile on my face. I look with admiration at men and women who spend their lives helping people in need, like nurses, social workers, therapists, and community organizers, wondering if I have the passion within me to do what they do.

I am also troubled by the contradictions in my life that do not leave me innocent: while I denounce the present capitalist economy for ethical reasons, I live a comfortable life thanks to a McGill

University pension, financed by capital investments that make me profit from the system I reject. I have often made the point that the cup of coffee in the morning relates us unfairly to the coffee pickers in the South, profiting as we do from the exploitative conditions inflicted upon them. In a gravely unjust world, the comfortable cannot claim to be wholly innocent.

For over two years now I have been receiving dialysis three times a week at the hospital, a treatment that allows me to survive and be well but that costs society an enormous amount of money – according to a recent article, about $80,000 a year.[1] Is it reasonable, is it ethical, to spend that sum on an old man in his nineties instead of investing it in the health and education of young people? My daily life is punctuated by an ethical question mark.

Still, like the widow of Sarepta, I am allowed to lead a happy life. I am cheerfully engaged in what I regard as my mission: the dialogue of theology with the social sciences in the service of the church's renewal and the reconstruction of society. In the old days we referred to this as "the intellectual apostolate." The Scottish philosopher John Macmurray expresses the emancipatory orientation of the intellectual life in this sentence: "All meaningful knowledge is for the sake of action, and all meaningful action is for the sake of friendship,"[2] meaning universal friendship in justice and peace. There is joy in this dedication because it is sustained by a transcendent mystery, the *missio Dei*.

29

The Humanism of Your Upbringing

Philip: *You tell us in "My Theological Pathway" that, when you first became deeply committed to faith in God, responding to the* Confessions of Saint Augustine, *you adopted an exclusivist stance, acknowledging salvation in the church and not beyond it. At that time you were troubled by St Thomas's proposal that divine grace was offered to every child as he or she reaches the age of reason. Later, you gradually moved to a more generous understanding of the Christian Gospel, the promise of God's redemptive presence promoting in every culture a humanism of love and justice. I wonder whether your journey is not, at least in part, a return to the moral ideal, the humanism you were taught as a child.*

I think there is some truth in your suggestion. My family embraced the ethos of the German Enlightenment, guided by thinkers like Herder, Lessing, Mendelssohn, and Kant, who praised the moral flourishing of persons in selfless service, just practices, loving behaviour, and the toleration of otherness. I was taken to the plays of Schiller – Wilhelm Tell, die Räuber, Don Carlos, die Jungfrau von Orleans, and Mary Stuart – all of which celebrate the resistance of courageous persons to the oppression inflicted by the powerful.

This is how Moses Mendelssohn summarized his ethical teaching:

Das Wahre suchen,
das Gute wollen,
das Schöne lieben,
das Rechte tun.

To seek the truth,
to will the good,
to love the beautiful,
to do the right thing.

We did not realize that this ideal of *Humanität* represented the highest aspirations of a particular social class, the cultured bourgeoisie (*Bildungsbürgertum*), leaving us indifferent to the disadvantaged. Yet I did recognize that this ethos offered us no guidance when Hitler came to power and, a few years later, chased us from the fatherland we loved. This is how I described my experience as a refugee in England:

> I felt that my world had gone under. The people I knew, my family and friends, had become mute. They had nothing to say. None of the inherited values shed light on the new situation. Life had lost all meaning. I well remember how amazed I was at the silence of my elders. It was soon afterwards that I began to search for a view of life and a source of wisdom that could outlast catastrophe.[1]

When I became a critical thinker, I recognized that the bourgeois ethics of *Humanität* had problematic political implications. It did not draw attention to the lot of the labouring classes and the poor, nor did it produce indignation at society's crass inequalities. The great ethical tradition of *Humanität* created – unintentionally – a strong class consciousness of the educated middle classes. In my family in the 1920s and 1930s, workers and servants, while respected, were seen as culturally inferior. The German they spoke, the clothes they wore, the food they ate, the newspapers they read, the entertainment they sought – they were all different from the way we lived. In "My Theological Pathway" I mention a childhood experience, sitting in my stepfather's car, looking at a street cleaner bending down, and feeling a deep sorrow over the humiliation inflicted upon the poor, an indignation I had not learned from my family.[2] The significance of this unforgettable experience dawned on me much later, in the late 1960s, when I became a critical thinker.

Philip, I am now able to reply to your question. The new Catholic humanism – universal solidarity and the respect for pluralism – in the emergence of which I was allowed to participate, has a certain affinity with the bourgeois humanism with which I was brought up, yet it is also quite different. Catholic humanism listens to the radical demand of Jesus that our love and solidarity exclude no one. Pope Francis reminds us that "our faith in Christ, who became poor, and was always close to the poor and the outcast, is the basis of our concern for the integral development of society's most neglected members."[3] Christ's special love for the disadvantaged remains a sting in our conscience, constantly demanding that we question ourselves.

30

Troubled Theism

Philip: *If I remember correctly, you wrote somewhere that a sting in our conscience also accompanies our faith in God. Am I right?*

In "My Theological Pathway" I raise the question of whether it is possible to believe in God after Auschwitz.[1] Rabbi Irving Greenberg argues that the Holocaust has spelled "the end of untroubled theism."[2] We are now troubled by doubt. I mentioned above that Jewish and Christian theologians, wrestling with this question, have spoken of God's *kenosis*, God's freely chosen powerlessness, assigning to humans the task of creating a just and peaceful world.[3] This is of course no final answer. Since God is mysterious, there is no final answer. We continue to find ourselves challenged by doubts.

There are other doubts that arise in the life of faith. Fernand Dumont has shown that faith is not a stable orientation of the soul but, rather, a trusting surrender to the Gospel that keeps on being questioned and that needs to be rethought in response to new insights and new religious experiences.[4] He mentions in particular that, as Christians move from one culture to another or from one historical context to another, they must discover the meaning of the Gospel for their new situation. That is why Dumont holds that doubt is not a sin, an expression of infidelity, as preached by the Church in the past; doubt is, rather, a dimension of the spiritual process that allows believers, challenged by new questions, to reaffirm their faith. Doubt makes us reread the Scriptures and rethink the church's witnesses throughout its history, to hear in them a redemptive message relevant to the present. If we refuse to ask questions and repress our doubts, we gradually become blind fundamentalists or lonely non-believers.

31

Deeply Rooted in the Catholic Tradition

Philip: *You say that you are deeply rooted in the Catholic tradition. But since you are known as a critical Catholic publicly disagreeing with certain official teachings and, second, because you have, as an ecumenist, great respect for all Christian churches, you have to explain what precisely you mean by being rooted in the Catholic tradition.*

As an ecumenical believer I have great respect for all Christian traditions. I am inclined to agree with Ernst Troeltsch that God's revelation in Jesus Christ is so rich in meaning and power that it cannot be embodied in a single ecclesiastical tradition. All the churches seek to be faithful to their understandings of the biblical message; at the same time, all of them are ambiguous historical communities, embodying movements inspired by the Gospel and others obscuring its true meaning. According to Fernand Dumont, all large organizations, including the churches, produce ideologies to protect their institutional interests, and, for this reason, churches are always tempted to proclaim their ideology as part of the divine message. For instance, the ancient Catholic doctrine *Extra ecclesiam nulla salus* (No salvation outside the church) was an ideology that concealed the work of the Holy Spirit outside the church's boundaries. Acknowledging the signs of God's presence in the world religions and in humanistic traditions, the Second Vatican Council transcended this ideology, giving the doctrine *Extra ecclesiam nulla salus* a new meaning, proposing that God's grace, to whomever it is given, creates a spiritual relationship to the church.

Since claiming that the Catholic Church is "the one true Church" conceals the work of the Holy Spirit in other Christian churches, theologians – following the spirit of the Second Vatican Council – will have to give it a new meaning. So far they have hesitated to do this. There are four empirical positions that lead me to claim that the Roman Catholic tradition is unique, different from the other Christian traditions and yet embodying within itself an echo of these traditions.

1 The Catholic tradition recognizes God's redemptive presence in the church, especially in the Scriptures, the sacramental liturgy, the sacred art and architecture, and the marvellous lives of sainted men and women. In spite of the world's sinfulness, Catholics are summoned to be joyful, surrounded as they are by signs of God's presence. Beauty in nature and art can be experienced as sacramental: a Mozart symphony or a bed of flowers and sunshine on the hills across the valley can mediate a sense of God's goodness. Catholics with a strong sense of God's redemptive immanence regard human life itself as sacramental. On this basis Catholics, in response to the pluralism of society, have – after a long resistance – rethought their relationship to outsiders, recognizing an echo of God's Word and an inkling of the Spirit in the world religions and all traditions of wisdom.

2 The Catholic tradition has, from the beginning, been in critical dialogue with philosophy, in particular with the Platonism widely accepted in Hellenistic culture. Traces of this philosophy are already found in the Old Testament, especially in the Book of Wisdom, and in the New Testament, especially in the Gospel of John. Catholics had no hesitation modifying ideas and practices taken from pagan cultures to announce the meaning of the

Gospel in a new society. We adopted Christmas trees and Easter eggs, bending these practices to have Christian meaning. In the thirteenth century, Catholic theologians turned to the thought of Aristotle to explore the intelligibility of the Catholic faith. Since the popes saw emerging modernity in a totally negative light, they condemned Catholic thinkers engaged in a creative dialogue with modern thought. In 1879, in the encyclical *Aeterni Patris*, Leo XIII made neo-scholasticism the unique basis for the church's philosophical and theological thinking, a monopoly that excluded Catholics from participating in the intellectual debate carried on in their society. To renew the relevance of the Gospel the Second Vatican Council asked Catholics to enter into dialogue with their culture and make use of its truths and values to articulate the Christian message, a process called "the inculturation" of the Gospel, a theological approach subsequently emphasized by John Paul II. In the 1998 encyclical *Faith and Reason*, the Pope returned to the classical Roman Catholic tradition by welcoming the dialogue of believers with the philosophers of their culture. Today, the Catholic Church enjoys philosophical pluralism.

3 The Catholic tradition, suspicious of wealth and power, has had a spiritual preference for poverty and the humble life. The institutional expression of this preference was the communal life of religious orders and congregations: here Catholics choose to forego married life and personal property and live as communities obedient to an appointed superior. The church recognized two distinct Christian vocations: life in the world and life in a religious order, the latter being the more radical form of discipleship. Yet all Catholics were called upon to practise the corporal works of mercy: to feed the hungry, to give drink to the thirsty, to clothe the naked, to shelter the homeless, to visit the sick, and to ransom captives. Following the emergence of soci-

ological thinking in the nineteenth century, the church's social teaching began to look upon society from the perspective of the proletariat (Leo XIII used this word) and to interpret the corporal works of mercy as support for political reform, a more just organization of labour, and the redistribution of wealth. Solidarity with the poor led Catholic social teaching in the 1960s and 1970s to follow Latin American liberation theology in denouncing the globalization of unregulated capitalism. Pope Francis reconfirmed this radical option for the poor. He writes in his exhortation *Evangelii gaudium*: "Each individual Christian and every [Christian] community is called to be an instrument of God for the liberation and promotion of the poor and for enabling them to be fully part of society. This demands that we be docile and attentive to the cry of the poor and to come to their aid."[1] The church's radical social teaching is received only by a minority in the church. Most bishops and priests turn a deaf ear to it. To embrace it, I have argued, requires a conversion of mind and heart, a divine gift available to some but not to others.

4 The Catholic tradition appreciates the practice of contemplative prayer, the silent turn to thanksgiving and worship, the patient waiting for union with God. Catholics honour the mystical dimension of religion. The English word "mysticism" is unfortunate: ending in "ism," it sounds like an ideology. The French say, more simply, "la mystique," and the Germans, "*die Mystik*." Catholic mystics, affected by Neo-Platonism, strove in their prayer to be united with God in a cloud of unknowing. They developed the *via negativa*, briefly discussed in "My Theological Pathway,"[2] which recognizes God's otherness and incomprehensibility. The predications of God in the biblical literature must first be negated: they are true only according to a certain analogy. Christian doctrine only hints at the truth, makes us see

through a glass darkly (1 Cor. 13:12), is knowledge only *secundum quid*, and provides indispensable metaphors of God's glory. I mentioned that the Fourth Lateran Council (1215) recognized that, between the Creator and the created order, the difference is always greater than the similarity (*Denzinger*, no. 806), implying that our language about God, which is part of the created order, can never be literally true but true only as hint, symbol, figure of speech, and/or metaphor. We know in a strict sense only what God is not: God is not finite, not material, not limited, not mortal, not unjust, not violent, not evil, and so forth. Our eyes are unable to see, the church fathers said, because the light is either too dark or too glaring. Being excessive light, God is to us the incomprehensible divine mystery.

These four theological positions explain what I refer to when I claim to be rooted in the Catholic tradition: (1) faith in God's redemptive presence in church and society; (2) the dialogue with philosophy and contemporary culture; (3) solidarity with the poor, the oppressed, and the excluded; and (4) the mystical tradition and the *via negativa*. I note that my understanding of rootedness in the Catholic tradition corresponds with Fernand Dumont's understanding of belonging to the church by *référence*,[3] that is, by identification with the witnesses of faith and the redemptive events in the Catholic past and present. These redemptive events include the ecclesiastical institution to the extent to which it serves the faith of the believing community.

These four theological positions also allow me to describe the uniqueness of the Roman Catholic Church among Christian churches. All the churches see themselves as faithful embodiments of the message and the gifts of Christ. In this sense, they all see themselves in apostolic succession, even if they do so humbly, recognizing their many failures. Yet the Catholic Church appears to me significantly different from the other churches and, at the same time, open to certain of these churches' values and practices that it presently lacks.

To argue this thesis carefully would require an entire book. Still, I allow myself to make the following suggestions. The Catholic Church shares with the Orthodox churches the claim to unbroken institutional continuity, but it differs from the Orthodox churches in its critical openness to the Enlightenment and to the rethinking of its relationship to outsiders, religious and secular. The Orthodox churches recognize the relative autonomy of the local church and base the unity of the church universal not on bureaucratic centralization but, rather, on the collegiality of the bishops and their communities. Their notion of collegiality exists as an echo in the Roman Catholic Church, an ideal that inspired the Second Vatican Council but, in the end, failed to find approval.

The Protestant churches do not share with Roman Catholicism either its faith in the sacramentality of life and worship or its appreciation of the mystical tradition. The Anglican Church has a greater affinity with the Roman Catholic Church than do other Protestant churches. At the same time, however, these other churches have insights and practices that the Catholic Church is lacking: trusting that the Spirit addresses all members of the believing community, these churches have governing institutions that allow their members to be heard and to participate in the formulation of the church's pastoral policies.

I conclude from these brief reflections that the time has come for the Catholic Church to rethink its understanding of being "the one true Church" by turning to a more historical understanding of its ecclesial identity, seeing itself empirically as an altogether unique Christian church. This is the Petrine tradition.

In never forgot the theological thesis of Solovyev, the Russian religious thinker who predicted that the Orthodox churches (in the Johannine tradition), the Roman Catholic Church (in the Petrine tradition), and the Protestant churches (in the Pauline tradition) would resist the powers of darkness, remain faithful to the Gospel, and, in that fidelity, be reconciled with one another. I was introduced to

Solovyev's proposal in the 1940s by an older German friend, Egbert Munzer, mentioned earlier,[4] who was writing a book on this Russian religious thinker.[5]

I am firmly rooted in the Petrine tradition. At the same time, the preaching of Jesus calls me to be critical of the ideological deformations of this tradition and its unchristian practices. Catholic women have rightly lamented the church's embrace of patriarchy and its ongoing unwillingness to acknowledge the equality between men and women. Latin American Christians have brought to light the Doctrine of Discovery, the set of fifteenth-century papal bulls approving the colonial conquest of pagan lands, the confiscation of the people's wealth, and the enslavement of the population.[6] Unforgettable for contemporary Catholics is the reactionary stance adopted by the Vatican in the nineteenth century, when it defended the feudal-aristocratic order against democracy and human rights, and the closeness of the Catholic Church to fascism in several countries in the twentieth century. It took the Holocaust to make the church recognize its anti-Jewish discourse and acknowledge its destructive cultural consequences. Sometimes I feel guilty for remaining a Catholic.

Since the Catholic Church regards itself as holy and without sin, it finds it difficult to come to self-knowledge and recognize the human damage produced by its policies and practices. John Paul II wrestled with this problem as no pope had done before him. He apologized on many occasions for the wrong done by the church in its long history.[7] In January 2000, he published *Memory and Reconciliation: The Church and the Faults of the Past*, the report of the International Theological Commission. And on 12 March 2000, he celebrated a solemn liturgy of repentance at St Peter's Basilica in Rome, asking God's forgiveness for the sins committed in the name of the church.[8] In the service these sins were divided into six categories: (1) sins committed in the service of the truth; (2) sins that have harmed the unity of the church; (3) sins against the Jews; (4) sins committed against love, peace, the rights of peoples, and the respect for cultures and religions; (5) sins against the dignity of women and the unity of the human race; and (5) sins violating the fundamental rights of persons. In these and many other apologies, the pope confesses the sins of Catholics in the name of the Church, but he still shies away from admitting that the church itself has sinned.

It is altogether in keeping with Catholic theology to say that the church has sinned or that the church is sinful, if one confesses at the same time that this same church proclaims and celebrates the truth and the gifts of Jesus Christ, by which it is forgiven and summoned to renew and reform itself. That is why Francis does not hesitate to acknowledge the sins of the church. He humbly apologizes for the Crusades, for the church's association with colonialism and its treatment of Indigenous peoples, and for the church's hostile attitude towards outsiders: Jews, Waldensians, Protestants, Pentecostals, and the followers of non-Christian religions. According to the Second Vatican Council:

> Christ summons the Church, as she goes her pilgrim way, to the continual reformation of which she always has need, insofar as she is an institution of men here on earth. Therefore, if the influence of events and of the times has led to deficiencies in conduct, in Church disciple, or even in the formulation of doctrine ... these should be appropriately rectified at the proper moment.[9]

I am firmly rooted in this Catholic tradition. Because it continues to be addressed by God's Word, the Catholic tradition is alive, creative, ready to respond to new challenges, and capable of communicating the Gospel to the contemporary world.

32

Your Homosexual Orientation

Philip: *Now I wish to turn to something quite personal. You mention in "My Theological Pathway" that you are homosexual and that you have been married – for thirty years. Don't you think that this calls for an explanation?*

I knew that I loved men since I was twelve years old. I was totally perplexed by this. What was happening to me did not make sense. I mentioned my attraction to an older student who, I thought, knew more about life than I did, but he was equally puzzled. When I hinted at my experience to my mother, she said that such inclinations do exist. She called it *Liebe unter Knaben* (love among young men). She probably thought that the same-sex love of youth would eventually be overcome in full maturity. I soon learned to accept my natural inclination, loving men from a distance, delighted by their presence and wishing them well.

Much later, in the internment camp, I fell passionately in love with a sailor, a man of intelligence and generosity. Hans Sturm was his name. He was a German refugee because, as a Jehovah's Witness, he had suffered persecution under Hitler's regime. While I was possessed by my devotion to him day and night, I had the discipline not to say a single word or make a single gesture that would reveal my feelings. That I was homosexual would have embarrassed Hans and put an unhappy strain on our relationship. In subsequent years I fell in love with men on several occasions with a passion that was both joyful and painful at the same time: I had great joy in the presence of the beloved and great pain because my love could not be received. Again God gave me the discipline to hide my feelings. Since the men I loved were straight, the awareness of my homosexuality would have made them uncomfortable. Because there was no future for the love I experienced, I decided not to explore the sexual dimension of my personality. This was undoubtedly one of the reasons that the idea of celibate life in a monastery attracted me.

I was forty years old when I had my first sexual encounter with a man. I met him in a restaurant in London. This was exciting and at the same time disappointing, for I knew what love was and what I really wanted was to share my life with a partner. I was capable of selfless love, but there was in those days no space in society to meet a seriously minded gay man. Looking back I began to realize that my vow of celibacy had not been a meaningful religious commitment but simply a promise to bracket my homosexuality, to refuse to explore its meaning and power.

In "My Theological Pathway" I mention that, in the 1960s, I came to disagree with the church's official sexual ethics and that, in 1974, I revealed my thinking about homosexual love in *Commonweal*.[1] I did not profess my own homosexuality in public because such an act of honesty would have reduced my influence as a critical theologian. I was eager to be heard as a theologian trusting in God as *salvator mundi* and committed to social justice, liberation theology, and global solidarity. Yet, since I no longer agreed with the church's official sexual ethics and was exploring my sexuality in non-conformist ways, I thought that resigning from the priesthood was the right thing to do. I published a short article in a University of Toronto student paper in which I expressed my disagreement with papal teaching, realizing that this would provoke an official reprimand. This was the right moment, I thought, for leaving the priesthood and the religious order, even as I remained committed to the Catholic tradition and my work as a Catholic theologian. Responding to my decision, Father

John Kelly, the president of St Michael's College, a man of great generosity, told me that I could keep my position of professor of theology and religious studies.

Living alone as a layman did not appeal to me. I was worried that I would waste my time looking for company. What I needed as a theologian was discipline, a regular life committed to study, reflection, and public witness. I talked about these matters with Shirley, a former nun, who had been, with me, a participant in the Therafields movement and had become a close personal friend. After leaving the convent Shirley had had a brief unhappy experience of marriage: she discovered that physical intimacy disturbed rather than fulfilled her. Aware of our friendship and our different sexual biases, we discussed the possibility of living together and getting married, and this is what we did. We celebrated our friendship in a happy union for thirty years, until Shirley's passing in 2007. People invited to our apartment often told us that they noticed the respect and tender concern we had for one another.

Shirley did not mind that, when we moved to Montreal in 1986, I met Normand, a former priest, with whom I fell in love. Committed to liberation theology, we share the same religious and political orientation. Shirley was fond of Normand, enjoyed his company, and trusted him. She was pleased that Normand would keep her company whenever I travelled to give lectures in Canada, the United States, and Germany. My love for Normand has never changed: his presence delights me to this day. While Normand is gay and welcomed my sexual embrace when we were younger (I was sixty-three when I met him, he was forty-six), he did not love me as I did him: he simply regards me as a great friend for whom he makes room in his life. I fully accept this. I discipline myself not to tell him my feelings: I don't put into words what he means to me nor do I articulate the joy that his presence gives me – except at certain very rare moments. The unwavering love of Normand, which has given stability to my life as a theologian, has been a gift of God.

What does theology have to say about the homosexual condition? I have avoided studying the persecution of homosexuals and the cruel punishments inflicted upon them throughout the ages, fuelled by the teaching and the hatred of the church. While I studied the anti-Jewish rhetoric of Christian preaching, I had no wish to face the sadistic treatment to which homosexuals have been exposed in Christian societies over the centuries. Gay scholars who study this story of torture and violence often come to look upon the God of Christians as their enemy. Instead of dealing with this cruel past, I have preferred to address the contemporary situation, offering theological arguments that allow gays and lesbians to be reconciled to their condition and recognize that Christ loves them as much as he does heterosexuals.

I have asked myself if there is a special meaning in the homosexual condition. God creates the great majority of humans heterosexual and only a small minority homosexual. Is there a special task associated with the condition of the latter? Since they are an oppressed minority, aware of the hypocrisy of society and the damage done by the dominant culture, I have suggested that gays and lesbians are intended to extend their solidarity to all marginalized groups and demand greater justice.[2] Because homosexuals are largely invisible in society, their prophetic vocation will have a cultural impact and support the struggle for human emancipation.

33

A Poem for Your Ninetieth Birthday

Philip: *Since you have had the courage to talk about very personal matters, I ask you to allow me to cite the poem about you that I wrote for the celebration of your ninetieth birthday at le Centre justice et foi in Montreal.*

GREGORY BAUM AT 90

Forced from his home
He never seemed to weep of loss
But always found
A workable belonging,
Expecting ever to be heard and liked
Because originary love –
God's in a mother's –
Kept the abyss of fear away,
Sustaining his élan
For traverse of four tongues
And more forms of life
Than I can tell.

Yet with these riches
And his workable belonging
He always was apart as well,
Remembering, I surmise, his kin

Exterminated for a Name.
He never could rest
With knowledge of the self,
But must be a voice
Of the silent dead
And silent warriors.
A journeyman voice,
He always said,
For the faith and justice
Workers of this lovely world
Besmirched by greed
And carelessness.

He spoke to me once
So bodily brought low
All he could do
Was lie in a darkened room
And say the Jesus prayer –
Son of David
Have mercy on me.
Now I hear the Lord
Has asked him to drop by
Three times a week
For a quiet chat.
Perhaps the next book
Will somehow emerge
As topic of that conversation.

Thank you Grégoire
Père et Frère
For dear long friendship,
Your witness in a darkened world,
And ever ready joy in life.
and peace.

34

Your Identity as a Man of Many Affinities

Philip: *I have often wondered how you define yourself. Since you were born in Berlin, a German of Jewish and Protestant background, a refugee in England, an immigrant in Canada, a Catholic theologian, and now a Néo-Québécois, you have belonged to several cultures. Does this confuse you? Who are you? How do you define your identity?*

The question you raise touches not only the manner in which I define my own identity but also the wider issue of the identity-formation of refugees and immigrants. Since this is a topic that interests me, my reply to you will be somewhat rambling. According to psychoanalysts, people's identity is largely created by the experiences they had as babies, while sociologists and anthropologists hold that people's identities are largely cultural creations – a supposition that I fully share. The language we speak, the food we eat, he clothes we wear, and the ideas that help us to interpret the world are all mediated by the culture in which we are born.

Many immigrants and refugees suffer because they have been severed from their cultural roots and experience themselves as marginal in their new society. The wife of a rabbi friend of mine, who had lived successively in several countries, once said to me, "We are all cut flowers." She meant by this, I think, that we are not plants rooted in the ground, flourishing ever anew as the spring arrives. Cut flowers do not reawaken. In her autobiographical reflections, *The Butterfly Healing,*[1] Julia Ching, the internationally respected scholar of Chinese religion, reveals the insecurity of her identity. Born in China, she had moved for her education to Hong Kong and Australia and eventually became a professor in Canada. She was a colleague of mine at the University of Toronto. Reading her autobiography, I discovered that she was torn and troubled by the question of whether she was an Asian woman or a Western woman. Because she felt that one could not be both, she did not know who she was. But personal identity can be multiple: we can be nourished by the participation in several cultural currents.

Today's neoliberal economy and culture offer a superficial solution to the identity problem of immigrants and refugees. With the rest of the population, the new arrivals learn to see themselves as customers and consumers, looking upon society as a vast supermarket. In one of his books Zygmunt Bauman draws an ironic picture of society as a giant shopping centre uniting people of all classes: it offers them free choice and consumption as their common values and reconciles the rich and the poor in the desire for the same goods – goods that the rich can buy and the poor can at least look at and touch. This caricature contains a grain of truth. I remember that, at a breakfast I had in a Toronto hotel, I heard the animated conversation among three waiters, an Asian, an African, and a Latin American, about the electronic gadget they wanted to buy if they could save enough money. The consumer-oriented lifestyle is one of the reasons that some immigrants resist integration into their new society, preferring to cling to their inherited culture, an option that leads to their marginalization.

Being rooted in a culture is of great importance: it provides the ideas and values we need to interpret the world we live in and to act in it. But this cultural identity must be open to engaging in dialogue with new cultural experiences in changed historical conditions. In modern society, this openness is essential not only for immigrants but also for all men and women. A national culture remains alive by responding creatively to the evolving social conditions by which it is challenged. The refusal to engage in dialogue leads to rigidity, immobility, and death. Immigrants unwilling to engage in dialogue with the culture of their new society isolate themselves, making their cultural inheritance into a straight-jacket. I hold that attentive conversation with the different cultural currents that surround immigrants allows them to be responsible citizens and to embrace their inherited values in a new way.

Openness to dialogue and the creativity of religious cultures has been of special interest to me. In "My Theological Pathway" I mention Robert Bellah's study of how East Asian religious cultures reacted to modernity. In it he shows that religious leaders who opposed new conditions began to cling rigidly to their traditions, while the leaders who were open to a dialogue were able to find a way of being faithful to their inherited traditions while becoming participants in their new society. In my own studies of the response of Catholic cultures to the challenge of modernity, I arrived at a similar conclusion: creative dialogue enabled the church, after a long period of pure resistance, to affirm a Catholic way of life, faithful to the truth received, that made an important contribution to contemporary society. While some people use the word "tradition" to refer to old ideas and customs that are obstacles to social progress, I have become convinced of the usefulness of traditions and their capacity to create the new under changed historical circumstances. I agree with Fernand Dumont, who defines tradition as the memory of past events that helps us to resolve the problems of the present.

The great event in my life, rescuing me from the experience of uncertainty, was my entry into a life of faith within the Catholic Church. I recount this in "My Theological Pathway." Becoming a Catholic in the year 1946 was more than the quest for personal salvation: it was an entry into a living tradition with roots in the distant past. I was aware at the time that the Catholic Church supported conservative forces in several countries and fascist governments in a few, yet what I embraced was not the political Catholicism of those days but the classical Catholic tradition: the living reality of the Scriptures, the sacramental liturgy, the early ecumenical councils, and the Community of Saints. I joined the spiritual world of Augustine and the church fathers, of Thomas and the medieval theologians, and of the Romanesque and Gothic churches I had visited as a child. In the library of my German friends in Toronto, Egbert Munzer and his wife Margo, I found books representing the creative German Catholicism following the First World War – the writings of Karl Adam, Romano Guardini, Gertrud von Lefort, Pius Parsch, Erich Przywara, and many others. Rooting myself in the Catholic tradition gave me a strong sense of personal identity that allowed me to be open to various cultures. I rewove my connection to Germany, I embraced a major cultural current in European history, and I participated in the movement to make Catholics open to ecumenism.

Fernand Dumont, as I only read quite recently, proposes that we belong to the Catholic tradition by *référence*, by remembering the redemptive events of the past, the life and teaching of Jesus, his death and resurrection, the gift of the Spirit, and the cloud of witnesses throughout the church's history – which give us hope for its renewal in the future. His theological proposal corresponds to my own experience.

At the end of the 1960s, as I mention in "My Theological Pathway," I was influenced by liberation theology and Rosemary Ruether's critical thought, I became a man of the left, in dialogue with socialist ideas and practices, critical of the dominant Catholic ideology, yet remaining fully within the Catholic tradition. When I visited Germany, I attended left-wing Catholic and secular meetings that dealt with the same issues that preoccupied me and my friends in Canada. Belonging to the board of directors of the international Catholic theological review *Concilium*, I met theologians from various parts of the world and discovered that they were wrestling with very similar issues. We were all part, in one way or another, of the faith and justice movement in the church. Despite this experience of universal solidarity, I do not see myself as cosmopolitan or as a citizen of the world: I have been locally involved, socially engaged in the society in which I live, and related to it emotionally, happy to see its cultural achievements and its entry into greater justice, and saddened by its decline and increasing social inequalities.

Rooted in the Catholic tradition, I find that I can be both at home and a stranger in several societies – at home because I share the values and aspirations of the humanistic left and support its activities, and a stranger because I am in disagreement with the dominant ideology. As a Catholic remembering his Jewish and Protestant background, I have no conflict in being a Berliner, a German, a Canadian, and a Québécois. Because these identities are in constant dialogue with one another, they do not tear me apart but, rather, stimulate new thinking and enrich my life.

Having multiple identities is the fate of vast numbers of people in the present age. For some this is a debilitating experience: they feel like "cut flowers," they have no cultural home, are torn by inner conflicts and have no roots to nourish their creativity. In my experience and in the experience of many others of immigrant background, multiple identities are enriching if they engage in an ongoing internal dialogue.

My reflection on this issue has been helped by the writings of Naïm Kattan, a Jewish immigrant from Iraq, who arrived in Montreal in 1956 and became a highly respected Quebec literary critic, novelist, and thinker. He sees himself as a Québécois committed to the flourishing of his society and faithful to his Jewish and Arab roots. He writes, "immigration is either an exile or a new birth."[2] Many immigrants look upon their situation as an exile: they are strangers in a society that does not understand them and assigns them to the margins. Many are forced to spend all their energy in the daily struggle of making a living, while others, attached to their cultural inheritance, prefer to remain uninvolved in their new society. Yet there are immigrants for whom the entry into a new society leads to unexpected discoveries. They enter into dialogue with thoughtful men and women, try to understand the history of their nation, learn to appreciate their cultural expressions, and become socially involved in order to achieve greater justice and equality. They find a new context for understanding their own ideas and values and begin to participate in the joys and sorrows of the people who love their nation. Naïm Katan calls this a new birth. Here immigrants learn to participate in the dynamism of their new society and make a contribution to its flourishing based, in part, on the cultural values of their country of origin. The prejudices from which they suffer on occasion do not stop them from contributing to the well-being of their society. This contribution is prominent in the fields of music, literature, painting, architecture, dancing, and the visual arts. It is also observable in the sciences, the intellectual life, the teaching profession, commerce and trade, and the social involvement in politics, civil issues, and human rights.

I have no hesitation in applying Naïm Kattan's category of new birth to my own experience: it happened to me as I settled in Canada, and it happened a second time, quite unexpectedly, when I moved to Quebec.

A contribution of immigrants that I forgot to mention is their work in building and serving society. They often take the burdensome and low-paying jobs that the older inhabitants do not want. John Paul II once said that, whenever he crosses a bridge, he thinks with gratitude of the labourers who built it. I wish I had learned something from this remark. While I see all over Montreal workers of immigrant origin, male and female, performing manual labour and offering the services that sustain the life of this city, even under exploitative conditions, I rarely stop to reflect on this, to appreciate their work and to be grateful to them.

Dialogue between cultural and religious identities is also recommended by Zijad Delic, a learned imam who serves at a mosque in Ottawa. In his *Canadian Islam: Belonging and Loyalty*,[3] he reflects on the question of how Muslim immigrants settled in Canada can avoid being torn apart by their religious and secular identities. He argues that people of multiple identities must come to recognize their identities as dynamic realities that are engaged in dialogue with one another and that affect one another creatively. Delic, a Canadian of

Bosnian origin, recalls that Bosnia was integrated into the Austrian Empire in the nineteenth century, thus rendering Muslims a small minority in a European society and confronting them with the question of whether to resist Western thought or enter into dialogue with it. Opting for dialogue, Bosnia's spiritual leaders fostered a European Islam open to critical thought and religious pluralism, while remaining faithful to the divine truth they inherited. His Bosnian background persuades Delic that he can help Canadian Muslims to engage in dialogue with their new society, feel at home in Canada, and remain committed to Islam. Yet he insists that asking Canadian Muslims whether their primary identity is Muslim or Canadian is misleading since doing so assumes that the two identities are in competition with one another. I agree that to ask people of faith to identify their primary loyalty – their religion or their society – is unfair. If there should arise a conflict between the two, the answer to the question would not be the theoretical priority of one or the other but, rather, what one decides after discerning the concrete issues involved.

35

You Continue to See Yourself as a German

Philip: *That multiple identities are enriching if they are engaged in dialogue with one another is a thesis with which I fully agree. I was born and raised in Australia and have lived in Canada for over fifty years. Yet I still have two questions related to your identity. First, how do you explain your strong sense of being a Berliner and a German, even though Germany expelled you and your family as Jews and planned and organized the Holocaust during the war?*

Refugees react to their past in many different ways. Abraham Heschel writes, "If I should go to Poland or Germany, every stone, every tree would remind me of contempt, hatred, murder, of children killed, of mothers burned alive, of human beings asphyxiated."[1] My own experiences have led me in a very different direction. I was brought up as a German in a patriotic family, proud of its German identity. Looking back, I think that the Jewish bourgeoisie that fully assimilated into German culture in the second part of the nineteenth century, often becoming secular or baptized, embraced an ardent patriotism as a response to the anti-Semitic prejudice that held that they could not be good Germans. The educated Jewish middle class loved German culture, the arts and the sciences, and did its best to contribute to it and make it flourish. German Jewish thinkers and intellectuals fully supported the First World War, at least at the beginning, and young German Jews were proud to be soldiers, ready to risk their lives fighting at the Front. My own father, as I mentioned above, was an officer in the German Army and worked with Fritz Haber, also a Protestant of Jewish origin, organizing the gas attacks on the British forces. When Hitler later declared that we were not Germans, we were confused and puzzled. With many others, I refused to allow Hitler to define my identity. I remained a German and treasured the German language. My sister, who fled to England in 1939, reacted quite differently: having been kicked out of Germany, she now wanted to forget her German and speak only English. I never exchanged a German word with her.

In "My Theological Pathway" I mention that, in my religious search as a student in Canada, I was greatly impressed by German Catholic theological and liturgical literature, to which I had access in the library of Egbert Munzer, a German friend of mine in Toronto. When I decided to enter a religious community, I chose the German province of the Augustinian Order, which, at that time, had a vice-province in Canada. When the Order sent me to Fribourg, Switzerland, for my theological education – I was to stay there for nine years – I had occasion to spend time in Germany, living in the monasteries or our parish in Berlin, meeting many Germans who were humbled, ashamed of the past, and ready, with their sleeves rolled up, to build a new, democratic Germany. These Catholics had not been Nazis; they had supported the Catholic party, *das Zentrum*, until it was suppressed in 1933. They had not been resisters under the Nazi regime; they had reluctantly obeyed and, when obliged, fought as soldiers in the army. It never occurred to me to associate them with the horrendous inhuman crimes of the Nazis. Guilty of these crimes, I then thought, were the Germans who devised them, participated in them, or even simply approved of them.

I learned much later that the question of German guilt had caused anguished debates in the German churches, leading to slightly different verdicts. The declaration by the Protestant Church confessed that Germany started the war and committed mass murder, a guilt shared by all Germans, even by those who were opposed to Hitler: as Germans are bonded by national solidarity, they must now assume their collective guilt and look upon the heavy reparations imposed by the victors as God's punishment.[2] This declaration was challenged by many Protestants. Many of the Catholic bishops did not agree with this understanding of collective guilt. They argued instead that the guilt of Germans depended upon the degree of their participation in these crimes, which implied that the Germans who simply conformed and obeyed, without inner consent, were free of guilt. As I mentioned above, this is what I thought

Today, having reflected a long time on social and/or structural sin, I am inclined to say that both of these verdicts are true in their own ways. As I argue in "My Theological Pathway," Canadians are not personally guilty of inflicting colonial oppression upon Aboriginal peoples, yet we are not totally innocent as we participate in a society that profits from the wealth derived from stolen lands.[3]

It was my theology that created a strong link to Germany. I learned a great deal from progressive German theologians, especially from Rahner, Metz, and Küng (a Swiss citizen teaching in Germany). I met these three once a year at the board meeting of *Concilium*, to which I belonged between 1970 and 1990. In the 1980s and 1990s, I was invited almost every year to give lectures in Berlin at a Catholic school of social work and a Protestant catechetical institute. Fascinated by the bold stance taken by the Protestant Church in communist East Germany, I studied the literature produced by its synods and its theologians, interviewed many active participants, and wrote *The Church for Others*, a book about the original self-understanding of this church in the communist society. Since I remained close to what happened in Germany, even while variously involved in Canada and Quebec, I asked to have my German passport restored, a request that was immediately granted. On the television in my apartment in Montreal, I have access to *Deutsche Welle*, the German channel, which allows me to follow the political and cultural debates in Germany. My German identity is in sustained dialogue with my theological thinking and my social engagement as a Canadian and a Quebecer.

36

As a Quebecer Have You Become a Sovereignist?

Philip: *My second question is related to your identity as a Quebecer. Reading your recent publications, I have the impression that the flourishing of Quebec society has become an important issue in your life. Have you become a sovereignist – that is, a supporter of Quebec's independence?*

I am fascinated by Quebec society, admire the cultural and intellectual creativity of this small nation, and am troubled by its vulnerability due to a variety of factors – among them, the cultural weight of the English language in North America and the lack of sympathetic understanding on the part of the federal government and the other Canadian provinces. Quebecers have come to see themselves as a nation, enjoying, according to International Law,[1] the right of cultural and political self-determination. I write about these matters in "My Theological Pathway." What I want for Quebec I have outlined in the afterword of *Nationalism, Religion, and Ethics*: my dream is the rewriting of the Canadian Constitution to make Canada an asymmetrical confederation that recognizes Quebec's status as a nation. A certain hope for this existed in the early 1960s when all political parties favoured a special status for the Province of Quebec, but Pierre Elliott Trudeau, elected prime minister in 1968, a passionate opponent of Quebec nationalism, encouraged the creation of a new constitutional statement – the Canada Act, 1982 – that failed to recognize Quebec's national aspirations. In fact, Quebec did not sign the Canada Act. In my opinion, the realization of René Lévesque's proposal of "sovereignty association" would have been of benefit to

Quebec as well as to Canada: it would have given the two national communities a stronger sense of who they are and made both of them more culturally and politically adventurous.

Quebec's cultural inheritance of solidarity and cooperation is also threatened by the global impact of the neoliberal economy and neoliberal values, favoured by Philippe Couillard, the present Liberal premier of the province.[2] My association with le Centre justice et foi, sponsored by the Jesuits, has taught me to think and feel with Quebec. Since its foundation in 2006, I have been a member of Québec Solidaire, a humanistic socialist party that advocates justice and equality for women and cultural minorities, and favours Quebec's independence if this promises greater justice, more equality, and greater openness to pluralism.

Over the last few years I have become more conscious of the colonial oppression inflicted by the Canadian government upon Aboriginal peoples. These peoples constitute nations and want to be treated as such. The recommendations of the 1996 Royal Commission on Aboriginal Peoples were ignored by the federal government and exerted little influence on public opinion. I shamefully admit that I, too, regarded the status of the First Nations as a minor issue. My eyes were opened at the 2011 meeting of la Société canadienne de théologie, which dealt with the colonial structure imposed upon Aboriginals and the ominous silence of the Catholic theological community. Since then there has been the Idle No More movement and, in 2014, the Canadian Truth and Reconciliation Commission. I regret that I have never taken the time to become personally acquainted with a First Nations community, never listened to their stories, and never tried to bring their message to a wider audience in Quebec and Canada. John Ralston Saul's recent book, *The Comeback*,[3] argues that a turning point has occurred: having acquired knowledge and power, the First Nations are about to overcome their colonial status, achieve a mode of self-determination within the Canadian Confederation, and come to occupy their honoured place in a history of the nations.

37

Stephen Harper's Remaking of Canada

In some of your articles you mentioned that you were unhappy with what Canada had become under Stephen Harper's Conservative government. What precisely were your complaints?[1]

Stephen Harper was Canada's prime minister from 2006 to 2015, a period of nine years in which he transformed Canada's social identity and its image in the world. With many Canadians I sorrowed over this. This is how the policies of Harper's Conservative government changed Canada, moving it:

• *from* respect for democratic participation – *to* the neglect of Parliament, the repression of critical voices, and the unchallenged power of the Prime Minister's Office;
• *from* supporting the welfare state and granting public funds to assist people in need – *to* eliminating social programs, lowering taxes on the rich, increasing social inequality, building bigger prisons, and serving the interests of powerful corporations;
• *from* a foreign policy aimed at the reconciliation of conflicts – *to* one-sided support for the policies of "our friends," such as the United States' policy in the Middle East, Israel's colonial rule over the Palestinians, and Saudi Arabia's religio-political influence in the Muslim world;
• *from* a society dedicated to peace and peace-keeping – *to* a military power, increasing its armed forces, glorifying the battles of the past, assigning new weight to the monarchy, selling Canadian-made weapons

indiscriminately to other governments, and becoming paranoid with regard to the enemy from within;

- *from* assisting self-directed economic development in the Third World – *to* support for economic enterprises in the South that are profitable for Canadian companies;
- *from* sharing the world's ecological concern – *to* refusing to adopt common norms and promoting Alberta's polluting tar sands industry; and
- *from* public support for women's organizations and human rights agencies – *to* the cutting of funds for groups with a critical message, including scientific research.

This sad story has been told in detail in several books.[2] Vast numbers of Canadians were greatly relieved when the Conservative government was defeated in the election of October 2015. Justin Trudeau, the new Liberal prime minister, immediately made speeches and public gestures announcing to Canadians and the world that Canada is returning to the best of its political tradition. We hope that Prime Minister Trudeau will put his promises into practice.

38

In Dark Times We Pray for God's Deliverance

Philip: *Writing about the dark times in which we find ourselves, you analyze the present crisis and mention four ways in which critical citizens, and Christians in particular, can involve themselves in resisting the forces that are threatening us. Do you think we should also pray for rescue?*

In a few pages of "My Theological Pathway" I draw a picture of the civilizational crisis that is upon us and suggest four ways in which people, Christians among them, can resist the dominant culture and try to rebuild society from the bottom up.[1] I recommend four activities in which people, driven by their conscience, can become socially involved: (1) promoting a critical culture through commitment to alternative values, through works of art and literature that challenge society or through the adoption of a simple lifestyle; (2) participating in reformist or radical social movements; (3) supporting the vision of the United Nations and calling for respect for International Law; and (4) becoming involved in community development and the social economy. I then add that we also resist by praying to God for rescue, redemption, and the newness of life. This proposal calls for some commentary.

Petitionary prayer is impossible to justify philosophically. Does God have to be reminded of people's suffering? Do their oppression and their misery have to be explained to the Almighty? Is God the omnipotent heavenly ruler of the universe who, in response to our prayers, may decide to intervene miraculously to rescue us from the evil that besets us? The answer to these two questions is: "No." What we know without a doubt is that, in the Bible, petitionary prayer is part and parcel of people's life of faith and their trust in God's goodness. On every page of the Old Testament and the New Testament we read prayers calling upon God for help, rescue, restoration, and divine blessing. Jesus asked us to pray that God's reign may come, that God's will be done on earth, that people everywhere will have their daily bread, and that we be delivered from the evil that destroys us. We offer prayers of intercession because this is what God wants us to do. I read this in an article by Abraham Heschel,[2] and it immediately answered for me an unresolved question. In every book of the Bible, people of faith offer prayers of intercession for their well-being and their rescue from hostile powers and, more universally, for the liberation of people tormented by violence, hunger, or oppression. Petitionary prayer, it can be argued, manifests confidence in God's compassion and is therefore an act of worship. The biblical God even seems to be pleased with people's complaints and lamentations before the divine throne. While we have no clear idea, no theological theory, why God wants us to pray for help in times of need and for divine blessing of our human endeavours, the biblical teaching is quite clear and the practice of these prayers convinces us that they bring us close to God. A theological argument could perhaps be made that God wants us to offer intercessory prayers because, through them, we participate in the *missio Dei*, the humanization of humankind and the salvation of the world.

If prayer is understood in its full sense, including intercession for the world's salvation, then contemplative life in a religious orders or in one's own home is a form of resistance to the oppressive features of society and, thus, has liberationist political meaning. This is the message of Thomas Merton – mystic, poet, and spiritual guide – who has taught contemplation to North American Catholics.

39

The Meaning of Prayer in Your Life

Philip: *I now wish to ask a more personal question: What has prayer meant in your daily life? Has your theology been a guide in your prayer life?*

When I entered the monastery in 1947, I believed I was called to a deep life of prayer. I enjoyed the joint recitation of the breviary, the meditation in the morning before the mass, and the many prayers throughout the day. I read with great longing the rich mystical literature, the inspiring testimonies of the great men and women of prayer. But this period came to a close after a few years.

In "My Theological Pathway" I mention that, as I left the monastery to do pastoral work in Neuchâtel, I became convinced that the internal drama of human existence was similar both inside and outside the monastery and even inside and outside the church. I was greatly helped by Karl Rahner, who saw God's implicit presence in people's lives: all of us are sinners, blinded by egotism, and all of us are addressed by God's Word and offered light by the Spirit. The mystery of redemption revealed in Jesus Christ touches the whole of humanity, with no one left out. Because I felt that God sustained me by my daily life – by the people I met, the books I read, the pastoral work I did, and my conversation with friends – I neglected the practice of meditative prayer I had learned to enjoy.

In a little book I published in 1969, I even theorize my secular interpretation of the Gospel.[1] To answer the question why people become and remain Christian, I introduce the concept of "depth experience"[2] – that is, an experience that is memorable, unifies one's personal life, and is the starting point of many practical decisions. Depth experiences enhance our human potential: they are steps leading us to greater self-realization. There are specifically religious depth experiences, such as the experience of the holy (studied by Rudolf Otto) or the experience of total dependency on God (invoked by Friedrich Schleiermacher). Yet many people become and remain Christian believers without having had these specifically religious experiences. Their depth experiences have been secular, such as listening to the voice of conscience, a creative encounter with "the other," the celebration of friendship, the conversion to truth, compassion for the wounded, and solidarity with the disadvantaged. My theological proposal is that people become and remain Christians if the Gospel explains, purifies, and multiplies their depth experiences. The Gospel *explains* that these experiences are memorable and humanizing because they are sustained by the Holy Spirit; the Gospel *purifies* these experiences because it delivers them of their self-seeking dimension; and the Gospel *multiplies* these experiences because the Spirit accompanies believers in their daily lives. I am still convinced that some people become and remain Christian because the Gospel makes their lives meaningful, selfless, and abundant.

Because I felt sustained, awakened, and empowered by God's implicit presence in my life, I neglected the practice of meditation and paid less attention to liturgical worship. I admit that other factors were involved in this neglect. As I mentioned above, I had begun to explore my sexuality in non-conformist ways, a practice that was harmful to my spiritual life. More important, my conversion to critical thinking and liberation theology produced two disturbing spiritual problems, which I described in *Compassion and Solidarity* and mention in "My Theological Pathway."[3] Solidarity with the poor and oppressed, accompanied by a keen awareness of their suffering, can lead to painful spiritual experiences, to which I refer as "the breakdown of trust" and "the dread of ideological distortion." We ask ourselves whether we can we say "Trust in God!" to people despised, oppressed, and near starvation. Can we trust in God after Auschwitz? And we also pose the question whether our faith in God's goodness is grounded in the comfortable and secure living conditions proper to the middle-class societies of the North. Is our faith a subtle defence of our privileged circumstances? The preferential option for the poor, I argue, has led believers to "the dark night of the soul" in a manner not known to the mystics of the past. Some believers get stuck in the dark night and lose their faith altogether, while others, waiting patiently in the dark, hear the divine call to a new spiritual life mindful of human misery and despair. They now live their faith with joy, though troubled by many unanswered questions. The peace they find in God is now a blessed restlessness.

As I became older and more thoughtful, and grieved over the dark times starting in the 1990s, I became again a man of prayer. I was moved by the total gratuity of God's gifts, by the marvellous things that have happened in my life, being gifted with faith, rescued from one snare after another, and appointed to a creative ministry that gave me joys and sorrows. I was and am embarrassed by my happiness in a world of so much suffering. As I write at the beginning of "My Theological Pathway," I feel like the widow of Sarepta, saved from starvation by the oil that does not run out.[4] Thanksgiving accompanies me throughout the day and serves as the starting point of my longer meditations. I turn to God as rescuer or saviour of the world, who does not allow me to forget the misery inflicted upon the multitudes.

What I write in "My Theological Pathway" about panentheism and the *via negativa* has guided my meditative prayer. Let me make a few remarks explaining what this guidance has meant to me. According to the *via negativa* the hidden God revealed in Jesus Christ can be known only in a non-literal, analogical sense, interpreting the adjectives attributed to God – good, just, and compassionate –

as insinuations of divine glory. God can be spoken of only in paradoxical terms. God is therefore never simply a Thou that is facing us, the merciful father protecting us, or the invisible friend accompanying us; God is at the same time the ground of our being (*der Lebensgrund*), the matrix of our vital existence, and the grace sustaining our commitment to truth and goodness. Panentheism, as we saw, images God as the great insider of human history and as a redemptive presence in personal life. Some authors refer to God as "the totally Other," which, in the Catholic tradition, is qualified by the paradoxical affirmation that God is not totally other because God is present in human flourishing. In meditative prayer, God is sometimes imagined as the gracious power that carries us, and at other times – paradoxically – as the divine person addressing us. Since we are told in Scripture that God is Love (1 John 4:8) and that God is the Truth (John 14:6), panentheistic theology allows us to see our own loving and our commitment to truth as participating, despite our fragility, in the divine mystery. Meditation is therefore not limited to an inner concentration on the divine Other; it also includes a letting go, a readiness to be carried by a power not our own, analogous to a swimmer upheld by the sea.

Because God is *salvator mundi*, saviour of the world, in preferential solidarity with the poor, the oppressed, and the despised, meditation in the panentheistic perspective finds itself time and again interrupted by intercessions for the multitudes, victims of injustice. Contemplation, as I write above, is a form of resistance. Because I lead a comfortable, happy, and productive life for which I am immensely grateful, my meditation humbles me, making me aware of how far away I am – an infinite distance – from the passion of Jesus Christ, his embrace of great suffering in defence of the truth out of love for self-afflicted humanity, a passion shared by many of the saints.

40

Thinking of Death and Resurrection

Philip: *Since you are now over ninety years old, I wish to ask: What are your thoughts about death, in particular about your own death?*

Your question compels me to address a number of questions. First, I wish to mention the criticism I have often made of a pastoral theology that helps people to face their own death. In the New Testament the focus is on the death of "the other," the violent death of Jesus, innocent, tortured, and crucified, a redemptive event that makes us think of all men and women, soldiers and civilians, killed in wars and other forms of violent conflict. Seventeen million were killed in First World War, 60 million in the Second World War,[1] and the killing continues. To die in one's bed after a long life, I suggest, is a privilege that calls for thanksgiving.

In the same vein, I am dissatisfied that the effort of Catholic bishops to protect and save human lives focuses on the private acts of abortion and suicide, without critiquing the collective acts of killing in wars and military interventions. The Canadian bishops did not feel that Canada's military presence in Afghanistan merited ethical reflection from a Catholic perspective. While bishops speak with authority against abortion and suicide, they offer no ethical teaching on the weapons industry, the production and sale of arms, the instruments of mass killing. I am grateful that Pope Francis's pastoral effort to protect human life includes the censure of the weapons industry. In an unscripted speech given at Turin on June 2015, he denounced the arms trade as "the industry of death." Why is it that so many powerful people do not want peace? Because, the pope said, they make more money with war. He lamented that industrialists, managers, and businesspeople who call themselves Christians are involved in the production and sale of arms. He sorrowed over the cynicism spreading in today's world.

My second remark touches upon the observation that most people in contemporary society are afraid, not of death, but of dying. They dread the possibility of becoming helpless in old age, racked by pain, dependent upon others for the most basic needs or living for years in mental darkness unable to recognize their children. Urged by a lively public debate about medically assisted suicide, the government of Quebec created a commission to study the issue, consult physicians and nurses, listen to the experience of ordinary people, and then produce a policy recommendation for the government. Since the hearings were broadcast on television, I spent many hours following the testimonies given to the commission. The medical doctors I heard were opposed to a law permitting medically assisted suicide: they believe that palliative care offers sufficient help for the dying. If a dying patient is in great pain, the doctor is allowed to give him or her sedative medication, even if this hastens death. The passionate advocates of medically assisted suicide were ordinary people: they described the suffering of a parent or a spouse who had lived for years without clear consciousness and without the ability to feed and clean themselves, a profound humiliation for the patient and a heavy burden for the caretakers, sometimes preventing them from living a life of their own. These witnesses asked that the law be changed, allowing people moving into an increasingly debilitating disease to end their lives with the help of a medical doctor. Catholic teaching is opposed to this, insisting that people disabled and unconscious retain their human dignity and deserve to be upheld in life. Yet the voices of ordinary people and public opinion in Quebec convinced the commission to recommend that the government adopt a law recognizing people's right, under clearly defined circumstances, to ask for medical help to die with dignity as they conceive it. Such a law was adopted by the national assembly on 4 June 2014.

The Catholic Church is opposed to medically assisted suicide, a teaching most Catholics fully endorse. Yet my own experience has made me raise a difficult question. I am a dialysis patient: since my kidneys no longer function, I survive because dialysis given three times a week allows me to live and be well. I am very grateful for this. But if my health should collapse, leave me in great pain, and make me totally dependent upon others, I could simply discontinue my dialysis and rapidly move into death. That would be both legal and fully approved by Catholic teaching. Having this emergency door at the end delivers me from anxiety and gives me a great sense of freedom. Should I not wish that all people have such liberty?

My own experience also persuades me that there are situations in which suicide is ethically justified. As a child in Nazi Germany I was surrounded by Jews ready to commit suicide rather than be arrested, humiliated, tortured, and very possibly killed in a concentration camp. Beginning on 9 November 1938, after a short stay in a concentration camp, my stepfather carried a cyanide pill until he left Germany in April 1939. An uncle of mine, a medical doctor, took the pill when he was arrested. Suicide was a widely spread practice. The Protestant poet and theologian Jochen Klepper, a vocal opponent of the Nazi regime, married to a Jewish woman, committed suicide with her during the war to escape the humiliation of the death camps. I have not come across a Christian moralist who criticized their choice. In fact, Klepper is venerated in the German Protestant Church and the hymns written by him are today part of the public liturgy.

Philip, the above remarks are prompted by your question about death. I now turn to my faith in life beyond the grave. In the ancient liturgy, the life after death of the redeemed was described by three beautiful words – *pax*, *requies*, and *lux* (peace, rest, and light) – a consoling message, serene and simple, discouraging curiosity about future conditions. In the Middle Ages this attitude changed. The funeral mass now included the hymn *Dies irae* (day of wrath), expressing the fear and trembling experienced by Christians as they anticipate meeting their stern divine Judge after death. I am grateful to Benedict XVI for correcting this misguided piety. Reflecting on the end of earthly life in his encyclical *Spe salvi*, he writes that, before God's judgment, the attitude is not horror but hope, a hope nourished by faith in God's mercy. With a contrite heart we need not live in fear. We are called to approach death with serenity.

I hardly ever think about what happens to me after I die; I simply leave this to God. Some words of Jesus even suggest that, for me, there may be no life after death. Jesus remarked that the rich and successful "have had their reward,"[2] implying that eternal life with God is granted to the poor and disadvantaged as the glorious compensation for their great deprivation. Because, as an unwarranted gift, I have had a life of light and happiness in the darkness of an unjust world, I may well "have had my reward."

While I do not speculate about what happens to me when I die, I cling to the message of Christ's resurrection whenever I think of the men, women, and children killed in genocides, armed conflicts, and famines. Rabbi Irving Greenberg proposed that a theological *statement* is valid only if it can be repeated in the presence of burning children – a horror that was part of the Holocaust.[3] Looking at them I could not say God is all powerful, nor that God is good. The one utterance I could make is *resurrexit*.

Resurrexit, Christ is risen, is a good note on which to close the story of my theological pathway.

Personal Bibliography

That They May Be One. New York: Newman Press, 1958.

The Jews and the Gospel. New York: Newman Press, 1961.

Progress and Perspective. New York: Sheed and Ward, 1962.

Ecumenical Theology Today. New York: Paulist Press, 1965.

The Credibility of the Church Today. New York: Herder and Herder, 1968.

Faith and Doctrine. New York: Newman Press, 1969.

Man Becoming. New York: Herder and Herder, 1970.

New Horizon. New York: Paulist Press, 1972.

Religion and Alienation. New York: Paulist Press, 1975. 2nd ed., Ottawa: Novalis, 2007.

Truth beyond Relativity: Karl Mannheim's Sociology of Knowledge (Marquette Lecture). Milwaukee, WI: Marquette University Press, 1977.

The Social Imperative. New York: Paulist Press, 1979.

Catholics and Canadian Socialism. Halifax: James Lorimer, 1980

The Priority of Labour: Commentary on John Paul II's Laborem exercens. New York: Paulist Press, 1982.

Ethics and Economics (with Duncan Cameron). Halifax: James Lorimer, 1984.

Theology and Society. New York: Paulist Press, 1986.

Solidarity and Compassion. Toronto: Anansi Press, 1988.

The Church in Quebec. Ottawa: Novalis, 1992.
Essays in Critical Theology. Kansas City: Sheed and Ward, 1994.
Karl Polanyi on Ethics and Economics. Montreal and Kingston: McGill-Queen's University Press, 1996.
The Church for Others: Protestant Theology in Communist East Germany. Grand Rapids: Eerdsman, 1996.
Nationalism, Religion and Ethics. Montreal and Kingston: McGill-Queen's University Press, 2001.
Frieden für Israel: Israeli Peace-and-Human Rights Groups in Israel (in German). Paderborn: Bonifatius Verlag, 2002.
Amazing Church. Toronto: Novalis, 2005.
Signs of the Times. Toronto: Novalis, 2006.
The Theology of Tariq Ramadan: A Catholic Perspective. Toronto: Novalis, 2009.
Truth and Relevance: Catholic Theology in French Quebec since the Quiet Revolution. Montreal and Kingston: McGill-Queen's University Press, 2014.
Fernand Dumont: A Sociologist Turns to Theology. Montreal and Kingston: McGill-Queen's University Press, 2015

Notes

Part One

1 I wrote two brief autobiographical essays, "Personal Experience and Styles of Thought," in Gregory Baum, ed., *Journeys* (New York: Paulist Press, 1975), 5–33; and "My Entry into Critical Political Consciousness," *Canadian Dimension*, May/June 2004, 20–3.

Chapter One

1 Amos Elon, *The Pity of It All: Portrait of the Jews in Germany 1743–1933* (New York: Picador-Henry Holt, 2002).
2 Ps. 12:5; Prov. 14:31; Eccles. 5:8; Is. 1:178.

Chapter Two

1 Vernon Brooks, "Brigadoon," *McGill News Alumni Magazine*, winter 2001–02.

Chapter Three

1 *Denzinger* (Henricus Denzinger, ed., *Enchiridion Symbolorum*), no. 373.
2 Gregory Baum, *Religion and Alienation* (Ottawa: Novalis, 2007 [1975]), 211.
3 Gregory Baum, *Man Becoming* (New York: Seabury Press, 1979 [1970]), viii.
4 *Denzinger*, no. 806: "inter creatorem et creaturam non potest

similitudo notari, quin inter eos maior sit dissimilitudo notanda."

Chapter Four

1 Pius XI, encyclical *Mortalium animos* (1928).
2 Pius XII, encyclical *Mystici corporis* (1943), no. 22.
3 Gregory Baum, ed., *Journeys* (New York: Paulist Press, 1975), 5–33.
4 Joseph Ratzinger, *Theological Highlights of Vatican II* (New York: Paulist Press, 2009 [1966]), 113.
5 Joint Declaration on the Doctrine of Justification by the Lutheran World Council and the Catholic Church, http://en.wikipedia.org/wiki/Joint_Declaration_on_the_Doctrine_of_Justification.
6 The Second Vatican Council, Decree on Ecumenism, no. 1.

Chapter Five

1 Jules Isaac, *Jésus et Israël* (Paris: Albin Michel, 1947).
2 Gregory Baum, *The Jews and the Gospel* (New York: Newman Press, 1961).
3 Rosemary Ruether, *Faith and Fratricide* (New York: Seabury Press, 1974).
4 Norman Tobias, *Jewish Conscience of the Church: Jules Isaac and the Second Vatican Council* (forthcoming).
5 Norman Tobias, "The Thought and Methodologies of Jules Isaac and James Parkes," paper delivered at "Jewish/Non-Jewish Relations from Antiquity to the Present," the Parkes Institute Jubilee Conference, University of Southampton, 7 September 2015.
6 See the ten points of the Seelisberg Conference at http://en.wikipedia.org/wiki/Seelisberg_Conference.
7 J.-M. Vereb, *Because He Was a German! Cardinal Bea and the Origins of Roman Catholic Engagement in the Ecumenical Movement* (Grand Rapids, MI: Eerdmans, 2006).
8 John Connelly, *From Enemy to Brother: The Revolution in Catholic Teaching on the Jews, 1933–1965* (Cambridge, MA: Harvard University Press, 2012).

Chapter Six

1 Gregory Baum, "Un souvenir de *Nostra aetate*," in *Vatican II au Canada: Enracinement et réception*, ed. Gilles Routier, 449–60 (Montréal: Fides, 2001).
2 Gregory Baum, "Vatican II: A Turning Point in the Church's History," in *Vatican II*, ed. Michael Attridge, Catherine Clifford, and Gilles Routhier, 366–7 (Ottawa: University of Ottawa Press., 2011).
3 Benedict XV, apostolic letter, *Maximum illud* (1919), no. 31.
4 Thomas Aquinas, *Summa Theologica*, III:8,3.
5 *The Ratzinger Report: Interview with Vittorio Messori* (San Francisco: Ignatius Press, 1985), 147. See also http://www.catholicnews.com/data/stories/cns/0506867.htm.
6 Gregory Baum, *Faith and Doctrine* (New York: Paulist Press, 1969), 103–19.
7 Hans Küng, *Christianity: Essence, History and Future* (New York: Continuum, 1996).
8 Hans Küng, *Judaism: Between Yesterday and Tomorrow* (New York: Crossroad, 1992).
9 Hans Küng, *Der Islam: Geschichte, Gegenwart und Zukunft* (München: Pieper, 2004).
10 Benedict XVI, Christmas Address to Roman Curia, 22 December 2005.
11 See page 161.

Chapter Seven

1 See my Significant Dates, page xi.
2 Charles Taylor, *A Secular Age* (Cambridge, MA: Harvard University Press, 2007), 115–30.
3 Gregory Baum, *Man Becoming* (New York: Seabury Press, 1979 [1970]), x.
4 The Second Vatican Council, Constitution *Gaudium et spes*, no. 16.

Chapter Eight

1 Gregory Baum, *Truth and Relevance: Catholic Theology in French Quebec since the Quiet Revolution* (Montreal and

Kingston: McGill-Queen's University Press, 2014), 38–42, 46–52, 204–5.

2 Gregory Baum, *Man Becoming* (New York: Seabury Press, 1979 [1970]), 1–3.6

3 Ibid., 118–26.

4 Grant Goodbrand, *Therafields* (Toronto: ECW Press, 2010).

Chapter Nine

1 Gregory Baum, *Signs of the Times* (Toronto: Novalis, 2007), 87–106.

2 Simone Weil, *Pensés sans ordre concernant l'amour de Dieu* (Paris: Gallimard, 2013), 23.

3 Hans Urs von Balthasar, *Do We Hope That All May Be Saved?* and *A Short Discourse on Hell* (San Francisco: Ignatius Press, 1988).

Chapter Ten

1 Gregory Baum, *Religion and Alienation* (Ottawa: Novalis, 2007 [1975]), 154–6.

2 Pius XI, encyclical *Quadragesimo anno* (1931), no. 77.

3 Robert Bellah, ed., *Religion and Progress in Modern Asia* (Glencoe, IL: Free Press, 1965). See his epilogue, 168–229.

4 John XXIII, Opening Speech to the Council, 11 October 1962, in *The Documents of Vatican II*, ed. Walter Abbott (New York: Herder and Herder, 1966), 700–19, 715.

5 Decree on Ecumenism, no.6.

6 Baum, *Religion and Alienation*, 173–7.

7 Canadian Bishops, "Sharing Daily Bread," Labour Day Message 1974, in *Do Justice: The Social Teaching of the Canadian Catholic Bishops*, ed. E.F. Sheridan, 258–66 (Montreal: Éditions Paulines, 1987).

8 Baum, *Religion and Alienation*, 65–104.

9 Gregory Baum, *The Credibility of the Church Today* (New York: Herder & Herder, 1968).

Chapter Eleven

1 Joseph Gremillion, ed., *The Gospel of Justice and Peace* (Maryknoll, NY: Orbis Books, 1975), 466 (Medellin Conclusions, "On Class Division," nos. 477–85; Medellin Conclusions, "Justice," no. 3).
2 Gremillion, *Gospel of Justice and Peace*, 461 (Medellin Conclusions, "Peace," no. 18).
3 Paul VI, encyclical *Populorum progression* (1967), no. 31.
4 Gremillion, *Gospel of Justice and Peace*, 461 (Medellin Conclusion, "Peace," no. 18).
5 Ibid., 514 (World Synod of Bishops 1971, *Justitia in mundo*, nos. 4, 5, 6).
6 E.F. Sheridan, ed., *Do Justice: The Social Teaching of the Canadian Catholic Bishops* (Montreal: Paulines, 1987), 314–21 (Labour Day Message of 1976 "From Word to Action"); and 399–410 (Bishops' Statement of 1982, "Ethical Reflections on the Economic Crisis").
7 Gregory Baum, *Compassion and Solidarity* (Toronto: Anansi, 1992 [1987]), 76, 77.
8 Cardinal Ratzinger, Congregation of the Doctrine of the Faith, "Instruction Concerning Certain Aspects of Liberal Theology," 6 August 1984. http://www.vatican.va/roman_curia/congregations/cfaith/documents/rc_con_cfaith_doc_19840806_theology-liberation_en.html.
9 Joseph Ratzinger, *The Ratzinger Report* (San Francisco: Ignatius Press, 1986), 174.
10 See http://www.catholicnews.com/data/stories/cns/1303902.htm.

Chapter Twelve

1 See pages 37–8.
2 Johann Baptist Metz, "Facing the Jews: Christian Theology after Auschwitz," in *The Holocaust as Interruption*, *Concilium* 175/5, ed. E. Schüssler-Fiorenza and D. Tracy, 26–33 (Edinburgh: T&T Clark, 1984).
3 See pages 59–61.

4 Eva Fleischner, ed., *Auschwitz: Beginning of a New Era?* (New York: KTAV Publishing, 1977) ; Gregory Baum, "Theology after Auschwitz," in *The Social Imperative*, 70–98 (New York: Paulist Press, 1979).
5 Fleischner, *Auschwitz*, 417–19.
6 Max Horkheimer and Theodor Adorno, *Dialectic of Enlightenment* (Stanford, CA: Stanford University Press, 2002 [1946]), 169.
7 This thesis is developed in detail in Zygmunt Bauman, *Modernity and the* Holocaust (Ithaca, NY: Cornell University Press, 1989).
8 Gregory Baum, *Man Becoming* (New York: Seabury Press, 1979 [1970]), 1–36.
9 Gregory Baum, *Catholics and Canadian Socialism* (Toronto: James Lorimer, 1980), 1–70.
10 B.B.Y. Scott and Gregory Vlastos, eds. *Toward a Christian Revolution* (Chicago: Willett and Clark, 1936). This book was republished in 1989 by R.P. Frey (Kingston, ON), with an introduction by Roger Hutchinson and Harold Wells.
11 Gregory Baum, "Politisés chrétiens," in *The Church in Quebec* (Ottawa: Novalis, 1991), 67–90.
12 Baum, *Catholics and Canadian Socialism*.
13 Gregory Baum, "Political Theology in Canada," in *The Social Imperative* (New York: Paulist Press, 1979), 70–98.
14 See pages 59–61.
15 E.F. Sheridan, ed., *Do Justice: The Social Teaching of the Canadian Catholic Bishops* (Montreal: Paulines, 1987), 122–34.

Chapter Thirteen

1 The Winnipeg Statement of the Canadian Bishops, http://www.u.arizona.edu/~aversa/modernism/winnipeg.html.
2 Herbert Doms, *The Meaning of Marriage* (London: Sheed and Ward, 1939 [1935]); Dietrich von Hildebrand, *In Defence of Purity* (London: Longmans, 1935 [1928]).
3 Robert Kaiser, *The Politics of Sex and Religion: A Case*

History in the Development of Doctrine, 1962–1984 (Kansas City, MO: Leaven Press, 1985).

4 https://en.wikipedia.org/wiki/Winnipeg–Statement.

5 The English translation of this dialogue is published as *The Dialectics of Secularization: On Reason and Religion* (San Francisco: Ignatius Press, 2010). See Gregory Baum, *The Ecumenist* 45 (Summer 2008): 22–3.

6 I cannot find the newsletter from which this quote is taken.

7 See pages 67–8.

8 See pages 160–7.

9 André Guindon, *The Sexual Creators* (Lanham, MD: University Press of America, 1986); Margaret Farley, *Just Love: A Framework for Christian Sexual Ethics* (New York: Continuum, 2006); and Todd Salzman and Michael Lawler, *The Sexual Person: Toward a Renewed Catholic Anthropology* (Washington: Georgetown University Press, 2008).

10 Stephan Pfürtner, *Kirche und Sexualität* (Reinbek: Rowohlt, 1972).

Chapter Fourteen

1 John Coleman, "The Homosexual Revolution," *The Sexual Revolution: Concilium* 173 (March 1984): 55–64.

2 Gregory Baum, "Les personnes homosexuelles devraient-elles rester catholiques?" *Présence Magazine*, June–July 2005.

Chapter Fifteen

1 "Our Mission Today: Service of Faith and the Promotion of Justice," *Decree* 4, March 1975, http://onlineministries.creighton.edu/CollaborativeMinistry/our-mission-today.html.

2 Gregory Baum, "How Moving to Quebec Has Affected My Theology," *Toronto Journal of Theology* 26, 1 (2010): 33–46.

3 E.F. Sheridan, *Do Justice: The Social Teaching of the Canadian Catholic Bishops* (Montreal: Éditions Paulines, 1987), 233–8, 295–306, 314–21, 399–410, 411–34.

4 Francis, Homily at Lampedusa, 8 July 2013.

5 In 1963, the Quebec government appointed the Parent

Commission to elaborate a reform of the educational system that would reflect the values fostered by the Quiet Revolution.

6 Gregory Baum, *The Church in Quebec* (Ottawa: Novalis, 1991), 49–66.

7 Gregory Baum, *Truth and Relevance* (Montreal and Kingston: McGill-Queen's University Press, 2014), 133–6.

Chapter Sixteen

1 Gregory Baum, *Nationalism, Religion and Ethics* (Montreal and Kingston: McGill-Queen's University Press, 2001).

2 "Le people québécois et son avenir politique," in *La justice comme bonne nouvelle: Message sociaux, économiques et politiques des évêques du Québec*, ed. G. Rochais, 137–44 (Montréal: Bellarmin, 1984).

3 Jacques Grand'Maison, *Nationalisme et religion*, 2 vols. (Montreal: Beauchemin, 1970).

4 Walter Laqueur, ed. *The Human Rights Reader* (New York: New American Library, 1990), 215–24.

Chapter Seventeen

1 Karl Polanyi became a friend of John Macmurray, worked with members of the Christian left, and collaborated in the publication of *Christianity and the Social Revolution* (London: Victor Gollancz, 1937).

2 Karl Polanyi's classic, *The Great Transformation*, first published in 1944, is available today in many editions. Cf. Gregory Baum, *Karl Polanyi on Ethics and Economics*, McGill-Queen's University Press, 1996.

3 Leonardo Boff, "Challenges of The Great Transformation," *Página Inicial*, 18 October 2014, https://leonardoboff.wordpress.com.

4 Margie Mendel, "The Social Economy in Quebec," 2003 Conference of Latin American Centre for Development and Public Administration, http://www.envision.ca/pdf/SocialEconomy/SocialEconomyinQuebecMendell.pdf.

5 Nancy Neamtan, "The Social Economy," Tamarack, Institute

for Community Engagement, 2006, http://tamarackcommunity.ca/g3s10_M4C2.html.

6 John Paul II, encyclical *Laborem exercens*, no. 6.

7 Gregory Baum, "Tracing the Affinity between the Social Thought of Karl Polanyi and Pope Francis," paper presented at the 13th International Polanyi Conference, Concordia University, Montreal, November 2014.

Chapter Eighteen

1 See Rudolf Siebert's website http://www.rudolfjsiebert.org/publications.htm.

2 See Gregory Baum, "The Originality of Catholic Social Teaching," *Concilium* 5 (1991): 55–62; and Baum, "Towards a Canadian Catholic Social Theory," *Theology and Society* (New York: Paulist Press, 1987), 66–87.

Chapter Nineteen

1 Gregory Baum, "Good-Bye to the *Ecumenist*," *Ecumenist* 26 (Spring 1990): 1–3.

2 Francis, exhortation *Evangelii gaudium*, no. 53.

3 Gregory Baum, *Signs of the Times* (Toronto: Novalis, 2007), 163–6.

4 Gregory Baum, "Pope Francis's Censure of Neoliberal Capitalism," *Ecumenist* 52 (Summer 2015): 8–10.

5 In E.F. Sheridan, ed., *Do Justice: The Social Teaching of the Canadian Catholic Bishops* (Montreal: Paulines, 1987), see the following bishops letters: "A Society to Be Transformed" (1977); "Unemployment: The Human Cost" (1980); and "Ethical Choices and Political Challenges" (1983).

6 Eric Shragge and Jean-Marc Fontan, eds., *Social Economy: International Debates and Perspectives* (Montreal: Black Rose Books, 2000).

Chapter Twenty

1 Rosemary Ruether and Herman Ruether, *The Wrath of Jonas* (New York: Harper and Row, 1989).

2 Gregory Baum, "The Kairos Palestine Declaration," *Ecumenist* 47 (Summer 2010): 1–5.
3 Gregory Baum, "The United Church: Moderate and Courageous," *Ecumenist* 49 (Summer 2012): 13–14.
4 Gregory Baum and Hubert Frankemölle, eds., *Frieden für Israel: Israeli Peace and Human Rights Groups in Israel* (Paderborn: Bonifatius Verlag, 2002).
5 Peter Beinart, *The Crisis of Zionism* (New York: Picador-Macmillan, 2013).
6 Shlomo Sand, *The Invention of the Land of Israel* (London: Verso, 2012).
7 Judith Butler, *Parting Ways: Jewishness and the Critique of Zionism* (New York: Columbia University Press, 2012).
8 Gregory Baum, "The Judaism of Judith Butler," *Ecumenist* 51 (Fall 2014): 1–4.
9 Dov Waxman, *Trouble in the Tribe: The American Jewish Conflict over Israel* (Princeton, NJ: Princeton University Press, 2016).

Chapter Twenty-One
1 Gregory Baum, *Signs of the Times* (Toronto: Novalis, 2007), 17–33, 18.
2 "Preventive detention" means that someone can be held without charge for up to three days just on suspicion of being involved in terrorism. The person can then be bound by certain probationary conditions for up to a year and, if he or she refuses these conditions, can be jailed for twelve months.
3 Tariq Ramadan, *Aux sources du renouveau musulman* (Paris: Bayard, 1998).
4 Gregory Baum, "La réponse de l'islam à la modernité: La pensée religieuse de Fethullah Gülen," *Théologiques* 19, 2 (2011): 173–88.
5 For instance, see the works of Mohammed Arkoun and Malek Chabel.
6 Gregory Baum, *The Theology of Tariq Ramadan* (Toronto/Notre Dame: Novalis/Notre Dame University Press, 2009).

7 Gregory Baum, *Islam et modernité: La pensée de Tariq Ramadan* (Montreal: Fides, 2010).
8 Abou El Fadl, *The Great Theft: Wrestling Islam from the Extremists* (New York: Harper, 2005).

Chapter Twenty-Two

1 Cardinal Joseph Ratzinger, *Glaube, Wahrheit Toleranz* (Freiburg: Herder, 2009), 60.
2 Gregory Baum, "L'Église catholique et le dialogue interreligieux: Un Magistère incertain," in *Le dialogue interreligieux*, ed. Fabrice Blée and Achiel Peelman, 201–18 (Montreal: Novalis, 2013).
3 Gregory Baum, *Amazing Church* (Toronto: Novalis, 2005): 129–33.
4 See page 60.
5 See http://religionsforpeaceinternational.org/sites/default/files/pubications/Second%20World%20Assembly.pdf.
6 The English translation of this dialogue is published as *The Dialectics of Secularization: On Reason and Religion* (San Francisco: Ignatius Press, 2010). See Gregory Baum, *Ecumenist* 45 (Summer 2008): 22–3.
7 This quotation from the eighteenth volume of Herder's *Werke* is cited in F.M. Barnard, *Herder's Social and Political Thought* (Oxford: Clarendon Press, 1963), 100.
8 Steven Lukes, *Moral Relativism* (New York: St Martin's Press, 2008), 104.
9 Gregory Baum, *Signs of the Times* (Toronto: Novalis, 2007), 57.

Chapter Twenty-Three

1 Gregory Baum, "*Le Devoir*: Forum for the Exchange of Ideas," in *The Public Intellectual in Canada*, ed. Nelson Wiseman, 83–97 (Toronto: University of Toronto Press, 2013).
2 Gregory Baum, *Truth and Relevance: Catholic Theology in French Quebec since the Quiet Revolution* (Montreal and Kingston: McGill-Queen's University Press, 2014).
3 Gregory Baum, *Fernand Dumont: A Sociologist Turns to*

Theology (Montreal and Kingston: McGill-Queen's University Press, 2015).

4 Gregory Baum, *Amazing Church* (Toronto: Novalis, 2005), 8–9.

5 Fernand Dumont, *Œuvres complètes*. Vol. 14: *L'institution de la théologie* (Montreal: Les presses de l'Université Laval, 2008), 149–408, esp. 226.

6 Francis, exhortation *Evangelii gaudium*, no. 35.

Chapter Twenty-Four

1 *America*, 30 September 2013, http://americamagazine.org/pope-interview.

2 Francis, exhortation *Evangelii gaudium*, no. 53.

3 Francis, speech delivered at the meeting of popular movements in Rome, 28 October 2014.

4 Francis, exhortation *Evangelii gaudium*, no. 188.

5 A shorter version of this paper is contained in my article "Karl Polanyi and Pope Francis," *Ecumenist* 53 (Winter 2016): 11–14.

6 Francis, address given at the workshop "Toward a More Inclusive Economy," held in Rome on 12 July 2014.

7 Francis, exhortation *Evangelii gaudium*, no. 11.

8 Ibid.

9 Francis, a message transmitted on 3 September 2015 to the International Congress of Theology held in Buenos Aires. See a brief analysis of his message in my article "Pope Francis on Theology," *Ecumenist* 53 (Winter 2016): 1–4.

10 Francis, exhortation *Evangelii gaudium*, no. 35.

11 Ibid., no. 41.

Chapter Twenty-Five

1 I follow the French version of the Synod's Preliminary Report of 18 October 2014, http://www.vatican.va/roman_curia/synod/documents/rc_synod_doc_20141018_relatio-synodi-familia_fr.html. The English version was somewhat different. In my article "The Synod of 2014: A Radical New Theological Proposal" (*The Ecumenist*, summer, 2015, p. 20), I note that the Preliminary Report now available on the internet is quite different from the original version which I saved in my computer: the present version leaves out the paragraphs that

introduce the new theological approach. Conservative voices at the Vatican had the power to make these changes.

2 Francis, *Amoris laetitia*, no. 3

3 Gaudium et spes, 44.

4 *National Catholic Reporter*, 3–16 June 2016.

Part Two

1 Gregory Baum, *Truth and Relevance: Catholic Theology in French Quebec since the Quiet Revolution* (Montreal and Kingston: McGill-Queen's University Press, 2014). This is published in French as *Vérité et pertinence: Un regard sur la théologie catholique au Québec depuis la Révolution tranquille* (Montreal: Fides, 2014).

2 Gregory Baum, *Fernand Dumont: A Sociologist Turns to Theology* (Montreal and Kingston: McGill-Queen's University Press, 2015). This is published in French as *Fernand Dumont: Un sociologue se fait théologien* (Montreal: Novalis, 2014).

Chapter Twenty-Six

1 Francis, exhortation *Evangelii gaudium*, no. 53.

Chapter Twenty-Seven

1 Gregory Baum, "The Dumont Report: Democratizing the Catholic Church," in *The Church in Quebec* (Ottawa: Novalis, 1991), 49–66.

Chapter Twenty-Eight

1 Karl Rettino-Parazetti, "Soigner le monde … et le Trésor québécois," *le Devoir*, 4 March 2015.

2 John Costello, *John Macmurray: A Biography* (Edinburgh: Floris Books, 2002), 325.

Chapter Twenty-Nine

1 Gregory Baum, "Personal Experiences and Styles of Thought," in *Journeys* (New York: Paulist Press, 1975), 5–33, 6.

2 See pages 10–11.

3 Francis, exhortation *Evangelii gaudium*, no. 186.

Chapter Thirty

1 See pages 59–61.

2 Irving Greenberg, "Cloud of Hope, Pillar of Fire" in *Auschwitz: Beginning or End of an Era?*, ed. Eva Fleischner (New York: KTAV Publishing House, 1977), 33.

3 See page 60.

4 Fernand Dumont, *Œuvres complètes.* Vol. 14: *L'institution de la théologie* (Montréal: Les presses de l'Université Laval, 2008), 158–9.

Chapter Thirty-One

1 Francis, exhortation *Evangelii gaudium*, no. 187.

2 See pages 24–5.

3 See pages 171–3.

4 See page 17.

5 Egbert Munzer, *Solovyev* (London: Hollis and Carter, 1956). Munzer's wife saw to the publication of this book after her husband's death.

6 Doctrine of Discovery, http://www.doctrineofdiscovery.org/.

7 See https://en.wikipedia.org/wiki/List_of_apologies_made_by_Pope_John_Paul_II

8 Gregory Baum, "An Extraordinary Ecclesiastical Event," *Ecumenist*, 37 (Fall 2000), 16–18.

9 The Decree on Ecumenism, no. 6.

Chapter Thirty-Two

1 Gregory Baum, "Catholic Homosexuals," *Commonweal*, 15 February 1974, 479–82.

2 Gregory Baum, "The Homosexual Condition and Political Responsibility," in *A Challenge to Love: Gays and Lesbians in the Church*, ed. Roger Nugent, 38–51 (New York: Crossroads, 1983).

Chapter Thirty-Four

1 Julia Ching, *The Butterfly Healing: A Life Between East and West* (Ottawa: Novalis, 1998).

2 Naïm Kattan, "Immigrant, déplacé ou réfugié," *Relations*, September 2013.
3 Zijad Delic, *Canadian Islam: Belonging and Loyalty* (Ottawa: Kirtas Publishing, 2014).

Chapter Thirty-Five

1 See Susannah Heschel's account of her father's thinking at http://home.versatel.nl/heschel/Susannah.htm.
2 Gregory Baum, *The Church for Others: Protestant Theology in Communist East Germany* (Grand Rapids, MI: Eerdmans, 1996), 46–9.
3 See pages 74–5.

Chapter Thirty-Six

1 International Covenant on Economic, Social and Cultural Rights, United Nations, December 1966, part 1, article 1: "All peoples have the right of self-determination. By virtue of that right they freely determine their political status and freely pursue their economic, social and cultural development." See http://www.ohchr.org/EN/ProfessionalInterest/Pages/CESCR.aspx.
2 The book that guides his political thinking, Coulliard says, is John Micklethwait and Adrian Woodridge's *The Fourth Revolution* (London: Penguin, 2014).
3 John Ralston Saul, *The Comeback* (Toronto: Penguin, 2014).

Chapter Thirty-Seven

1 In the federal election of 19 October 2015, Stephen Harper's Conservative government was defeated and Justin Trudeau's Liberal Party was elected.
2 Christian Nadeau, *Rogue in Power: Stephen Harper Is Remaking Canada by Stealth* (Toronto: Lorimer, 2011); Michael Harris, *Party of One: Stephen Harper and Canada's Radical Makeover* (Toronto: Penguin, 2015).

Chapter Thirty-Eight

1 See pages 146–8.
2 Abraham Heschel, "The Spirit of Jewish Prayer," in *Moral Grandeur and Spiritual Audacity* (New York: Farrar, Straus and Giroux, 1996), 100–26.

Chapter Thirty-Nine

1 Gregory Baum, *Faith and Doctrine* (New York: Paulist Press, 1969), 51–90.
2 This concept is taken from Donald Evans, "Differences between Scientific and Religious Assertions," in *Science and Religion*, ed. Ian Babour, 102–7 (New York: Harper and Row, 1968).
3 See pages 82–3.
4 See page 4.

Chapter Forty

1 See https://en.wikipedia.org/wiki/World_War_II_casualties.
2 Matt. 6:2, 6:5; Luke 6:24.
3 Irving Greenberg, "Cloud of Hope, Pillar of Fire," in *Auschwitz: Beginning or End of an Era?*, ed. Eva Fleischner (New York: KTAV Publishing House, 1977), 23.

Index

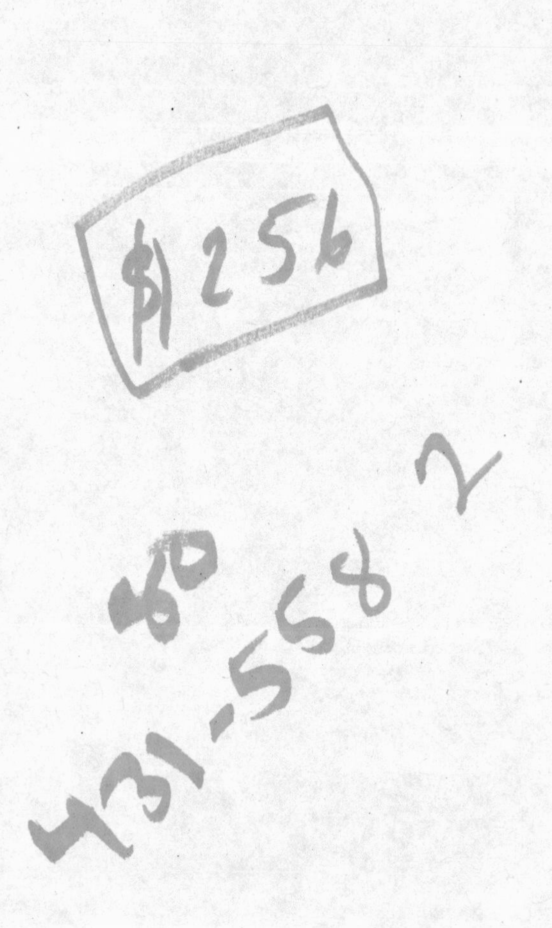